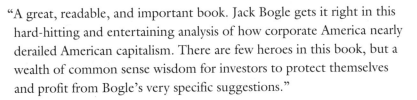

Praise for *The Battle for the Soul of Capitalism*

"A great, readable, and important book. Jack Bogle gets it right in this hard-hitting and entertaining analysis of how corporate America nearly derailed American capitalism. There are few heroes in this book, but a wealth of common sense wisdom for investors to protect themselves and profit from Bogle's very specific suggestions."

—Arthur Levitt, 25th Chairman of the U.S. Securities and Exchange Commission

"This book is a gift to the reading and investing public that holds a lifetime's wisdom. Bogle uniquely understands mutual funds and everyone needs to listen when he warns of the deceptions that have plagued the industry. Investors will profit if they follow his simple straightforward advice."

—Robert A. G. Monks, author of *Corporate Governance*

"Jack Bogle says exactly what needs to be said, and he does it with gusto. He knows what he's talking about, he loves capitalism, and he is eager to punch out those who would abuse the system. His tales and lessons should be required reading for any business leader, plus they offer great insights for smart investors."

—Walter Isaacson, President of the Aspen Institute

"Over the past half century, American capitalism nearly lost its soul. One of the few who noticed was Jack Bogle. Now, for the first time, he tells the whole tale as only Jack Bogle can: just what happened, just how it happened, and just how to fix it. Written in his trademark compelling style, this is mandatory reading for anyone with a dollar to invest or an interest in the future of American capitalism."

—William Bernstein, author of *The Birth of Plenty*

"Jack Bogle has written a brilliant and insightful book that highlights the many ways that our economy has suffered because managers have placed their own economic interests ahead of those of owners and investors. Bogle offers prescriptions that, if enacted, will help prevent a repeat of the scandals that we have witnessed over the past five years."

—Eliot Spitzer, Attorney General of New York

"The low-cost revolution Jack Bogle has led, both vocationally and intellectually, has improved the lives of investors everywhere. Simply put, capitalism has too many characters and not enough men of character. When one of the few tells us that the system he loves is ailing, and how he'd fix it, we had best listen."

—Cliff Asness, Ph.D., Managing and Founding Principal, AQR Capital Management

"John Bogle, whom I regard as the conscience of the mutual fund industry, has written an insightful book with great historical and contemporary perspective. His analysis of what has gone wrong and what needs to be done should be required reading for students, financial practitioners, and official policy makers."

—Henry Kaufman, President of Henry Kaufman and Company Inc.

"A wake-up call to policy makers. Anyone who cares about the future of America needs to read this book."

—Jack Treynor, President of Treynor Capital Management Inc.

"This is a must-read book for anyone interested in how to restore badly needed integrity, and efficiency, to our capital markets.".

—The Honorable Peter G. Peterson

"Jack Bogle has done more to protect corporate shareholders from mounting abuses at the hands of greedy and negligent CEOs, directors, and money managers than anyone in America. The case he makes here is so powerful and well reasoned that our Washington politicians will be hard pressed to ignore it."

—Mario Cuomo, 52nd Governor, New York State

"Jack Bogle's *The Battle for the Soul of Capitalism* is arguably the most important treatise on the bubble era. Policy makers, investment fiduciaries, and individual investors should read and act upon Bogle's prescriptions. The stakes are high: our collective financial souls."

—Steve Galbraith, Limited Partner, Maverick Capital

"This is an important book for the post-Enron era. In his characteristic hard-hitting style, one of the legends of the mutual fund industry presents an insider's view of what's wrong with corporate America and what can be done to improve it."

—Burton G. Malkiel, Princeton University

"Bogle describes the continuous struggle for control of our capitalistic system, the odds being heavily in favor of the managers. Individual investors and beneficiaries remain helpless, intermediaries are passive or conflicted, and Boards not yet effective. You owe it to yourself to read this book and reflect on his call for further Federal intervention to restore some balance."

—Ira Millstein, Senior Partner, Weil, Gotshal & Manges LLP

"In this tour de force, Bogle subjects corporate America to a forceful critique. Keen insights, rich experience, and moral courage shine throughout. Anyone interested in our corporate system should read this book, and those who do will never see corporate America the same again."

—Lucian Bebchuk, Harvard University

"The American wage earners' pension and 401(k) savings are now a major source of capital. Incredibly, although the source of capital is democratized, wealth is more concentrated. Jack Bogle finds this contradiction unacceptable and in this book shows us how to democratize the rewards of capitalism."

—Ray Carey, author of *Democratic Capitalism: The Way to a World of Peace and Plenty*

"John Bogle has done more to help ordinary investors than any other person in America today. He continues his battle on behalf of shareholders with this impassioned new book. Every investor and every policy maker should read his ideas for reform."

—Peter Fitzgerald, U.S. Senator for Illinois, 1999–2005

"Jack Bogle's brilliant tour de force provides the first integrated view of how our system of investing often destroys more value than it creates. Bogle clearly understands how the system works and how perverse motivations are undermining value creation. Always a pragmatic, he offers workable and practical solutions of how to get back on track."

—William W. George, Former Chairman and CEO
  of Medtronic, Inc.

"Once again Jack Bogle is the clearest and most courageous voice pointing out critical flaws in our governance and financial system but also showing, in constructive, brilliant ways, how to make the timely repairs. This book presents a rare blend of erudition, experience, and utility. It should be required reading for CEOs, public policy leaders, and MBA students—if not all informed investors."

—Jeffrey Sonnenfeld, Yale University

"This superb book should be a required reading for every business student in college. Like a fine surgeon, Jack Bogle dissects what is wrong with the capital markets from an investor's view, and at the same time provides a well-reasoned cure."

—Lynn Turner, Former Chief Accountant of the U.S. Securities
  and Exchange Commission

"In his characteristic style, Bogle delivers strong medicine for what ails our capital markets and corporate governance framework. Not all will agree with everything that he has written, but they would be wise to take note, as his message is resounding and his proposals go to the heart of crucial debates about management, ownership, and value creation."

—Devin Wenig, President, Business Divisions, Reuters Group

THE BATTLE FOR THE SOUL OF CAPITALISM

JOHN C. BOGLE

THE BATTLE
FOR THE
SOUL OF
CAPITALISM

YALE UNIVERSITY PRESS / NEW HAVEN & LONDON

Designed by Mary Valencia.

Set in ITC Galliard type by Integrated Publishing Solutions.

Printed in the United States of America.

The Library of Congress has cataloged the hardcover edition as follows:

Bogle, John C.
  The battle for the soul of capitalism / John C. Bogle.
    p. cm.
  Includes bibliographical references and index.
  ISBN 0-300-10990-3 (alk. paper)
    1. Capitalism—United States. 2. Corporations—United States.
3. Investments—United States. 4. Mutual funds—United States.
I. Title.
  HB501.B655 2005
  330.12'2'0973—dc22   2005013193

A catalogue record for this book is available from the British Library.

The paper in this book meets the guidelines for permanence and
durability of the Committee on Production Guidelines for Book
Longevity of the Council on Library Resources.

  ISBN-13: 978-0-300-11971-8 (pbk. : alk. paper)
  ISBN-10: 0-300-11971-2 (pbk. : alk. paper)

10 9 8 7 6 5 4 3 2 1

To my twelve grandchildren—
Peter, David, Rebecca, Sarah, Christina, Ashley,
Andrew, Molly, Christopher, John, Alex, and Blair—
and to all the other fine young citizens of their generation.

My generation has left America with much to be set right;
you have the opportunity of a lifetime to fix what has
been broken. Hold high your idealism and your values.
Remember always that even one person can make a difference.
And do your part "to begin the world anew."

*If the trumpet give an uncertain sound, who shall prepare himself
to the battle?*   —St. Paul, I Corinthians

*This above all: To thine own self be true, and it shall follow, as the
night the day, thou cans't not then be false to any man.*
       —William Shakespeare, *Hamlet*

A prophet is not without honor, save in his own country.
       —Matthew 13

*We are not afraid to follow truth wherever it may lead, nor to
tolerate any error so long as reason is left free to combat it.*
       —Thomas Jefferson

*Sometimes people call me an idealist. Well, that is the way I know
I am an American. America is the only idealistic nation in the
world.*   —Woodrow Wilson

CONTENTS

FOREWORD

Some, particularly those from the financial services industry, might say that Jack Bogle is cantankerous. Perhaps, but we now know that had we heeded his persistent warnings about a troubled financial system we may well have avoided the stock market losses and corporate scandals we have witnessed in recent years. We now know that on many matters he was right and others were wrong.

"Cantankerous" simply may be a hapless attempt by some with interests to protect to dismiss a man who has done so much to elevate the standards of conduct in business over the years. Indeed, if cantankerous, he is far more than that. He is straight talking, straight thinking. He is tough on all of us: corporate executives, board members, and ultimately the owners of equities. But he also tries hard to be fair minded.

He is concerned and caring. Concerned because he knows that our current account deficits are at unheard-of levels—now running at a staggering annual rate of $700 billion a year. He knows that the United States is starved for savings and is outsourcing our need for capital to foreign sources at reckless and dysfunctional levels. He knows that foreign investor confidence and, of course, domestic confidence, in the integrity of our capital markets is crucial to the health of our economy. To restore that integrity, he knows that fundamental reforms are needed in our corporations and our financial institutions as well.

It did not take this book to convince me of all this. I got to know Jack Bogle very well as a member of the Conference Board Commission on Public Trust and Private Enterprise that John Snow and I co-chaired along with an extraordinary group of ten other respected Americans.* Jack was

---

*Other distinguished members were TIAA-CREF's John H. Biggs; former comptroller-general Charles A. Bowsher; former SEC chairman Arthur Levitt, Jr.; Peter M. Gilbert of the Pennsylvania State Retirement System; Intel's Andrew S. Grove; Johnson and Johnson's CEO Ralph S. Larsen; Harvard professor Lynn Sharp Paine; former U.S. senator Warren B. Rudman, and the Honorable Paul A. Volcker.

a firm advocate of directly confronting the really tough issues—such as the expensing of stock options, the need for an independent chairman (as he puts it in this book, companies need both a "boss of the business" and "a boss of the board"), executive compensation based on long-term operating performance, truly independent compensation and audit committees that have the will and authority not only to hire and fire outside advisers but also to assure themselves that these advisers are not conflicted by providing services, such as consulting services by auditing firms where their perceived client is not the board but the management, and on and on.

Jack also has a stylish pen (one I wish I had!). He is a rarity, at least within our industry. He is highly literate. Who else could quote so easily and so relevantly from the likes of Demosthenes, Edward Gibbon, Alexander Hamilton, Thomas Jefferson, and Oscar Wilde?

His writing is also memorable. Jack has a knack for the colorful headline that helps the reader understand and remember the relevant observation or reform.

- To make the point that we have too few long term investors, he reminds us of how we have gone from an "own-a-stock" to a "rent-a-stock industry."
- To crystallize what went wrong he describes our descent from "owners' capitalism" to "managers' capitalism."
- To punctuate the notion that many advisers have become too beholden to managements who hire them for fees for related services, he quotes Descartes, "A man is incapable of comprehending any argument that interferes with his revenue."
- To suggest the possibility that inappropriate behavior in the marketplace may have metastasized more than we may wish to acknowledge, he raises the provocative question, "Bad apples or bad barrel?"
- To decry the state of affairs in the mutual fund industry, he says that these funds have gone from the "stewardship of shareholder investments to the salesmanship of asset gathering."

He rigorously defines the problems. He clearly outlines the needed reforms. This is a must-read book for anyone interested in how to restore badly needed integrity, and efficiency, to our capital markets.

THE HONORABLE PETER G. PETERSON

A C K N O W L E D G M E N T S

It is no accident that this book begins with an initial epigraph
that both incorporates the word *battle* that begins the book's title and
warns the reader that the trumpet that I sound will be certain. In an age of
temporizing, this is a book with a clear point of view: capitalism has been
moving in the wrong direction. We need to reverse its course so that the
system is once again run in the interest of stockholder-owners rather than
in the interest of managers. If this clear message makes readers—including
the movers and shakers of America—see things a new way, *The Battle for
the Soul of Capitalism* will have accomplished its purpose.

The issues go far beyond the importance of returning capitalism to its
owners. Once empowered, the owners themselves must be both motivated
to exercise their rights of corporate citizenship and required to observe their
responsibilities as good corporate citizens. This will be no small task, for,
in a sea change that has been largely unrecognized, we have moved from
being a society in which stock ownership was held directly by individual investors to one overwhelmingly constituted by investment intermediaries
who hold indirect ownership on behalf of the beneficiaries they represent.

Our society today, then, is no longer an "ownership society." It has become an "intermediation society," and it is not going back. In the ideal, if
we all work long enough and hard enough at the task, it will become a "fiduciary society," one in which the citizen-investors of America will at last
receive the fair shake they have always deserved from our corporations, our
investment markets, and our mutual fund industry. Public, private, and individual retirement savings are the backbone of our financial system, but
our intermediaries consume far too large a portion of whatever returns our
financial markets are generous enough to provide, with far too small a portion going to the last-line investors who put up all of the capital and assume all of the risks.

Given the contentious nature of these issues, the powerful economic interests of the oligarchs, and the urgent need to face up to the changing

world of capitalism, it is remarkable that so little public discourse exists on most of the issues tackled in this book. (Notable exceptions would be the responsibilities of corporate directors, the Sarbanes-Oxley Act, and the reform of Social Security, which have been widely discussed.)

But in the investment community, I have seen no defense of the inadequate returns delivered by mutual funds nor of the industry's archaic and bizarre structure; no attempt by institutions to explain why the rights of ownership that one would think are implicit in holding shares of stock remain largely unexercised; no serious criticism of the virtually unrecognized turn away from the once-conventional and pervasive investment strategies that relied on the wisdom of long-term investing toward strategies that increasingly rely on the folly of short-term speculation. If my book helps to open the door to the analysis and introspection by our corporate and financial leaders that is so long overdue, perhaps the needed changes will be hastened.

The many gracious and generous comments that I have received about *The Battle for the Soul of Capitalism* give me hope that change is on the way. I am greatly encouraged (and I confess to being somewhat stunned) by the positive opinions of so many thoughtful and respected citizens from a wide range of careers and perspectives:

- Across the political spectrum—Democrats Mario Cuomo and Eliot Spitzer, and Republicans Peter Fitzgerald and Pete Peterson.
- From the world of investing—economist Henry Kaufman, investment theory pioneer Jack Treynor, financial adviser (and neurologist) Bill Bernstein, equity strategist Steve Galbraith, and hedge fund manager Cliff Asness.
- From the world of business—Medtronic's Bill George, ADT's Ray Carey, and Reuters's Devin Wenig.
- From the U.S. Securities and Exchange Commission—former chairman Arthur Levitt and former chief accountant Lynn Turner.
- From the world of academe—Princeton's Burton Malkiel, Yale's Jeffrey Sonnenfeld, and Harvard's Lucian Bebchuk.
- From the world of public policy, Aspen Institute's Walter Isaacson, legendary corporate attorney Ira Millstein, and governance pioneer Robert Monks.

These categorizations themselves are unfairly confining. For example, the list includes fourteen successful authors in their own right—Messrs. Bebchuk, Bernstein, Carey, Cuomo, George, Isaacson, Kaufman, Levitt, Malkiel, Millstein, Monks, Peterson, Sonnenfeld, and Treynor.

Hesitant as I am to identify any *primus inter pares* among these commenters, I extend special thanks to three of them:

- To my wonderful friend the Honorable Peter G. Peterson, with whom I served during 2002–3 on the Conference Board Commission on Public Trust and Private Enterprise, for his infinitely kind foreword.
- To my new friend Peter Fitzgerald, former senator from Illinois, for his useful suggestions both on the general concepts and on the specific content of the book, reflections all of his disciplined Benedictine education.
- To my longtime friend and colleague Burton Malkiel, for his thorough reading of the text and his pungent commentary. Both helped me to balance the arguments I present and encouraged me to cover several areas that I had initially ignored. I've known Burt since he joined our Vanguard board of directors in 1977, where he has served with distinction ever since. He is the very paradigm of the intelligence, experience, objectivity, independence, and even passion that, were they to be widely shared among fund directors, would make the mutual fund industry a far better place for our citizens to invest.

I also want to extend my deepest appreciation for the hard work, commitment, loyalty, patience, and friendship of the other two crew members who serve with me at Vanguard's Bogle Financial Markets Research Center. Emily Snyder, my dependable assistant for fifteen years, was the indefatigable organizer, typist, and circulator of the many drafts of the text. Right up until the printing press began to roll, she incorporated an infinite number of edits and corrections, all extra duty over her regular responsibilities of keeping our office working and our budgets in line, and dealing with the daily barrage of phone calls, correspondence, and e-mails that continue even at this stage of my long career.

Kevin Laughlin, who has now worked with me for six years—one of the longer tours of duty among the thirteen people who have served with me as "assistant to the president" over the past four decades—was tireless in providing me with the statistics, research, and citations required for a book of this type. We've both gone over the text and the organization of the material numerous times, and his computer expertise has been a giant asset. I simply can't imagine having brought this book into being without Kevin at my side.

Of course there would be no book had I not experienced the second chance at life that came with the heart transplant I received on February 21, 1996. So I remain in the eternal debt of three of the splendid physicians who watched over me: Bernard Lown of the Harvard School of Public Health, who has given me tender and loving care, and helped me fight the battle against a failing heart ever since we first met in 1967; Rohaton Morris, the surgeon whose strong, delicate, and experienced hands did the transplant and who spoke the first words I heard thereafter ("Congratulations. You have a new heart. And it is young and strong"); and Susan Brozena, my cardiologist then and now, a lovely human being, a skilled professional, and a true angel who has supervised my remarkable recovery.

Finally, I want to thank Yale University Press for publishing the book, and editor Michael O'Malley for his constructive suggestions, his dedication, and his overall contribution. When Michael wrote to me in January 2004 suggesting Yale's interest in being the publisher of my next book, little did either of us imagine that only eighteen months later *The Battle for the Soul of Capitalism* would be a fait accompli.

I should make it clear that the strong opinions I have expressed in this book do not necessarily reflect the views of the present management of the Vanguard Group, the organization that I founded more than thirty years ago and led for more than two decades. The ideas and the words are mine alone, as are any faults or shortcomings.

However the book may be judged by its readers, I'm deeply humbled and profoundly honored to contribute to the debate on public policy that I hope and expect will be forthcoming. The business and ethical standards of corporate America, of investment America, and of mutual fund America have been gravely compromised. It is time to set out on a new course that, paradoxically enough, will lead us directly back to where we began, with the traditional values of capitalism—trusting, and being trusted.

Capitalism and American Society

As the twentieth century of the Christian Era ended, the United States of America comprehended the most powerful position on the earth and the wealthiest portion of mankind. The frontiers of the nation were guarded by two great oceans, and her values and ideals at once incurred the respect, the envy, and the ill-will of much of the rest of mankind. The gentle but powerful influence of her laws, her property rights, her manners, and her business institutions and financial institutions alike had combined to produce her power. Her peaceful inhabitants enjoyed and abused the advantages of wealth and luxury. Her free constitution had gradually cemented the union of the states and was preserved with decent reverence. *

As some readers will recognize, that paragraph, aptly describing our nation as the twenty-first century began on January 1, 2001, is a play on the words of the famous opening paragraph of Edward Gibbon's 1838 epic, *The Decline and Fall of the Roman Empire*. And yet, Gibbon continued, "the Roman Empire would decline and fall, a revolution which will be ever remembered and is still felt by the nations of the earth."[1] By the end of his epic, the Roman Empire was no more. Constantinople had fallen, the fruitful provinces overwhelmed by Vandals; Britain was lost; Gaul was overrun; and the brutal Goths had conquered Rome itself, as in

---

* The original version: "In the second century of the Christian era, the Empire of Rome comprehended the fairest part of the earth, and the most civilized portion of mankind. The frontiers of that extensive monarchy were guarded by ancient renown and disciplined valor. The gentle but powerful influence of laws and manners had gradually cemented the union of the provinces. Their peaceful inhabitants enjoyed and abused the advantages of wealth and luxury. The image of a free constitution was preserved with decent reverence."

410 A.D. the Imperial City was delivered to the licentious tribes of Germany and Sythia.

Why did the Roman Empire fall? One answer seems to lie in its citizens' unshaken demand for material goods ("bread") and the self-indulgence of its civic order ("circuses"); the acceptance of money as the measure of their worth, their wants, and the value of their property; their need for honor and recognition, even as their vision of freedom, liberty, and greatness was fading. As Saint Augustine suggested, it was self-love that led to the fall of the Roman Empire. Gibbon's conclusion is expressed in this profound warning: "O man! Place not thy confidence in this present world."[2]

Gibbon's history reminds us that no nation can take its greatness for granted. There are no exceptions. So I am concerned about the threats we face, not only the external threats to America's greatness in *this* present world, but the internal threats we face at home. This book is my attempt to address one of those major threats: the remarkable erosion that has taken place over the past two decades in the conduct and values of our business leaders, our investment bankers, and our money managers.

My vantage point is that of an American businessman (and a lifelong Republican) who has spent his entire half-century-plus career in the financial field—writing an idealistic thesis on the mutual fund industry during 1949–51; then spending a near-quarter century working at and finally heading fund pioneer Wellington Management Company; founding the Vanguard Group of Investment Companies in 1974 and serving as its CEO through early 1996; and subsequently, to this day, researching, writing, and lecturing on investment issues. For better or worse, my youthful idealism—the belief that any truly sound business endeavor must be built on a strong moral foundation—still remains today, at least as strong as it was all those years ago.

By the latter years of the twentieth century, our business values had eroded to a remarkable extent. Yes, we are a nation of prodigious energy, marvelous entrepreneurship, brilliant technology, creativity beyond imagination, and, at least in some corners of the business world, the idealism to make our nation and our world a better place. But I also see far too much greed, egoism, materialism, and waste to please my critical eye. I see an economy overly focused on the "haves" and not focused enough on the "have-nots," failing to allocate our nation's resources where they are most needed—to solve the problems of poverty and to provide quality education for all. I see our shocking misuse of the world's natural resources, as if they were ours to waste rather than ours to preserve as a sacred trust for future generations, and I see a political system corrupted by the staggering infusion of money that is, to be blunt about it, rarely given by disinterested citizens who expect no return on their investment.

America's Bread and Circuses

As the new millennium begins, America has her own bread and circuses. That they are not the same as those of ancient Rome is hardly surprising, but they exist nonetheless. Much of our bread, as it were, goes not to keep the masses peaceable but to a fairly small elite, including the fabulous compensation paid to corporate chief executives and star athletes and entertainers. (Shades of the Roman Empire!) Our bread was leavened even more with the incredible wealth creation of the stock market bubble of 1998–2000, enriching senior corporate officials, aggressive entrepreneurs, venturesome investors, investment bankers, financiers, and the managers of other people's money. During the subsequent 50 percent stock market crash, however, half of the paper wealth created for the investing public during the bubble went up in smoke. Despite the market's strong rebound in 2003–4, investor wealth in equities remains more than 20 percent below the peak it reached five years ago.

Too late, investors learned that, absent the delivery of the future cash flows, stock valuations are evanescent. For all its trumped-up promise, for example, the "new economy" of technology, science, and communications during the bubble era produced an earnings growth rate of just 8 percent per year, barely larger than the 7 percent growth rate of the "old economy" of traditional goods and services. The over-leavened bread of market values that accompanied that modest growth inevitably fell flattest in the new-economy sector, precisely where the extraordinary popular delusions and madness of the investing crowd had departed furthest from reality.

And our circuses abound, too. While our nation's largest arena, the stadium at the University of Michigan, holds but 107,501 citizens—one-third the 320,000 capacity of the Circus Maximus—television screens bring U.S. sports and entertainment to worldwide audiences that reach into the billions. As stocks became entertainment, perhaps our greatest circus became our financial markets. Electronic trading abounds; dealers and day traders move the market in spasms; stock market turnover has risen to the highest levels since 1929. CNBC and CNN and Bloomberg television alert opportunistic traders of stocks to the contemporaneous opinions of Wall

Street gurus about each merger, each earnings report, each uptick and each downtick in the stock market. And earnings are almost universally described in terms of how close they come to widely publicized "guidance" from management. Any deviations from expectations, positive or negative, can inexplicably mean billions of dollars, more or less, in the market capitalizations of large corporations. Not surprisingly, then, companies rarely report earnings that disappoint the omnipotent market.

When we should be teaching young students about long-term investing and the magic of compound interest, the stock-picking contests offered by our schools are in fact teaching them about short-term speculation. And the biggest financial circus of all—today's incarnation of the Circus Maximus—is the garish eight-story NASDAQ MarketSite Tower in Times Square, displaying stock prices on what is proudly billed as the "world's largest video screen." That display, it seems to me, is the visual paradigm of a stock market that has become not only a circus, but a casino for speculators. Yet as Lord Keynes warned us: "When the capital development of a country becomes the by-product of the activities of a casino, the job is likely to be ill-done."[3]

Beyond the Financial Markets

While our bread and circuses are different from those of ancient Rome, we'd best consider whether they bear the seeds of our own undoing. As Mark Twain reminded us, "history may not repeat itself, but it rhymes." So we would be wise to accept the hardly far-fetched analogy of ancient Rome with modern America as a warning to put our house in order. For while the situation I've described goes to the very heart of our wealth-oriented, things-fixated society, we still have the ability and the freedom to solve our problems and build a better world. All we need is the wisdom to recognize our challenges and the willpower to surmount them. It will not be easy. But as my marvelous cardiologist, Dr. Bernard Lown, wrote to me a few years ago, "the destination for a society deserving of human beings is still distant, but it is up to all of us to hasten the day of arrival."[4] So, I leave to my readers not only to decide whether I exaggerate our problems, but also to consider whether we have the will to solve them.

Beyond our borders, and now even within them, we are threatened by a malevolent war of terrorism. Radical elements of the Muslim world, operating in a globe that is now virtually without borders or meaningful protection, threaten our daily lives. While the type of massive attack that reduced our proud World Trade Towers to rubble four years ago has not been repeated, no one denies the possibility—even the likelihood—that we have not seen the final act of devastation take place on America's shores. Whether or not one agrees with our nation's policies and actions since September 11, 2001, our self-appointed role as the world's police force and the wars we launched in Afghanistan and Iraq have clearly inflamed the hatred of much of the Muslim world for America's values and her power, and have consumed an alarmingly high amount of our national resources ($300 billion through 2005) that might have been better expended on our needs at home, or even, in the name of fiscal rectitude, unexpended. For history is clear that economic power is the ultimate bulwark of political and military power and national dominion, and capitalism is its bulwark.

Enter Capitalism

It is not my province to address in this book the vast challenges that our nation now faces at home and abroad. But the example of the fall of the Roman Empire ought to be a strong wake-up call to all of those who share my respect and admiration for the vital role that capitalism has played in America's call to greatness. Thanks to our marvelous economic system, based on private ownership of productive facilities, on prices set in free markets, and on personal freedom, we are the most prosperous society in history, the most powerful nation on the face of the globe, and, most important of all, the highest exemplar of the values that, sooner or later, are shared by the human beings of all nations: the inalienable rights to life, liberty, and the pursuit of happiness.

Today's capitalism, however, has departed, not just in degree but in kind, from its proud traditional roots. Over the past century, a gradual move from *owners' capitalism*—providing the lion's share of the rewards of investment to those who put up the money and risk their own capital—has culminated in an extreme version of *managers' capitalism*—providing vastly disproportionate rewards to those whom we have trusted to manage our enterprises in the interest of their owners. Managers' capitalism is a betrayal of owners' capitalism, a system that worked, albeit imperfectly, with remarkable effectiveness for the better part of the past two centuries, beginning with the Industrial Revolution as the eighteenth century turned to the nineteenth.

The human soul, as Thomas Aquinas defined it, is the "form of the body, the vital power animating, pervading, and shaping an individual from the moment of conception, drawing all the energies of life into a unity."[5] In

our temporal world, the soul of capitalism is the vital power that has ani-
mated, pervaded, and shaped our economic system, drawing its energies
into a unity. In this sense, it is no overstatement to describe the effort we
must make to return the system to its proud roots with these words: *the
battle to restore the soul of capitalism.*

Part I—Corporate America

After the financial shenanigans of the stock market bubble; the
rife scandals best exemplified by the malfeasance at Enron, WorldCom,
and Tyco; the inflated balderdash fed to investors by the so-called research
analysts of Wall Street investment bankers; the grotesquely excessive compensation paid to chief executives, in cash and in the form of obscene
grants of stock options, awards that came at the direct expense of the
shareholders, though not even counted as an expense in the companies' income statements; and the focus of our stock market on the evanescent
prices of stocks rather than the durable intrinsic *values* of corporations, the
idea that companies have been run for the benefit of their managers at the
expense of their shareholders is hardly news. But in the first section of this
book I bring into sharp focus not only *what* went wrong with corporate
America, but *why* it went wrong.

Essentially, most of what went wrong can be described as an "agency
problem" characterized by:

- One, executive compensation. Driven by mega-grants of stock
  options, the total pay of the average CEO soared from 42 times that
  of the average worker in 1980 to 280 times in 2004, a staggering increase unjustified by any remotely comparable business achievement.
- Two, the onset of quarterly earnings guidance, accompanied by financial engineering designed to produce the promised results and abetted
  by the attendant laxity in traditional accounting standards. When the
  investment community demanded, and the business community
  provided, the illusion of "managed earnings" in order to inflate
  stock prices and enrich insiders, it was only a matter of time until
  the ensuing market bubble burst.

How could these aberrations in corporate America occur? The responsibility lies heavily upon the shoulders of the gatekeepers we trusted to pro-

tect investors—legislators, regulators, rating services, attorneys, public accountants, and, most importantly, corporate directors, who seemed unable
to recognize their responsibility for the stewardship of the corporation in
the interest of its owners. They failed to intercede appropriately on behalf
of the shareholders.

To reform this faltering system, I present a series of recommendations
designed to strengthen the independence of the board of directors, and to
bring a semblance of "corporate democracy" into the system by first enabling, and then encouraging, investors to exercise their voting franchise,
working with company directors to return capitalism to its owners so it can
function effectively in the nation's service.

Part II—Investment America

While much has been written about the shortcomings of corporate America, little has been written about the failure of its owners to
assert their ownership rights. So in the second section of the book I discuss in some depth the nature of the controlling ownership of our corporations today. The stockholders of investment America—dominated by
our giant financial institutions—hold awesome power. Yet, these firms all
too rarely exercise that power, in essence neglecting the legitimate interests of the ultimate stock owners, the beneficiaries whom they are duty-
bound to represent. The failure of these institutions to demand their
rights of ownership, as well as their failure to honor their responsibilities
of ownership, bears a heavy burden for what went wrong in investment
America.

Why did it go wrong? In part because of the profound conflicts of interest that permeated the field of financial intermediation, and in part because the behavior of these stockholders changed radically, from a traditional focus on the wisdom of long-term investing to the folly of short-term
speculation—a change in which the momentary precision of the price of a
corporation's stock came to overwhelm the eternal verity of the intrinsic
value of the corporation itself, however difficult to measure. Our nation's
financial institutions transmogrified themselves from members of an *own-
a-stock* industry into members of a *rent-a-stock* industry, enabling corporate
managers to run roughshod over their owners. This pervasive substitution
of direct owners of stocks—*principals*—by intermediaries—*agents*—has
created a host of new challenges to the return of owner's capitalism. While

there are no easy ways out of this morass, I again offer some constructive suggestions for reform.

Part III—Mutual Fund America

The third section of the book deals with the $8 trillion mutual fund industry, now our nation's largest financial institution. Mutual funds constitute the major portion of the missing link that enabled the managers of corporate America to assert their nearly unchecked power to place their own interests ahead of the interests of their owners. Paradoxically, however, it is in the very structure of the mutual fund industry itself where we find the greatest violation of owners' capitalism. In effect, the fund industry operates under an institutionalized system of managers' capitalism, one so deeply entrenched that it will be difficult to dislodge. An institution with its own serious governance problems and riddled with conflicts of interest is hardly in a preferred position to cast stones at others.

While the shareholder wealth consumed by the managers of corporate America has been far from trivial, the shareholder wealth consumed by the managers of mutual fund America has been enormous. More than one-fifth of the robust *annual* gross returns generated for investors in the financial markets—stock, bond, and money market alike—during the past two decades has been siphoned off by fund managers. The awesome *magic* of compounding *returns* has been overwhelmed by the *tyranny* of compounding *costs*. Without a major reduction in the share of market returns arrogated to themselves by our mutual fund intermediaries, more than three-quarters of the future *cumulative* financial wealth produced by stocks over an investment lifetime will be consumed by fund managers, leaving less than 25 percent for the investors. Yet it is the investors themselves who put up 100 percent of the capital and assume 100 percent of the risk.

As in the earlier cases of corporate America and investment America, I also describe why mutual fund America went wrong. The principal instigating factor has been a basic shift in orientation from a profession of stewardship to a business of salesmanship. How can it be fixed? Since the ownership of mutual fund America is held largely by 95 million individual investors, most of modest means and none with the kind of latent power that institutional investors hold over corporate America, my prescriptions for reform are more complex. But although these reforms will be far more difficult to accomplish, the winds of change are already beginning to blow in a positive direction.

Conclusion—American Capitalism in the Twenty-first Century

So all is hardly lost. In corporate America, investment America, and mutual fund America, owners are awakening. The disgusting scandals in business, on Wall Street, and in the fund industry have opened the door to reform that has already begun. Despite all their wealth and power, our corporate managers, our institutional investors, and our fund operators will be forced—haltingly, spasmodically, and slowly perhaps, but inevitably—to accept an idea whose time has come: the owner is king. In the fourth section of this book, I reflect on what it will take "to begin the world anew," including a return to the traditional values of mutual trust, responsibility, and stewardship.

During my own long career, I've done my best to honor these values and build an enterprise that honors the highest principles of fiduciary duty and the interests of investors—to put the owners, if you will, into the driver's seat once again. It all comes down to upholding the values that once made our corporate and financial enterprises so successful, fairly providing the rewards of investing to those who put up the capital and assume the risks involved. To win the battle to restore the soul of capitalism, it is these values that must prevail.

It is imperative that we succeed at this monumental task, for we require a powerful and equitable system of capital formation if our nation is to overcome the infinite, often seemingly intractable, challenges of our risk-fraught modern world. Our economic might, political freedom, military strength, social welfare, and even free religious values depend upon it.

In the conclusion, I present strong evidence not only that reform is necessary in our capitalistic system, but that reform is consistent with the ideas of our nation's great statesmen of the past as well as our wisest leaders of the present. Specifically, I call for the formation of a national commission to recommend policies that respond to the development of our "intermediation society" in which direct stockowners are an endangered species, and to the frightening shortfall in the expected future wealth of the "investment society," largely the public, private, and individual retirement plans that have become the foundation of our national savings. The reconciliation of the interests of these two societies lies in the creation of a "fiduciary society" in which intermediaries truly represent—first, last, and only—the interests of those they serve.

For our nation's vast business-financial complex to function the way it must for America to sustain her economic strength, her national power, and her global leadership—and to uphold the values expressed in our Declaration of Independence and our Constitution—it is high time we turn to the task of reforming our system of democratic capitalism. That is the challenge to which corporate America, investment America, and mutual fund America must rise. There is too much at stake for us to fail to do our part.

PART **ONE**

Corporate America

We begin with an analysis of what went wrong in corporate America, reflected in "a pathological mutation" from traditional owners' capitalism to a new form, managers' capitalism. While the modern world of business was built on a system of trusting and being trusted, societal changes produced a new "bottom line" society whose attributes included grossly excessive executive compensation and stock options, part of an enormous transfer of wealth from public investors to the hands of business leaders, corporate insiders, and financial intermediaries during the stock market boom and bust.

Much of the responsibility for this subversion of capitalism lies in the diffusion of ownership of corporate America, and the resultant vacuum of ownership power. Our traditional gatekeepers—corporate directors, auditors, the financial community, and regulators and legislators—failed to protect the owners against overreaching by managers, reinforcing the principle that, in the words of the second chapter's subtitle, "somebody's gotta keep an eye on these geniuses."

The final chapter in this section reviews the reaction to the faults of the recent era by governmental and private organizations, and presents seven specific recommendations designed to clearly define the distinctly different responsibilities of management and ownership. It calls for the restoration of shareholder rights in governance and makes the case for corporate democracy, urging investors to step forward and exercise their rights of ownership. The chapter closes with the exhortation "Owners of the World, Unite."

CHAPTER **I**

What Went Wrong
in Corporate America?
"A Pathological Mutation"

The great stock market bubble of 1997–2000, and the great crash that inevitably followed, are poignant reminders of the periodic but random aberrations described in Charles MacKay's 1885 epic history of speculation, *Extraordinary Popular Delusions and the Madness of Crowds.* Each burst of madness, of course, is different, but each yields similar adverse consequences. The most recent episode witnessed the culmination of an era in which our business corporations and our financial institutions, working in tacit harmony, corrupted the traditional nature of capitalism, shattering both confidence in the markets and the accumulated wealth of countless American families. Something went profoundly wrong, fundamentally and pervasively, in corporate America.

At the root of the problem, in the broadest sense, was a societal change aptly described by these words from the teacher Joseph Campbell: "In medieval times, as you approached the city, your eye was taken by the Cathedral. Today, it's the towers of commerce. It's business, business, business."[1] We had become what Campbell called a "bottom-line society." But our society came to measure the *wrong* bottom line: form over substance, prestige over virtue, money over achievement, charisma over character, the ephemeral over the enduring, even mammon over God.

Joseph Campbell's analogy proved to be ominous. On September 11, 2001, we witnessed the total destruction of the proudest towers of American commerce, the twin towers of New York's World Trade Center. While that tragic event reawakened the nation to many of our social values, it was too late to deter our financial system from its ruinous course. In the aftermath, the stock market continued its downward trajectory. When the plunge ended, the aggregate market value of America's corporations had dropped by a stunning 50 percent, the worst stock market crash since 1929–33. The value of U.S. stocks collapsed from $17 trillion to $9 trillion, before some $4 trillion of this paper wealth was recovered in the ensuing market rebound. New symbols of commerce arose from the ashes: no longer the proud towers of commerce, but beleaguered captains of industry. Too many of our business leaders were transmogrified from mighty lions of corporate success to self-serving and untrustworthy operators, with several doing "perp walks" for the television cameras.

Our bottom-line society has a good bit to answer for. As the United Kingdom's chief rabbi Jonathan Sacks put it: "When everything that matters can be bought and sold, when commitments can be broken because they are no longer to our advantage, when shopping becomes salvation and advertising slogans become our litany, when our worth is measured by how much we earn and spend, then the market is destroying the very virtues on which in the long run it depends."[2]

Capitalism—The Virtuous Circle

Capitalism, *Webster's Third International Dictionary* tells us, is "an economic system based on corporate ownership of capital goods, with investment determined by private decision, and with prices, production, and the distribution of goods and services determined mainly in a free market." Importantly, I would add, it is "a system founded on honesty, decency, and trust," for these attributes too have been clearly established in its modern history.

During the eighteenth and nineteenth centuries, as the world moved from its agrarian roots toward an industrial society, capitalism began to flourish. Local communities became part of national and, later, international commerce; trading expanded; and large accumulations of capital were required to build the factories, develop the transportation systems, and fund the banks on which the new economy would depend. Surprising as it may seem today, according to an article by James Surowiecki in *Forbes*, the Quakers were at the heart of this development.[3]

In the 1700s and early 1800s, Quakers dominated the British economy, probably because their legendary simplicity and thrift endowed them with the capital to invest. They owned more than half of the country's ironworks and played key roles in banking, consumer goods, and transatlantic trading. Their emphasis on reliability, absolute honesty, and rigorous record-keeping infused them with trust as they dealt with one another, and other observant merchants came to see that being trustworthy went hand in hand with business success. Self-interest demanded virtue.

This coincidence of virtue and value, of course, is exactly what the great Scottish economist and philosopher Adam Smith expected. In *The Wealth of Nations* in 1776, he famously wrote, "The uniform and uninterrupted effort to better his condition, the principle from which [both] public and private opulence is originally derived, is frequently powerful enough to maintain the natural progress of things toward improvement. . . . Each individual neither intends to promote the public interest, nor knows how much he is promoting it . . . [but] by directing his industry in such a matter as its produce may be of the greatest value, *he is led by an invisible hand to promote an end which was no part of his intention.*"[4]

And so it was to be, the *Forbes* essay continued, that "the evolution of capitalism has been in the direction of more trust and transparency and less [purely] self-serving behavior; not coincidentally, this evolution has brought with it greater productivity and economic growth. . . . Not because capitalists are naturally good people, [but] because the benefits of trust—of being trusting and of being trustworthy—are potentially immense, and because a successful market system teaches people to recognize those benefits . . . a virtuous cycle in which an everyday level of trustworthiness breeds an everyday level of trust."[5]

Said differently, capitalism requires a structure and a value system that people believe in and can depend on. We do not need a Pollyannaish faith in the goodwill of mankind, but we do need the confidence that promises and commitments, once made, will be kept. We also need assurances that the system as a whole does not unduly benefit some at the expense of others. It is these elements that led capitalism to flourish.

The Birth of Plenty

The flourishing of capitalism was central to the soaring prosperity that became the hallmark of the modern era. During the past two extraordinary centuries, the global economy has experienced increasing productivity and economic growth at rates never witnessed before in all human history. According to the brilliant investor, philosopher, and neurologist William J. Bernstein, author of *The Birth of Plenty: How the Prosperity of the Modern World Was Created*:

> [From] about A.D. 1000 . . . the improvement in human well-being was of a sort so slow and unreliable that it was not noticeable during the average person's *twenty-five-year* [italics added] life span. Then, not long after 1820, prosperity began flowing in an ever-increasing torrent. With each successive generation, the life of the son became observably more comfortable, informed, and predictable than that of the father . . . [the result] of the four essential ingredients that are necessary for igniting and sustaining economic growth and human progress:
>
> - *Property rights*—creators must have proper incentives to create, which go hand in hand with civil liberties.
> - *Scientific rationalism*—innovators must possess the proper intellectual tools in order to innovate, and must be able to do so without fear of retribution.
> - *Capital markets*—entrepreneurs must have access to sufficient capital to pursue their visions.
> - *Transportation/communication*—society must be able to rapidly and efficiently move information and finished products.[6]

It was only at the birth of modern capitalism in the early nineteenth century that all four of these elements began to flourish in concert. While the forces that drive economic growth are complex to evaluate, and often contested in academic circles, there was a timely convergence of human and physical capital, supported by a network of modern systems: legal, financial, commercial, educational, governmental, and the like. In any event, two centuries ago the world's standard of living began inexorably to improve, and the modern world was born.

A Pathological Mutation

The system worked. Or at least it *did* work. And then, late in the twentieth century, something went wrong. The system changed; one more aberration in the long course of capitalism. While each of its earlier failures was followed by safeguards put in place as defenses against future abuses, none of them contemplated the next step of scandal that perhaps almost inevitably would follow. What went wrong this time, as William Pfaff described it, was "a pathological mutation in capitalism." The classic system—*owners'* capitalism—had been based on a dedication to serving the interests of the corporation's owners in maximizing the return on their capital investment. But a new system developed—*managers'* capitalism—in which, Pfaff wrote, "the corporation came to be run to profit its managers, in complicity if not conspiracy with accountants and the managers of other corporations." Why did it happen? "Because the markets had so diffused corporate ownership *that no responsible owner exists.* This is morally unacceptable, but also a corruption of capitalism itself."[7]

The age of managers' capitalism has had dire consequences for our notion of some sort of fairness in American society, and is a major cause of the increase in the gap between America's rich and poor, between haves and have-nots. In the mid-1970s, for example, the wealthiest 1 percent of Americans owned about 18 percent of the nation's financial wealth. By the close of the twentieth century, the share owned by the top 1 percent had soared to 40 percent, the highest share in the nation's history, with the possible exception of the estimated 45 percent share reached around the turn of the previous century, the age of the Robber Barons—John D. Rockefeller, E. H. Harriman, Jay Gould, et al. Such concentration, most citizens would agree, is antithetical to the long-term stability of our society. Of course these inequalities won't be easily remedied by a return to owner's capitalism, for the issues are deeper and more complex than that. But I caution that a society that tolerates such differences in income and wealth is a society that faces long-term disruption.

The Long Boom

As the culmination of this change in the nature of capitalism drew near, the critical factors that affect the markets also were changing. Only recently, as 1999 was about to roll into 2000, the Y2K issue—an acronym now almost lost in the dustbin of history—was the major challenge of the day. Our nation's systems experts prevailed, and our computers clicked into the year 2000, and then, a year later, into the twenty-first century. A new century, billed as a new era of growth for our global economy, had begun. The spirit of the coming age was summarized in a 1997 article entitled, of all things, "The Long Boom." *Wired* magazine, the hottest publication geared to the "new economy" fantasy, headlined its lead story: "We're Facing Twenty-Five Years of Prosperity, Freedom, and a Better Environment for the Whole World. You Got a Problem with That?"

Who could *possibly* have a problem with that? Indeed, the readers of *Wired* must have salivated as they anticipated, in the article's words, "the beginnings of a global boom on a scale never experienced before . . . a period of sustained growth that could eventually double the world's economy every dozen years and bring increasing prosperity for billions of people on the planet . . . growth that will do much to solve seemingly intractable problems like poverty, and ease tensions throughout the world, all without blowing the lid off the environment."[8]

That wildly bullish thesis was based on the indisputable triumph of the United States as sole superpower, the end of major wars, waves of new technology, soaring productivity, an expanding global marketplace, and corporate restructuring—"a virtuous circle . . . driven by an open society in an integrated world." In all, a "radically optimistic *meme**."[9]

The Happy Conspiracy

The financial markets of the late 1990s seemed to accept the *Wired* thesis; if not in its entirety, surely in its spirit and its direction. From the start of 1997 to its high point in March 2000, the stock market doubled, valued at stratospheric multiples of earnings, dividends, and book values literally never seen before. The Great Bull Market fed on itself, a mania driven by the idea that we were in a New Era. Bolstered by that euphoria, our system of market capitalism—as all systems sometimes do—experienced a profound failure, with a whole variety of root causes, each interacting and reinforcing the other: the notion that our corporations were trees that could grow not only to the sky but beyond; the rise of the imperial chief executive officer; the legerdemain of financial engineering in corporate reporting; the failure of our gatekeepers—the auditors, regulators, legislators, investment managers, and boards of directors—who forgot to whom they owed their loyalty; the change in our financial institutions from being stock *owners* to being stock *traders;* the promotional hyperbole of Wall Street; the willingness of professional securities analysts

---

* *Meme:* A contagious idea that replicates like a virus, passed on from mind to mind through networks and face-to-face contacts . . . the basic unit of cultural evolution.

to put aside their skepticism; the frenzied excitement of the media; and, of course, the eager members of the investing public, reveling in the easy wealth that seemed like a cornucopia. It was this happy conspiracy among virtually all interested parties that drove business standards down even as it drove stock prices up. The victory of investors, insiders, and investment operators during the Great Bull Market had a thousand fathers.

The Great Bear Market

As Sir Isaac Newton warned us, for every action there is an equal and opposite reaction, and the reaction to the stock market boom and the mismanagement of so many of our corporations inevitably followed. The reaction to the Great Bull Market, of course, was the Great Bear Market, one that held us in its throes for two and a half years and from which we still feel the residual effects. From its high in March 2000 to its low in October 2002, the market lost fully one-half of its value, making it, with the Great Crash of 1929–33, one of the two largest drops of the entire century.

That combination of percentages—a market that rose 100 percent, then tumbled 50 percent—produces a net gain of *zero*. Even with the subsequent 50 percent recovery from the low through early 2005, stock prices remained more than 20 percent below the peak, about where they were in 1998. Nonetheless, taking dividends into account, investors who stayed the course during this seven-year period are far better off on balance than those who rushed in later to ride the wave of euphoria, only to experience heavy losses.

In a sense, the *Wired* forecast was right on the mark. We *were* moving into a New Era. But, so far at least, the New Era has been the diametrical opposite of its bullish predictions. Rather than a long boom in the stock market, we've seen a short bust. Rather than the end of war, the United States is now engaged in three wars, in Iraq, in Afghanistan, and on terrorism. The growth rate in information technology has slowed dramatically. Employment has increased only marginally, and the abatement of poverty is nowhere in view. Rather than the sustained economic growth that *Wired* anticipated, we've had a recession, from which our economy is recovering only fitfully. And, corporate malfeasance has shaken the confidence of investors to the point that the very nature of modern-day capitalism is—quite properly—being challenged. Each of these challenges reverberates across the entire financial services field.

Yet even after the Great Bear Market, the return on stocks for long-term investors has been remarkable. From 1982, when the long bull market began, to early 2005, the U.S. stock market provided a compound growth rate averaging 13 percent per year. Through the miracle of compounding, those who owned stocks in 1982 and still hold them today had multiplied their capital more than 16 *times* over. So for all of the stock market's breathtaking ups and downs, long-term owners who bought and held common stocks have been well compensated for the risks they assumed. For such investors, the coming of the bubble and then its going—the boom and then the bust—simply did not matter. Unfortunately, for far too many others, it was devastating to their wealth.

All that has transpired could be sparingly acknowledged if it weren't for the fact that there were winners and losers during the mania—and lots of both. Simply put, the winners were those who *sold* their stocks in the throes of the halcyon era that is now history; and our financial intermediaries, who prospered beyond the dreams of avarice. The losers were those who *bought* stocks, and those who paid the high intermediation costs that are part and parcel of participating in the stock market.

The Winners

Consider first the winners. A large proportion of the shares that were sold as the bubble soared to its peak were those held by corporate executives who had acquired vast holdings of their companies' stocks through options, and those of entrepreneurs whose companies had gone newly public as Wall Street investment banking firms underwrote huge volumes of initial stock offerings, many now worthless. Examining a group of executives in a mere twenty-five corporations in those categories, *Fortune* magazine placed sales of stock at $23 billion—nearly a billion dollars for the executives of each company.[10]

While hard data for all stock sales by executives in publicly traded companies are not available, it seems reasonable to estimate that total sales could have reached $200 billion or more. Initial public offerings (IPOs)—largely of "new economy" companies, most of which were bereft of earnings—totaled more than $800 billion from 1995 through 2001.[11] (An unknown, but doubtless enormous, portion of the proceeds of these sales was reinvested in stocks.) Thus, the wealth transfer to insiders and entrepreneurs who sold their stocks may well have totaled $1 trillion or more.

The other—and even bigger—recipients of the massive transfer of wealth were the financial intermediaries themselves—investment bankers and brokers who sold those high-flying stocks to their clients, and mutual fund managers who sold those speculative "new economy" funds to the public. Why were they winners? Because the investment banking, brokerage, and management fees paid by investors for their services reached staggering levels. More than a few individual investment bankers saw their annual compensation reach well into the tens of millions, and at least a half-dozen owners of fund management companies accumulated personal wealth in the billion-dollar range, including one family whose wealth is said to be at the $20 billion level. During 1997–2002 alone, the total revenues paid by investors to investment banking and brokerage firms exceeded $1 *trillion*, and payments to mutual funds exceeded $275 *billion*.

The Losers

If the winners raked in what we can roughly estimate as at least $2.275 trillion, who lost all that money? The losers, of course, were those who *bought* the stocks and who paid the intermediation costs. Most of the buying came from the great American public—sometimes directly by buying individual stocks; sometimes indirectly, through mutual funds; sometimes in their personal accounts; and frequently through the increasingly popular 401(k) thrift plans, themselves often treacherously loaded with the stock of the companies for which the investors themselves worked. "Greater fools?" Perhaps. Surely greed, naiveté, and the absence of common sense plagued too many stock buyers, and aggressive sellers capitalized on the popular delusions and madness of the investing crowds.

Millions of investors rushed into the stock market to buy the burgeoning number of speculative stocks—technology shares in Internet, telecommunications, and other companies—that were part of the ballyhooed "new economy." For example, during the peak two years of the bubble, $425 billion of investor capital flowed *into* "new economy" mutual funds, favoring those types of speculative growth stocks; $100 billion actually flowed *out* of those stodgy "old economy" value funds that would provide a peaceful refuge from the storm that was to come.

Ironically, the list of losers also included those same corporations. In order to avoid the dilution in their earnings that would otherwise have resulted from their issuance of options, the very corporations that issued those billions of options at dirt-cheap prices also bought them back—but at the inflated prices of the day. The real losers, of course, were not those corporations themselves, but their own shareholders, who lost twice: first because of the dilution in their interests caused by the options issuance, and second because the purchases of their stocks depleted corporate cash. The largest 100 companies in the S&P 500 Index actually bought back even *more* of their stocks than they issued in the form of stock option grants, while the 100 largest NASDAQ companies appear to have (wisely) bought back far smaller amounts.[12]

Stock Market Bubbles

This massive $2 trillion-plus transfer of wealth from public investors to corporate insiders and financial intermediaries during the late bubble years was hardly without precedent. Transfers of this nature and relative dimension happen over and over again whenever speculation takes precedence over investment. But a day of reckoning always follows. As the Roman orator Cato wrote some three thousand years ago: "There must certainly be a vast Fund of Stupidity in Human Nature, else Men would not be caught as they are, a thousand times over, by the same Snare, and while they yet remember their past Misfortunes, go on to court and encourage the Causes to which they were owing, and which will again produce them."[13]

While each financial bubble is different, most have been associated with the abandonment of traditional financial standards. As Edward Chancellor, author of *Devil Take the Hindmost: A History of Speculation,* reminds us, manias reflect the worst aspects of our system: "Speculative bubbles frequently occur during periods of financial innovation and deregulation . . . lax regulation is another common feature . . . there is a tendency for business to be managed for the immediate gratification of speculators rather than the long-term interests of investors."[14] What is more, bubbles often take on the attributes of castles built on sand, as sound business practices erode, integrity and ethics are compromised, and financial malfeasance creeps into the system.

One danger of such bubbles is that they undermine the notion that the stock market is an appropriate investment vehicle for long-term investors. The idea that common stocks were acceptable as investments—rather than merely speculative instruments—is said to have begun in 1925 with Edgar Lawrence Smith's *Common Stocks as Long-Term Investments.* Its most recent incarnation came in 1994, in Jeremy Siegel's *Stocks for the Long Run.*

Both books unabashedly state the case for equities and both, arguably, helped fuel the bull markets that ensued. Both books presented compelling statistical evidence that stocks were the ideal long-term investments.

Nevertheless, based on the impressive historical data on past stock returns that the books presented, the public seized on the idea that the market was somehow a risk-free venture, and that making money was inevitable. Ironically, while both books clearly emphasized the importance of long-term investing, they seemed to mute investors' apprehensions, inadvertently creating an atmosphere of short-term speculation. Apparently ignoring the inherent risk in stocks, investors of both eras seemed to make the implicit assumption that stock market history would repeat itself. When stocks are seen as a "sure thing" and prices are bid up to unsustainable levels, great bear markets follow. And so it was in the aftermath of the publication of both books.

Yet the only certainty about the equity returns that lie ahead is their very uncertainty, a lesson that, unfortunately, too often gets lost from one generation to the next. We simply do not know what the future holds, and we must accept the self-evident fact that historic stock market returns have absolutely nothing in common with actuarial tables (a point of view that is fully discussed in chapter five). "The past is history; the future's a mystery."

The Vicious Circle

The market boom and bust were based not only on the delusions of the day but on a mutation from virtuous to vicious circle—a failure of character, a triumph of hubris and greed over honesty and integrity in corporate America. It's facile to ascribe the wrongdoing of the era to just a few bad apples, and it's true that only a tiny minority of our business and financial leaders has been implicated in criminal behavior. But I believe that the barrel itself—the very structure that holds all those apples—is bad. While that may seem a harsh indictment, I believe it is a fair one.

Consider Reuters journalist Martin Howell's list of 175 "red flags," each of which describes a particular shortcoming in our recent business, financial, and investment practices.[15] I've personally observed many of these warning flags, twenty-four of which are listed in Box 1.1. They amply illustrate that those in privileged positions, corporate managers, and money managers alike who ought to have known better, rather than accepting uncritically the financial machinations and hyperbole of the so-called New Era, should have been issuing instead stern warnings to investors.

Box 1.1 Red Flags

Among the 175 "red flags" listed in Martin Howell's *Predators and Profits* are these twenty-four warning signs that trouble may be afoot in a corporation:

1. When you find the big lie, everything else crumbles around it.
2. If a technology stock is said to transform the world, it is being over-hyped.
3. When money is easy to raise, be alert to companies doomed to fail.
4. The Quitter: When a CEO leaves without an explanation.
5. Beware the worst combination of all: an aggressive CEO and a compliant CFO.
6. A CEO is known as a serial acquirer rather than a builder.
7. If a company rewards failure by repricing stock options.
8. Cross-board memberships can lead to conflicts of interest.
9. A company hides behind anti-takeover devices and ignores votes to change.
10. Companies dipping in and out of cookie-jar reserves.
11. When net profit is rising but cash flow is declining or negative.
12. Beware of accountants who are promoters of the latest business fad.
13. Don't get caught out by the latest fad; it probably won't last.
14. The SEC launches a full-scale probe into possible securities fraud.
15. A company is facing a large number of class-action law suits.
16. A CEO is built up as the new star who is going to fix everything.
17. When senior management includes the company's former auditor.
18. When CEO pay is not closely linked to performance.
19. When stock options are handed to executives like there's no to-morrow.
20. When top executives own very little of their company's stock.
21. Big payments are made to executives for their work on takeovers.
22. Companies that always meet or beat earnings expectations.
23. The use of one time earnings gains (or aggressive pension fund assumptions) to reach earnings targets.
24. A company restates its results.

Source: Martin Howell, Predators and Profits *(Upper Saddle River, N.J.: Reuters Prentice Hall, 2003). Quoted with permission. I wrote the foreword to this book.*

The Spark That Lit the Fire

It should hardly surprise us that one of the chief protagonists that sparked the fire that led to the rapid escalation in stock prices was executive compensation, closely linked with its fellow protagonist, managed earnings. Executive compensation, made manifest in the fixed-price stock option, rewarded executives for raising the price of their company's stock rather than for increasing their company's intrinsic value. (I discuss the issue of price versus value in greater depth in chapter five.) When that is what investors measure, in effect, that is what managers manage.

Executives don't need to be told what to do: achieve strong, steady earnings growth and tell Wall Street about it. Set "guidance" targets with public pronouncements of your expectations, and then meet your targets—and do it consistently, without fail. First, do it the old-fashioned way, by increasing volumes, cutting costs, raising productivity, embracing technology, and developing new products and services. Then, when *making it and doing it* isn't enough, meet your goals by *counting it,* pushing accounting principles to their very edge. And when that isn't enough, *cheat.* As we now know, too many firms did exactly that.

The stated rationale for fixed-price stock options is that they "link the interests of management with the interest of shareholders." This oft-repeated and widely accepted bromide turns out to be false. Managers don't *hold* the shares they acquire. They *sell* them, and promptly. Academic studies indicate that nearly *all* stock options are exercised as soon as they vest, and the stock is, in turn, sold *immediately.* Indeed, the term *cashless exercise*—in which the firm purchases the stock for the executive, sells it, and pays the difference to the executive when the proceeds of the sale are delivered—became commonplace. (Happily, the practice is no longer legal.) We rewarded our executives not for the reality of creating long-term economic value but for pumping up the perception of short-term stock market prices. The fact is that executives had created wealth for themselves, but not for their shareowners. Long before the stock market values melted away, executives had made a timely exodus from the market by selling much of their stock.*

---

*One caveat: Since executives have substantial human and economic capital tied up in their firms and some diversification is warranted, I recognize that moderate portions of their holdings may be sold from time to time. But they should retain holdings that are a substantial portion of their total compensation and wealth.

The Flaws of Stock Options

Even if executives were required to hold most of their stock for an extended period, however, the fixed-price stock option is fundamentally flawed as a method of aligning the interest of ownership and management:

- They are not adjusted for the cost of capital, providing a free ride even for executives who produce only humdrum returns.*
- They do not take into account dividends, so there is a perverse incentive to avoid paying dividends.
- Stock options reward the *absolute* performance of a stock rather than its performance *relative* to peers or to a stock market index.

As a result of these conceptual flaws, executive compensation takes on the appearance of a lottery, creating unworthy centimillionaires in bull markets and eliminating rewards even for worthy performers in bear markets. By making the incorrect presumption that stock price, and stock price alone, is the measure of executive performance, we produced undeserving executive celebrities and overlooked those who incrementally and consistently added real value to their corporations.

These problems were well known, and simple solutions to the executive compensation morass were readily available. Restricted stock, in which executives are awarded shares of the company and required to hold them to earn their rewards, were one obvious alternative. Companies also could have raised the option price each year or linked the stock performance with the performance of the overall market, or with a peer group. But such sensible programs were almost never used. Why? Because those alternative schemes would have required corporations to count the cost as an *expense*. This recognition of compensation expenses would have reduced the earnings that they were trying to drive ever upward. Largely because their costs were conspicuous by their absence on companies' expense statements, fixed-price options became the universal standard. Rather than consider compensation plans that made sense for the business, the self-imposed constraint of expense avoidance framed the discussion of executive pay.

As the compensation consultants are wont to say, these stock options are "free." That singular, simple anomaly bears much of the responsibility for

---

* The cost of corporate capital is generally described as the risk-free interest rate plus an equity premium. In early 2005, approximately 4¼ percent on the U.S. Treasury ten-year note, plus, say, 3 percent. Total cost of capital, 7¼ percent.

the staggering increase in these payments over the years. But stock *prices* are inherently flawed as a means of compensation. Uncritically, we came to accept stock prices as a measure of executive prowess and success, ignoring the fact that short-term fluctuations in stock prices are based only tangentially on the level of corporate earnings (even earnings that are accurately stated). Rather, short-term prices are driven by speculation, reflected in how many dollars investors are willing to pay for each dollar of earnings on any given day. But in the long run, as I will show in chapter five, virtually 100 percent of the return on stocks is determined by dividend yield and earnings growth.

Burgeoning Executive Compensation

The recent era, however, defied the long-run reality. When the S&P 500 Index rose from 130 in March 1981 to 1,527 in March of 2000, the return on investor capital, excluding dividends, was 13.8 percent per year. Earnings growth amounted to 6.2 percent annually, less than half of the return, with the remainder the result of a rise in the price-earnings ratio from eight times to thirty-two times. That increase alone accounted for 1,100 points of the 1,400-point gain, or 7.6 percent per year. If one were to attribute even a 5 percent corporate cost of capital as a threshold for a stock option grant—a return a company might have earned merely by placing all of its assets in a bank certificate of deposit—corporate management could claim responsibility for an extra return of only 1.2 percent per year. Yet when the Index reached 1,527, a stock option for ten thousand shares at $130 at the outset would have placed a cool $14 *million* on the executive's plate at its conclusion. Nice work if you can get it!

With huge option grants to corporate managers and overstated earnings, all the while disregarding the cost of these options as an expense, total executive compensation went through the roof. In 1980, the compensation of the average chief executive officer was forty-two times that of the average worker; by the year 2004, the ratio had soared to 280 times that of the average worker (down from an astonishing 531 times at the peak in 2000). Over the past quarter-century, as Table 1.1 shows, CEO compensation measured in current dollars rose nearly sixteen times over, while the compensation of the average worker slightly more than doubled. Measured in real (1980) dollars, however, the compensation of the average worker rose just 0.3 percent per year, barely enough to maintain his or her standard of living. Yet CEO compensation rose at a rate of 8.5 percent annually, increasing by more than seven times in real terms during the period.

Table 1.1. Annual salaries, the average CEO and the average worker.

	Current dollars		1980 dollars	
	CEO	Worker	CEO	Worker
1980	$625,000	$14,900	$625,000	$14,900
2004	9,840,000	35,100	4,500,000	15,900
Total increase	1,147%	136%	614%	7%
Annual rate	12.2%	3.6%	8.5%	0.3%

Sources: John A. Byrne, "Executive Pay: The Party Ain't Over Yet," Business Week, April 26, 1993; and Claudia H. Deutsch, "My Big Fat C.E.O. Paycheck," New York Times, April 3, 2005; and author's estimate.

The rationale was that these executives had "created wealth" for their shareholders. But were CEOs actually creating value commensurate with this huge increase in compensation? Certainly the average CEO was not. During that twenty-four-year period, corporations had *projected* their earnings growth at an average annual rate of 11½ percent. But they actually *delivered* growth of 6 percent per year—only half of their goal, and even less than the 6.2 percent nominal growth rate of the economy. In real terms, profits grew at an annual rate of just 2.9 percent, compared to 3.1 percent for our nation's economy, as represented by the Gross Domestic Product.[16] How that somewhat dispiriting lag can drive average CEO compensation to a cool $9.8 million in 2004 is one of the great anomalies of the age. If CEOs have failed to create value, there must be another explanation for such compensation. One can only wonder what it might be.

What is more, the staggering sums paid to CEOs are understated. The figures include only what is publicly disclosed as CEO compensation, and since our CEOs receive a host of perquisites to augment their lavish lifestyles, the reality is considerably higher. These "perks" are often undisclosed and excluded from the "total compensation" reported for officers in the proxy statement. Even the list in Box 1.2 does not exhaust the undisclosed special benefits extended to executives, such as bargain interest rates on their loans and high interest rates on their deferred compensation.

Bad Apples

Striking as they do at the heart of our capitalistic system, the corporate scandals of the recent era were unpleasant to witness. But even as "it's an ill wind that blows no good," when the bright spotlight of pub-

Box 1.2 Executive "Perks"

Since what is publicly disclosed as CEO compensation excludes the host of perquisites they receive to augment their lavish lifestyles, their compensation is actually understated. Even the list below does not exhaust the remarkable benefits paid to senior management. General Electric, for example, pays 9.5 to 14 percent interest on salary deferrals.[17]

- *Use of company aircraft for personal travel.* The cost of this most popular perk can easily run in the hundreds of thousands of dollars per executive per year. (In 2003, personal flights valued at $304,527 were paid by Citigroup for just one of its officers, executive committee chairman Robert E. Rubin, whose other pay came to $16.2 million.)
- *Payment of taxes on personal travel benefits.* A substantial extra perquisite, essentially doubling both the benefit to the executive and the cost to the shareholders.
- *Lending money to executives, then forgiving the loan.* While such loans are no longer legal, forgiveness of earlier loans can go on indefinitely. Home Depot lent $10 million to new CEO Robert Nardelli in 2000, and each year forgives one-fifth of it and the attendant interest, as well as pays the taxes on both, as "an incentive for him to stay with the company."
- *Providing "amenities."* Private boxes at sporting events, entertainment, luxury apartments, country club dues, home security systems, and so on, available only to the highest paid executives.
- *Payments to terminated executives.* As it has been said, "corporate America takes care of its own," but never more generously than the $140 million awarded to Michael Ovitz for his fourteen months of work at Walt Disney before being fired.
- *Stepped-up retirement benefits.* Generous termination bonuses and massive step-ups in pension benefits are often paid to executives when they retire, and thus slip through the reporting screen.
- *Charitable contributions* by corporations to the favorite causes of senior executives, which may even give credit to the CEO for his generosity.

In his detailed study of executive perquisites and personal aircraft usage, David Yermak of New York University suggests that the typical CEO fails to "recognize boundaries between the company's assets and his own."[18] However, Yermak also finds that perks are a useful, if inverse, diagnostic tool for investors—the higher the perquisites, the greater the likelihood the company will perform badly.

lic attention shines on major scandals, it also illuminates all the nibbling that has taken place around the edges of proper ethical practice. Were it not for the scandals, untoward practices may have persisted indefinitely. Because they call attention to a corporate barrel that itself is in need of considerable repair, we owe a certain perverse kind of debt to the fallen idols of capitalism, "bad apples" like these:

- *Kenneth Lay, Jeffrey Skilling, and Andrew Fastow* presided over the collapse of Enron, revealing a panoply of financial engineering that quickly turned to fraud. Enron's bankruptcy also turned the spotlight on the profound failings of a blue-chip board, the co-opting of its accounting firm (which also provided Enron with consulting services), and the active participation of its bankers in deals of dubious validity. Market value of Enron at pre-scandal high: $65 billion. Final market value: zero.
- *Bernard Ebbers,* CEO of the bankrupt WorldCom (later MCI), gained his position in the hall of shame when the firm cooked the books, resulting in an $11 billion accounting scandal. To avoid selling his own shares to meet margin calls, he had borrowed a stunning $408 million, which WorldCom's board guaranteed. (The Sarbanes-Oxley Act now bans corporate loans to executives.) Market value of WorldCom at pre-scandal high: $165 billion. Final market value: zero.
- *William Esrey and Ronald LeMay* of Sprint gained the spotlight with their receipt of $287 million in option compensation, paid to reward them for a merger (with the aforesaid WorldCom, of all choices) that in fact was never consummated. Their subsequent attempt to dodge taxes through an allegedly illegal tax shelter also raised the issue of collusion by the firm's independent auditor in the setting of executive compensation. Market value of Sprint at pre-scandal high: $58 billion. Market value in early 2005: $32 billion.
- *Dennis Kozlowski,* the CEO of Tyco, gained his first unwelcome attention with a clumsy attempt to illegally evade state sales taxes on $13 million of art purchases, quickly followed by disclosure of the $2 million Roman-theme party given in Sardinia for his wife's birthday. The fete included the now-famous ice statue of Michelangelo's *David* exuding, as it were, vodka. But the spotlight on those events quickly illuminated a classic case of a manager's confusing the share-

holders' money with his own, as he allegedly looted Tyco and its shareholders of $600 million. Market value of Tyco at pre-scandal high: $117 billion. Market value in early 2005: $68 billion.

- *Jack Welch* of General Electric gained an equally unwelcome spotlight for his extramarital peccadilloes. His divorce proceedings illuminated the "stealth" compensation typically awarded to retired chief executives but rarely disclosed. While his total compensation as GE's CEO surely approached $1 billion, his lavish retirement benefits, valued by one commentator at $2 million per year, included a New York apartment with daily flower deliveries and wine, and unlimited use of a company jet. He also was awarded a generous retirement stipend of $734,000 . . . *per month*. Nonetheless, he seems to have little to spare, given that his charitable giving came to just $614 per month.* Market value of GE at 2000 high, $600 billion. Market value in early 2005: $379 billion.

- *Steve Case* of AOL. In an extraordinary example of the delusions of grandeur that characterized the information age, the news of the marriage of the "new economy" AOL and the "old economy" Time Warner as 2000 began sent the price of Time Warner soaring to a then-all-time high of $90 per share. But AOL's revenues began to tumble almost immediately. Barely two years after the merger was announced, the firm reported losses totaling $98 *billion*. In the heady days before the bubble burst, Case, the founder of AOL (and the chairman of the merged company) sold nearly one-half *billion* dollars worth of his shares, mostly at boom-level prices. The stock value declined to a low of $9.64. Market value of AOL at pre-scandal high: $226 billion. Combined market value of Time Warner and AOL at merger, $240 billion. Market value in early 2005: $82 billion.

- *Richard Grasso,* chairman of the New York Stock Exchange, made news with the disclosure in 2004 of the staggeringly large compensation package ($187.5 million) bestowed on him by those he regulated. The spotlight also illuminated the salutary (if not explosive) effects of disclosure, the Big Board's flawed system of governance,

---

*While the Good Book says "judge not, lest ye be judged," the tight-fisted charitable giving of such fabulously wealthy executives appalls me. Another example is Sam Waksal, imprisoned for his crimes at ImClone. He earned $134 million in 1999–2001 and gave but $157,451 to charity, implicitly telling the world, "¹⁄10 of 1 percent for the greater good, 99.9 percent for me."

and the near-monopoly it maintains for its member firms and specialists, who operate each day with bountiful inside information about the buying power of, and selling pressure from, investors who intend to engage in trades. Value of seat on the New York Stock Exchange at 1999 high, $2.65 million. Value in early 2005, $975,000.

There are many other "bad apples" whom I might as easily have mentioned, but these seven examples should be enough to make the point that the scandals of the recent era have brought into sharp relief the painfully broad and baneful impact of managers' capitalism, and the financial shenanigans that it fomented.

The problem goes far beyond the few renegades I have listed as bad apples. The traditional nature of capitalism has been distorted, and today's version is riddled with problems reflected in serious manipulation of financial statements. Indeed, since the market crash, some 1,570 publicly owned firms have restated their earlier financial statements, including some of our largest global corporations, such as Royal Dutch/Shell, the giant oil company, Schering-Plough, Qwest, Bristol-Meyers Squibb, Xerox, and Halliburton. (See Box 1.3.)

Managers' Capitalism in the Driver's Seat

Clearly, owners' capitalism had been superseded by managers' capitalism, and managers' capitalism has created great distortions in our business world and our society alike. Our imperial chief executives, with all their fame, their jet planes, their perquisites, their pension plans, their club dues, their Park Avenue apartments, appear to have forgotten that they are employees of the corporation's owners. The owners seem to have forgotten it, too. But executive character has not gone unnoticed. CEOs are now close to the bottom of the barrel in public trust. One survey showed that while 75 percent of the general public trust shopkeepers, 73 percent trust the military, and 60 percent trust doctors, only 25 percent trust corporate executives—slightly above the 23 percent that trust used-car dealers.[19]

These self-styled lions of capitalism, often so powerful, charismatic, and demanding that they earned the title "imperial" CEOs, typically drew compensation that suggested that they alone controlled the fates of their companies. As silly as this claim is, more than a few were willing contributors to this fantasy, too often arrogant, greedy, and vainglorious, convinced that "they did it all by themselves" and are worth every penny they were paid.

Box 1.3 Bad Apples or Bad Barrel? Phase I

Corporate America Restates Its Earnings

While the miscreants of corporate America are often dismissed as a few "bad apples," the abuses of the barrel of capitalism have been pervasive. The corporations listed below, many with market capitalizations of $100 billion or more, have restated earnings or been involved in settlements with the Securities and Exchange Commission (without admitting or denying guilt). Their aggregate market value, measured at their individual highs, totaled some $3 trillion, an enormous part of the giant barrel of corporate capitalism.

Adelphia	Kodak
American International Group	Krispy Kreme
Avon	Legato Systems
Boeing	Lernout & Hauspie
Bristol-Myers Squibb	Lucent Technologies
Cendant	Marsh McClennan
Ceridian	MBIA
Citibank	Merrill Lynch
Coca-Cola	MGIC
Computer Associates	Micro Strategy
Conseco	Microsoft
Critical Path	Network Associates
Dynegy	Oxford Health Plans
Enron	Peregrine Systems
Fannie Mae	PNC Financial Services
Fleming Companies	Qwest Communications
Freddie Mac	Raytheon Corporation
Gateway	Reliant Resources/Energy
GemStar—TV Guide	Rite Aid
International	Royal Dutch/Shell
General Electric	Safety Kleen Corp
Global Crossing	Silicon Graphics
Halliburton	Spiegel
Hanover Compressor	Sunbeam
HBO McKesson Robbins	Symbol Technologies
HealthSouth	The Shell Transport Co.
Homestore	Time Warner
Household International	Trump Hotels & Casino Resorts
Informix	Tyco
Interpublic	Warnaco Group
Kimberly Clark	Waste Management
Kmart	WorldCom

But while so many business managers took the credit (and the cash) for themselves, it was our expanding national economy and our booming stock market that made them look good. So long as their own wealth was growing, investors accepted uncritically the idea that the high rewards generated in CEO compensation were well deserved.

The reality was far different: While our CEOs created enormous wealth for themselves, far beyond what our thriving economy delivered, they had failed to create extra wealth for their shareowners. And when the bubble burst and the stock market values melted away, these operators had long since sold hundreds of billions of dollars worth of their own stock to the public (and even to their own companies), leaving the new owners holding the bag.

Executive pay is out of control because compensation committees aren't doing their job. But the consultants *are* doing theirs. They are *paid* by management to *advise* management *how much* management should be paid. Small wonder that in 2000, for example, we observed awards for achievement for CEOs running from as high as $92 million, to $125 million, to $151 million, and to, believe it or not, $872 million. *For a single individual in a single year!* These numbers, of course, find their way into the great compensation database, which in turn ratchets up when awards for 2001 are considered, moving formerly *average* awards into *below average* territory. And so the compensation norms rise again. It is truly a sick system, all the more difficult to cure since "everyone is doing it," and the process has the superficial appearance of being rational.

Managers' capitalism, then, is more than just a provocative idea. It carries a high cost to corporate owners that can be measured. A study by two professors from Harvard Law School and Cornell University recently found that the compensation of the five highest-paid executives in each of the 1,500 companies included in the Standard & Poor's 500, Mid-Cap 400, and Small-Cap 600 indexes during 1993–2003 alone was in excess of $300 billion.[20] What is more, despite the fact that the reported corporate earnings grew at a puny 1.9 percent nominal annual rate during the period they examined, the share of corporate profits consumed by these executives not only rose, but more than doubled—from 4.8 percent of profits in 1993–95 to 10.3 percent in 2001–3. A long time ago, even as staunch a conservative as former president Herbert Hoover said, "You know, the only trouble with capitalism is capitalists. They're too darn greedy."[21] Just imagine what he'd say today.

Extraordinary Compensation for Ordinary Performance

The record is clear that investors have a big stake in executive compensation. A study by Morgan Stanley's former chief strategist Steve Galbraith found that "one way [for CEOs] to rake in the dough has been to preside over a company with an underfunded pension plan, large layoffs, and mediocre stock performance."[22] (While Mr. Galbraith does not argue causality, more extensive studies may well make such a case.) Analyzing the 500 companies in the S&P Index, he found that the six companies whose CEOs made more than $50 million in 2002 provided average annualized returns in 2002–3 of *minus* 40 percent, compared to minus 3 percent for the remaining companies in the Index.

Galbraith argues that "the root appeal of capitalism revolves around extraordinary reward potential for extraordinary performance, [but] what is less understandable are extraordinary compensation packages handed out for ordinary performance."[23] Thus, despite wildly errant growth projections, these seemingly failed executives (or terrible forecasters) were rewarded with increases that took their average annual compensation to new heights—an amazing failure of prudent governance by corporate directors. Paraphrasing Churchill, never has so much been paid by so many to so few for so little.

Managed Earnings

Hand in hand with the excesses of CEO compensation came "managed earnings" as a major contributor to the stock market boom. Sleight-of-hand financial engineering produced quarterly profits that were viewed by investors as predictable and recurring. The result: handsome rewards to those projecting unprecedented levels of future earnings growth, and then, with the skill of the alchemist, delivering the results they had forecast.

During the 1990s, the idea of corporations providing quarterly earnings guidance took hold and quickly was followed by earnings management. "Exceeded expectations," or "met expectations" (or, heaven forbid, "failed to meet expectations") became the jargon of corporate America's financial reporting. Market participants anxiously awaited each company's quarterly announcement, quickly comparing it with the earlier "guidance." What was ultimately revealed, however, is what we always knew to be true: relying on the accrual accounting that is the basis for corporate financial statements is an act of faith, no more, no less. As the eminent economist Peter Bernstein has written: "The financial statement records as revenues money not yet received. It excludes from expenses money actually paid out if spent on assets expected to produce revenues in the future."[24] And when earnings guidance is given, there seem to have been few limits on the earliest possible recognition of revenues and the latest possible recognition of expenses. On some occasions, fraud was involved.

A 2004 study by Thomson Financial found that since 1998 companies have missed their analysts' expectations only 16 percent of the time. The remaining 84 percent of the time they at least met expectations—23 percent exactly, another 22 percent by an additional one penny per share, and 39 percent by more than one penny—remarkable predictability, during good times and bad times alike, in complicated businesses with many lines of endeavor. It was, of course, "too good to be true."

For such performance defies common sense. Thoughtful investors know that while business growth may follow rough trend lines, quarterly surprises are inevitable. Accounting results that show otherwise are nonsense. Although it seems absurd that a company that misses its guidance by a mere penny can see its market capitalization promptly plummet by several billions of dollars, in a certain way the logic is unexceptionable: if, with all that financial pushing and pulling and stretching, the company nonetheless falls short of its guidance, it is only a matter of time before the chickens come home to roost in the form of a major negative surprise.

Such surprises, it turns out, can be measured. At least some overaggressive accounting is often uncovered later by federal and state regulators, requiring the kinds of earnings restatements catalogued in Box 1.3. In total, some 1,570 public companies restated their earnings from 2000 to 2004, seven times the 218 companies that restated their earnings from 1990 to 1994.[25] While many corporate executives have already been paid huge bonuses based on those engineered earnings, I have not heard of a single instance in which their bonuses have been recalculated and the overpayments returned to the stockholders.

Future Pension Fund Returns

Nowhere is the fiction of managed earnings more apparent than in the assumptions of future returns made by corporate pension funds. Over the past decade the yield on the ten-year U.S. Treasury bond has plummeted from 7.9 percent to 4.2 percent—a drop of 45 percent—and the prospective investment return on stocks (dividend yield plus assumed 5 percent earnings growth) has fallen by 15 percent, to 6.8 percent. For a typical pension portfolio (60 percent stocks, 40 percent bonds), the expected market return would be 5.8 percent. Yet in 2004, the average corporate pension fund assumed a future annual return of 8.6 percent, 35 percent higher. To make a bad situation worse, neither return takes into account investment costs, nor leaves a reserve against the unexpected. The fact is that pension funds should probably be counting on future annual long-term returns, net of investment costs, of something like 5 percent per year. (I cover this subject in greater depth in chapter five.)

Manipulating pension returns has played a major role in enabling corporations to manage their earnings, for in few other places on the corporate books are unbridled estimates of assets and liabilities so easy to adjust. Yet, it is only in recent years that pension projections have become the stuff of scandal—"pension deficit disorder," using the inspired phrase of Morgan Stanley strategist Henry H. McVey—and the Securities and Exchange Commission (SEC) is investigating the issue. We shall learn much more about how corporations—in league with their highly paid actuarial consultants—have managed earnings by managing their pension assumptions.

Changing pension assumptions can make an astonishing difference in corporate earnings. Consider this example:

> In 2001, Verizon Communications reported a net income of $389 million and awarded its executives bonuses based on that amount. Net income would have been negative, however, had the company not included $1.8 billion of pension income. Thus, Verizon was able to use pension earnings to convert net income to profits, giving the firm cover to provide managers with higher bonuses. It gets worse. It turns out that Verizon's pension funds did not generate *any* real income in 2001; they had negative investment returns, losing $3.1 billion in value. How, then, could Verizon report income of $1.8 billion from its pension assets? The company merely increased its projection of future returns on pension assets to 9.25 percent, a move allowed under the accounting rules then in effect. Thus, the $1.8 billion in pension income used to move Verizon into the black did not even reflect actual returns generated by the pension funds. The pension income was simply the result of a change in the accounting assumptions. This certainly did not create any value for the firm or its shareholders.[26]

A New Kind of Capitalism

The change from traditional owners' capitalism to the new managers' capitalism is at the heart of what went wrong in corporate America. It was reflected in the stock market bubble and the subsequent market burst, during which at least $2 trillion of wealth was transferred from public investors to corporate insiders, entrepreneurs, and financial intermediaries. Largely through stock options, executive compensation reached extraordinary levels, despite the production of corporate profits that were in fact, measured by the growth of our economy, *less* than ordinary. Managed earnings was an important engine of the system, and its goal, at least implicitly, was to raise corporate stock prices whether or not increases in intrinsic corporate values were achieved. It is that pathological mutation in capitalism that largely explains what went wrong. Explaining why it went wrong is the province of the next chapter.

Why Did Corporate America Go Wrong?

"Somebody's Gotta Keep an Eye on These Geniuses"

The failure of corporate governance lies at the heart of why corporate America went astray. As James Madison wrote in *The Federalist Papers* in 1788, "If men were angels, no government would be necessary." Similarly, in describing capitalism today, we could aptly say, "If business executives were angels, no corporate governance would be necessary."

The analogy between national and corporate governance is fitting. Just as the United States is not a pure *democracy,* controlled directly by its citizens, neither is the American corporation. (Even approvals of corporate resolutions by shareholders are often nonbinding.) Rather, like our nation, the corporation is a *republic,* with supreme power vested in its shareholders, who exercise their power through the directors they elect, who are charged with representing their ownership interests. In the search for productivity and efficiency the shareholders, perhaps because of their knowledge of their own limitations, cede control to those who will act in their behalf. Indeed, in both our national and our corporate republics, sometimes the trust of the constituency is honored, sometimes betrayed. But while our republican federal government operates under a system of checks and balances, similar limits rarely prevail among our republican corporations.

Indeed, we have come perilously close to accepting a system of *dictatorship* in corporate America, a system in which the power of the CEO seems virtually unfettered. My peer business leaders of course don't look at their jobs in those terms. When I raised this topic in a speech to the Business Council in 2003, the assembled group of CEOs was not particularly smitten by the analogy. But it holds more than a grain of truth.

The republican system of corporate governance has broken down. Too many boards have failed to adequately exercise their responsibilities of managerial oversight. Worse, it was only the rare institutional investor that exercised its responsibilities of corporate citizenship and demanded such oversight, insisting that managers operate not in their own interest, but in the interest of the owners. In short, the owners didn't seem to care. When the *owners* of corporate America don't care about governance, who on earth *should* care?

Writing in *The New Yorker* a few years ago, business columnist James Surowiecki gave us an amusing but perceptive answer. He used the example of the 1956 comedy *The Solid Gold Cadillac,* in which Judy Holliday played Laura Partridge, a small investor. Her continual harassment of the board of directors finally forces the company to put her on the payroll as its first director of investor relations. She quickly uses the position to organize a shareholder revolt that topples the corrupt CEO. As Surowiecki concludes: "American companies are the most productive and inventive in the world, but a little adult supervision [by the owners] wouldn't hurt. Laura Partridge had it right a half a century ago: 'Somebody's gotta keep an eye on these geniuses.'"[1]

Under our governance system, the board of directors is the first "somebody." It is the board that is charged with holding management responsible to represent the interests of shareholders. And when the directors don't fulfill that responsibility, the second "somebody" must hold the board accountable: the shareholders themselves. If the directors do not provide the necessary "adult supervision" required to move us away from the existing system of managers' capitalism that we never should have allowed to come into existence in the first place, then it is up to the shareholders to do so. As owners, they have the right to vigorously demand a return to the system that began all those years ago, a system in which trusting and being trusted created a virtuous circle of progress. Only the owners can return us to owners' capitalism.

This is not to say that the long history of capitalism has been bereft of aberrations. The Robber Barons of the late nineteenth century, the competition-stifling business trusts of the early twentieth century, the utility-holding companies of the 1920s, all were betrayals of trust. But the ugly deviations from fair play in the recent era represent a new breed of corruption. It required only two ingredients:

1. The diffusion of corporate ownership among a large number of investors, none holding a controlling share of the voting power.
2. The unwillingness of the agents of the owners—the boards of directors—to honor their responsibility to serve, above all else, the interests of their principals—the shareowners themselves.

The Modern Corporation and Private Property

The issue of widely diffused corporate ownership was first examined systematically in 1932, as the stock market was tumbling to its nadir in the Great Crash of 1929–33. During this period, an astonishing 90 percent of the market value of U.S. equities was erased. The examiners were Adolph A. Berle and Gardiner C. Means, professors at Columbia University whose seminal work on this topic, *The Modern Corporation and Private Property*, has become enshrined as an enduring business classic. They were concerned about the separation of the ownership from the control of publicly held corporations. With corporate ownership becoming more widely diffused among legions of individual investors, none of whom, in most cases, held anything resembling a controlling interest (there was then virtually no institutional ownership of stocks), they posited that the door was wide open for senior managers to operate companies in their own self-interest.

Their principal conclusions:

- Most fundamental of all, the position of ownership has changed from that of an active to that of a passive agent. The owner now holds a piece of paper representing a set of rights and expectations with respect to an enterprise, but [he] has little control. The owner is practically powerless to affect the underlying property through his own efforts.
- The spiritual values that formerly went with ownership have been separated from it. Physical property capable of being shaped by its owner could bring to him direct satisfaction apart from the income it yielded in more concrete form.

- The value of an individual's wealth is determined on the one hand by the actions of the individuals in command of the enterprise— individuals over whom the typical owner has no control—and on the other hand, by the actions of others in a sensitive and often capricious market. The value is thus subject to the vagaries and manipulations characteristic of the marketplace.
- The value of the individual's wealth not only fluctuates constantly, but is subject to a constant appraisal. The individual can see the change in the appraised value of his estate from moment to moment, a fact which may markedly affect both the expenditure of his income and his enjoyment of that income.
- Individual wealth has become extremely liquid through the organized markets, convertible into other forms of wealth at a moment's notice.
- Finally, in the corporate system, the "owner" of industrial wealth is left with a mere symbol of ownership while the power, the responsibility, and the substance which have been an integral part of ownership in the past are being transferred to a separate group in whose hands lies control.[2]

Berle and Means, insightful prophets of how corporate control would evolve, had identified a problem that would plague modern capitalism, a problem that has yet to be resolved. But in that era of deeply depressed stock prices, with corporations struggling to achieve profitability, perhaps even an era in which standards of business conduct were higher (albeit not without some notorious abusers), their warnings gained little public notice. Only decades later, in a booming stock market environment that was aided and abetted by the happy conspiracy among virtually all market participants, did we realize the residual effects that arose from passive ownership by shareholders, including excessive management compensation, managed earnings, and merger mania. The worst potential abuses of managers' capitalism became stark realities.

When most owners either don't or won't or can't stand up for their rights, when directors lose sight of whom they represent, and when financial manipulation is unchecked by the system's gatekeepers, corporate managers quickly step in to fill the void, confirming Spinoza's claim that "nature abhors a vacuum." Little good is likely to result when the CEO becomes not only boss of the business but boss of the board, erasing the bright line that common sense tells us ought to exist between management and governance. Put more harshly, in an unattributed quote that I came across a few years ago, "when we have strong managers, weak directors, and passive owners, don't be surprised when the looting begins."

Adam Smith, that patron saint of capitalism, would not have been surprised by this outcome. More than two centuries ago, he wrote: "It cannot be well expected that the directors of companies, being the managers rather of other people's money than of their own, should watch over it with the same anxious vigilance with which partners in a private copartnery frequently watch over their own. Like the stewards of a rich man, they . . . very easily give themselves a dispensation. Negligence and profusion must always prevail."[3]

Adam Smith's words presciently describe corporate America in the recent era. While the actual looting we know about has been limited, negligence and profusion have been rife, and managers have given themselves, using Smith's word, "dispensations" that would have appalled the thrifty Scot. But the malfeasance in our capitalistic system has spread far beyond executive compensation to the very financial integrity of our corporations. The contradictions of managers' capitalism lie behind the failures of the system that we've witnessed.

The Failure of the Gatekeepers: Directors

Stock owners have traditionally relied on a whole bevy of gatekeepers to ensure that corporations would be operated with honesty and integrity, and in their interests. During the Great Bull Market of 1997–2000, however, we witnessed a fatal breakdown among all of these gatekeepers. Independent auditors became business partners of management. The investment community put aside its professionalism, its traditional skepticism, and even its independence. Government regulations were relaxed. Our elected public officials not only didn't care but actually stood by, aiding and abetting the malfeasance. Worst of all, corporate directors, who should have constituted the front line of defense against management overreaching, failed to fulfill their responsibilities.

Directors are the most important of the gatekeepers that society relies on to keep corporations functioning productively, efficiently, and honestly. Given the business savvy of board members, their joint perspective, and their intimacy with the particular organization they serve, they are well placed to intervene, when necessary, on behalf of shareholders. But corporate boards often seemed reluctant, unwilling, and perhaps even unable to govern with a firm hand. As a result, our directors must assume a major portion of the responsibility for the problems that developed in corporate America.

Despite being the elected representatives of the owners, boards of directors looked on the proceedings with benign neglect, apparently unmindful of the impending storm. Lightning first struck Enron. When the firm collapsed in November 2001, the *New York Times* described it as a "catastrophic corporate implosion . . . that encompassed the company's auditors, lawyers, and directors . . . regulators, financial analysts, credit rating agencies, the media, and Congress . . . a massive failure in the governance system."[4] Other dominoes soon fell, including WorldCom, Adelphia, Global Crossing, and Tyco. In the years that followed, still more disreputable companies were to surface.

Public Accountants as Gatekeepers

Next among the gatekeepers are our certified public accountants. The role of the CPA is to attest to the fact that a company's financial statements follow generally accepted accounting principles (GAAP), and to provide reasonable assurance that they are free of material misstatement. It would seem obvious, then, that our CPAs should have constituted a vital line of defense against pushing accounting standards to the edge and beyond, providing at least some protection against questionable financial practices and reporting. (While it is no easy matter to uncover outright fraud—after all, the perpetrators of fraud are clever at hiding it—too many borderline cases were not vigorously questioned.) Further, our accounting standards themselves had gradually become debased. "Cookie jar" reserves were created after corporate mergers and off-balance sheet special purpose enterprises flourished, creating debt that was invisible to the public eye and giving "financial engineering" a whole new meaning.

There always has been pressure on accountants to conform their opinions to those of the corporate clients who pay for their services. But over the past decade, to that seemingly unavoidable conflict of interest has been added the conflict of being business partners with their clients, providing management consulting services whose revenues often dwarfed their audit fees. In the year 2000, for example, U.S. corporations paid their auditors nearly $3 billion for auditing services, only one-half of the $6 billion paid for consulting. The profit from non-audit revenues almost certainly constituted an even higher proportion of these firms' net earnings.

How vigorous an advocate for truth-in-earnings, for example, could Motorola's auditor be? In 2000, the audit firm was paid a staggering $62.3 million for systems development and "all other services," more than fifteen *times* as much as the $3.9 million it received in audit fees. In that case, the firm's audit committee reported that such a disparity was nonetheless "compatible with maintaining the independence of such auditors." The same conclusion was drawn at Enron, where $29 million of consulting fees were paid to its accounting firm, even larger than its $23 million of audit fees. Any mix of consulting services with accounting services places pressure on the auditor to compromise its accounting probity with its business priorities. And when that mix is heavily overbalanced with consulting services, the pressure is close to irresistible.*

Yes, accountants argue that their "reputation risk" provides assurance to shareholders and the public that the attestation firm will hold fast to proper accounting standards. But those standards are technical, vague, and often easily subverted. Further, the auditors' position ignores the countervailing argument that a rigid, principled firm that garners the reputation of never compromising one iota with its client on matters that involve some subjectivity may be taking an even larger risk—not only the risk of losing the client who tires of their pesky primness, but of chasing away potential clients who feel the same way. In any event, reputation risk proved a weak reed on which to lean in maintaining audit standards. Even as Enron went down, so did its so-called independent auditor, Arthur Andersen.

As managers promised quarterly earnings growth that became impossible to deliver as an operating matter, the added pressure on accountants to accede to management's demands was multiplied. Consequently, a company's *numbers* became more important than a company's *business*. This change is a direct contradiction to the advice given to his professional colleagues by James Anyon, America's first accountant, way back in 1912:

---

*These are hardly unusual or hyperbolic examples. In the same year, Sprint paid Ernst and Young $2.5 million for audit services and $63.8 million for other services; GE paid KMPG $23.9 million for audit and $79.7 million for other services; and for J.P. Morgan Chase, the respective expenditures to Pricewaterhouse Coopers were $21.3 million and $84.2 million. After the Sarbanes-Oxley Act prohibited auditors from providing a wide range of non-audit services to clients, expenditures on other services tumbled. In 2004, direct audit expenditures by Motorola, GE, and J.P. Morgan Chase came to an average of just 67 percent of the total, with the remaining 33 percent allocated to audit-related fees (acquisitions, retirement plans, Sarbanes-Oxley costs, etc.) and tax services. Fees paid to auditors for other services by these representative firms were zero.

"Think and act upon facts, truths, and principles, and regard figures only as things to express them. . . . So proceeding, [you will be] a credit to one of the truest and finest professions in the land."[5] As we came to rely on figures to present facts, truths, and principles of shaky validity, the creative accounting of the recent era took us a long, long way from Mr. Anyon's eternal wisdom.

"Pro Forma Earnings"

Our accounting gatekeepers were silent partners with the managements they were obliged to audit in the acceptance of "pro forma earnings," the epitome of the era's financial shenanigans. As Humpty Dumpty might have told Alice, "When I report my earnings per share, it means just what I choose it to mean—neither more nor less . . . the question is who is to be the master—that's all." And so, for example, Yahoo! makes itself the master in this example: having telegraphed that its expected earnings for the third quarter of 2001 would break even, it reported in the first paragraph of its earnings release that its net income totaled one cent per share—"beating expectations." A footnote to the release pointed out that the pro forma earnings figure *excludes* "depreciation, amortization, payroll taxes on option exercises, investment gains and losses, stock compensation expenses, acquisition-related and restructuring costs."[6] The *Wall Street Journal* reported that investors were "encouraged" by the news, doubtless pleased that Yahoo! exceeded expectations, even though it didn't actually have any earnings; in fact, Yahoo! *lost* four cents per share.[7]

Yahoo! is not alone. The fact is that in 2001, 1,500 companies reported pro forma earnings—what their earnings *would* have been *if* all those bad things hadn't happened, and *if* all those customary costs of doing business had simply vanished. Ignoring the all-too-real costs of restructuring charges, asset write-downs from discontinued operations, stock option expenses, and research and development systems purchased from other companies, of course, results in the substantial overstatement of the earnings that corporations report. As a result, the gap between *reported* earnings and *operating* earnings (before write-offs) got completely out of hand. In the ten years that ended in 2000, for example, annual *operating* earnings per share for the S&P 500 Index typically exceeded *reported* earnings by 11 percent per year. What is more, while operating earnings as stated grew at a 9.0 percent rate, the growth rate tumbled to just 4.9 percent after adjustments only for pension and health care expenses and stock option grants, a reduction of 45 percent. Yet few voices were raised to challenge this chimera, and "operating earnings" remains the financial community's principal measure of a stock's value.

Enron put undisclosed off-balance-sheet items into the headlines. The firm created "special purpose enterprises" that were not shown on the balance sheet, relying on the loophole that if an outside owner holds 3 percent of the stock in a subsidiary, neither the debt incurred (even when guaranteed by the parent) nor the losses realized (or, for that matter, unrealized) need be reported. In retrospect, of course, that failure to disclose was absurd. Let us hope that with our eyes at last opened to the manipulation that is going on, we establish new accounting principles that will eliminate such a huge loophole and require that those hidden liabilities be reflected on the balance sheet.

In 2000, one year before Enron, I expressed this view in a lecture at New York University entitled "Public Accounting: Profession or Business?"

Sound securities markets require sound financial information. It is as simple as that. Investors require—and have a right to require—complete information about each and every security, *information that fairly and honestly represents every significant fact and figure that might be needed to evaluate the worth of a corporation.* Not only is accuracy required but, more than that, a broad sweep of information that provides *every appropriate figure that a prudent, probing, sophisticated professional investor might require* in the effort to decide whether a security should be purchased, held, or sold. *Full disclosure. Fair disclosure. Complete disclosure.* Those are the watchwords of the financial system that has contributed so much to our nation's growth, progress, and prosperity.[8]

Observing those disclosure standards—not merely generally accepted accounting principles but far more—surely would have helped to prevent the Enron bubble from inflating and then imploding, and spared investors and employees from the fallout. Under those standards, the special-purpose enterprises that lie unaccounted for on a firm's balance sheet would have been revealed. Similarly, the revenue assumptions based on projecting commodity prices ten years out would have been open to challenge by stockholders and security analysts. The wise investor's rule must be: *trust but verify.* But stockholders can only verify what is revealed.

The Financial Community as Gatekeeper

In an earlier era, professional security analysts might have been expected to help fill the void left by so many boards and auditors, calling attention to managed earnings, financial engineering, and auditor complicity. But the "sell-side" security analysts employed by Wall Street's giant brokerage and investment banking firms proved to be far more interested in making recommendations for buying stocks ("good news") rather than recommendations for selling them ("bad news"). Further, with the outpouring of lucrative initial public offerings during the market mania, many of no obvious inherent value, the pressure on these sell-side professionals to appraise the new issues with grossly excessive generosity was greatly intensified. They put aside their analytical training and joined the marketing arm of their firms, helping not only to sell new issues of stocks and bonds to the public but to attract new clients who would be prospects for "going public." Wall Street was a major participant in, and contributor to, the financial mischief of the day, and proved to be utterly worthless as a responsible gatekeeper that watched over corporate conduct.

We might have expected the "buy side" to do better. Some 75,000 professional security analysts now ply their trade in our giant financial institutions, including 62,000 who hold the designation "chartered financial analyst." But while their mandate is bereft of the conflicts inherent in the mix of investment banking, brokerage, and security analysis in a single firm, these independent analysts apparently succumbed to the mania as well. They set aside their education, their training, their skepticism, their independence, their responsibility, their duty, and often their integrity, accepting, if not aiding and abetting, the financial shenanigans. Of course, as money poured into the funds they managed, they were well compensated for their participation in the mania.

In retrospect, it's astonishing that the voices of concern among the members of money management community were barely raised. Indeed, these managers, like so many others, seemed to develop a vested interest in the short-term price of a stock, heavily influenced by whether or not the company's quarterly earnings were meeting the guidance given to Wall Street, and virtually ignoring what the company was actually worth—its intrinsic long-term value, measured largely by its fundamental earning power and its balance sheet. When Oscar Wilde described the cynic as "a man who knows the price of everything but the value of nothing," he could have as easily been describing our security analysts during the recent era.

Even as institutional owners were participants in the happy conspiracy to inflate stock prices during the boom, so they were leaders in the happy conspiracy of silence in its aftermath.

Regulators and Legislators as Gatekeepers

On the regulatory and legislative front, our public servants, who might otherwise have served as gatekeepers, were pressed into relaxing existing regulations for accounting standards and disclosure. When proposals for reform came—for example, requiring that stock options *actually be counted* as a compensation expense, or prohibiting accountants from providing consulting services to the firms they audit—the outrage of our legislators, inspired (if that's the right word) both by political contributions and by the fierce lobbying efforts of corporate America and the accounting profession, thwarted these long overdue changes. Too many of our elected officials abdicated their public duty in favor of the corporations that vigorously advocated their desire to preserve the status quo, and succeeded in large measure because of the "pay-to-play" standard that has come to dominate the political scene.

The power of our private managers over our public servants was exemplified by the ability of business lobbyists to persuade Congress to nullify the 1993 attempt by the Financial Accounting Standards Board (FASB) to require stock options to be expensed in corporate earnings statements. In June 1993, Senator Joseph Lieberman introduced a bill condemning the FASB's attempt, which passed the Senate overwhelmingly. He later introduced a side bill that would have put the FASB out of business if it implemented its option-expensing initiative. The FASB had little choice but to retreat, a sad example of legislation interfering in accounting decisions.

A similar event also took place when Congress forced the SEC to back down on its 1998 proposal to disallow a single firm to provide both auditing services and consulting services to the same client. When I testified before the SEC at the hearings on that issue, I was challenged to find a "smoking gun" in the form of data that linked the provision of consulting services to audit failures. I could only respond, "sometimes statistics cannot prove what common sense makes obvious." Confirming that judgment, the series of accounting scandals began to unfold only two years later.

Two centuries ago, Thomas Jefferson said, "I hope we shall crush in its birth the aristocracy of our moneyed corporations which dare already to challenge our government in a trial of strength, and bid defiance to the laws of our country."[9] The recent era of managers' capitalism presents one more example of the consequences of allowing "the aristocracy of our moneyed corporations" free rein. Rather than taking the risk of blatantly defying our laws, our moneyed corporations took the safer route of thwarting remedial legislation, thereby compromising the best interests of their own stockholders.

Stewardship: The Responsibility of the Board

Of all these gatekeepers, surely it is the board of directors that should have been the front line of defense. Why? Because it is the directors' job to be good stewards of the corporate property entrusted to it. In medieval England, the common use of the word *stewardship* was religious: the responsible use of the congregation's resources in the faithful service of God. In the secular world of corporate America, the word has come to mean the use of the enterprise's resources in the faithful service of its owners. Yet far too many corporate directors have been placed in positions of great power and authority without a full understanding of their fiduciary duty: to ensure that the corporation's assets are responsibly employed in the faithful service of the company's owners.

It is not clear exactly why boards turned away from their traditional stewardship role. But it's easy to hypothesize that during an era of remarkable prosperity and a booming stock market—when managers and investors alike were paying too much attention to stock prices and not enough attention to corporate values—directors relaxed their vigilance. After all, corporate profitability (or at least apparent corporate profitability) was soaring, and directors were largely unaware of the growing collusion between public accountants and company managers, and the retreat of much regulatory oversight.

What is more, the instant wealth amassed by the creators and leaders of new information age companies in a rush of IPOs created great pressure to allow the compensation of CEOs in other, often more mundane industries, to run amok. In boardrooms where collegiality rather than dissent remained the watchword and managers controlled the information presented to the directors, it would have been easier than ever for our increasingly prominent and ever-more-imperial CEOs to dominate the agenda. Indeed, the rise of the term *chief executive officer,* which itself goes back only to 1950, may well have been a factor in elevating the perceived importance of senior corporate managers, and hence their compensation.* But perhaps the onset of the "bottom line" society of our age was the most important factor of all in causing the notion of stewardship to recede.

As directors turned over the virtually unfettered power to the company's managers to place their own interests first, both the word *stewardship* and the concept of stewardship became conspicuous by their absence from corporate America's agenda. Managers drove their subordinates to cooperate in the financial engineering of the day. Some 60 percent of corporate employees, for example, report that they have observed violations of law or company policy at their firms, many that went unchallenged or were handled all too gently. Two hundred and seven of 300 "whistle-blowers" report they lost their jobs as a result of reporting violations they observed. In such an environment, the ethical culture that is an important and vital preventative that makes dishonest acts unthinkable gradually deteriorates.

When potential conflicts arise between the management and the shareholders, it is the board's duty to be the judicious mediator. Yet despite the failure of many boards to act as prudent stewards during the Great Bull Market, our society has lionized our boards of directors nearly as much as our vaunted CEOs. Late in 2000, for example, *Chief Executive* magazine told us that "dramatic improvements in corporate governance have swept through the American economic system, [thanks to] enlightened CEOs and directors who voluntarily put through so many [changes] designed to make the operations of boards more effective."[10] In particular, the magazine praised a certain "new economy" company, "with a board that works hard to keep up with things . . . and working committees with functional responsibilities where disinterested oversight is required," a company whose four highest values were "Communication; Respect; Excellence; and Integrity—open, honest, and sincere. . . . We continue to raise the bar for everyone [because] the great fun here will be for all of us to discover just how good we can really be."[11]

---

* An interesting sideline. In 1986, I wrote to *New York Times* "On Language" columnist William Safire suggesting that he research the origin of the use of "CEO." I had read a puzzling article about Motorola in which the company made it clear that while former CEO Robert Galvin had relinquished the CEO title, he would continue to "*lead* [emphasis in original] the company just as before." In an amusing essay entitled "Hail to the C.E.O.," Safire credited me ("chairman and chief you-know-what of the Vanguard Group") for my ability to "delegate the work to others" (William Safire, "Hail to the C.E.O.," *New York Times Magazine*, September 28, 1986).

As it happens, we now know just how good they could really be: The company, so good that its board was named the third best among all of corporate America's thousands of boards in the year 2000, is bankrupt. While its executives reaped billions in compensation, its employees are jobless, their retirement savings obliterated. The firm's name now serves as a national symbol for greed, excess, and deceit; its reputation is shredded beyond repair; some of its senior executives are in jail, others on trial for their alleged misconduct. The firm, of course, was Enron.

Yet the board of directors is the ultimate governing body of the corporation. Directors are the stewards who have the responsibility of overseeing the preservation and growth of the company over the long term. When corporate affairs were overseen by substantial owners, vigilant oversight by other corporate shareholders seemed unnecessary. Even in the recent era, society continued to trust directors to act properly without interference. We relied on directors to do their duty. Yet too many directors failed to consider that their overriding responsibility was to represent not the management but those largely faceless, voiceless shareholders who elected them. They failed, if you will, to honor the director's golden rule: "Behave as if the corporation you serve had a single absentee owner, and do your best to further his long-term interests in all proper ways."[12] Indeed, those were the words used by Warren Buffett in his Berkshire Hathaway Annual Report in 1993, more than a decade ago. As a group, alas, our corporate directors have failed to measure up to that standard.

Management, Measurement, and the Consequences

When managers are seduced by the siren song of unfathomable riches, largely unfettered by the notion of serving the interests of the corporation's long-term owners, they are easily tempted to focus on driving the stock price higher. When earnings growth goals are unrealistically high and the investment community brooks no interruptions in a regular progression of growth, the temptation to run the business around the numbers becomes overwhelming. To meet "the numbers," important long-term initiatives may be the first cost to be cut, with downsizing (artfully renamed as "rightsizing") next in line; then financial standards are pushed to the limit; finally, earnings become so illusory and subjective that credibility is lost. What can all too easily follow is the severe damage to the corporation's reputation and then its business, happening right under the noses of our traditional gatekeepers.

These gatekeepers, in short, failed to protect our corporate owners against managements that were all too eager to cast their firms' lot in terms of numbers rather than intrinsic values, corporate character, and meaningful self-appraisal. Even otherwise sound companies dwelt too heavily on what can be measured—market share, productivity, efficiency, product quality, costs—and set internal goals to achieve them. ("Six-Sigma"—less than 3.4 defects per million opportunities—is the current management vogue.) But business is hard and competitive, and when achieving these self-imposed measures proved impossible, it was only a matter of time until the measurements themselves were distorted and forced. When *measures* become *objectives,* they are often counterproductive and self-defeating—at times producing the very results that companies wished to avoid. The role of management should not be beating abstract numeric estimates but improving the operations and long-term prospects of organizations by providing forceful and lucid direction, and by demanding a moral and ethical framework for behavior.

The truth is that most business measurements are inherently short-term in nature. Far more durable qualities drive a corporation's success over the long term. While they cannot be measured, such traits as character, integrity, enthusiasm, conviction, and passion are every bit as important to a firm's success as precise measurements. *Human beings* are the prime instruments for implementing a corporation's strategy. Other things being equal (of course, they never are), if those who serve the corporation are inspired, motivated, cooperative, diligent, ethical, and creative, the stockholders will be well served.

Yet recent years have shown us that when ambitious chief executives set aggressive financial objectives, they place the achievement of those objectives above all else—above proper accounting principles and a sound balance sheet, even above their corporate character. Far too often, all of the means available—fair or foul—were harnessed to justify the ends. When the modus operandi of business managers becomes a ready acceptance of deceit and its shadow of self-deception, "everyone else is doing it, so I will too" becomes a sort of Gresham's law that comes to prevail in corporate standards, and good management practices are driven out by bad.

Clearly, "management by measurement" is easily taken too far. The management consultants' familiar bromide, "If you can measure it, you can manage it," is just plain wrong. Managing to a measure ignores the myriad manifestations of "the law of unintended consequences" that are sure to ensue. I recall reading of a chief executive who called for earnings growth from $6.15 per share to a nice round $10 per share five years later—an earnings increase of more than 10 percent per year—but without a word about how it would be done. I don't believe that the greater long-term good of shareholders is served by establishing such a precise yet abstract numeric goal, and then moving heaven and earth to meet it. Indeed what worries me is not that it *won't* be achieved, but that it *will*. For in an inevitably uncertain world, the company may meet its goal only by manipulating the numbers, or even worse, relying on cutbacks and false economies, and shaping everything that moves (including the human beings who will have to bend to the task) to achieve the goal. *But at what cost?*

The companies that will lead the way in their industries over the long term will be those that have made their earnings growth not the objective of their corporate strategy, but the consequence of their corporate performance. Only then will the product *makers* gain their ascension over the numbers *counters,* and deliver the value that their owners have every right to expect.

Rock, Paper, Scissors

The penalties for the recent financial mania are borne by our society as well. As Michael Jensen and Joseph Fuller argued in a perceptive piece in the *Wall Street Journal:* "Stock prices are not simply abstract numbers. [They] affect the nature of the strategies the firm adopts and hence its prospects for success, the company's cost of capital, its borrowing ability, and its ability to make acquisitions. *A valuation unhinged from the underlying realities of the business can rob investors of savings, cost people far more innocent than senior management their jobs, and undermine the viability of suppliers and communities.*" [13] (Italics added.) When business is seen as a "numbers game" by corporate managers, by directors and auditors, and by buy-side and sell-side analysts alike, it is our society as a whole that pays the price.

In the numbers-driven environment of the day, many so-called industrial companies have become financial companies—companies that *count* rather than companies that *make.* (Witness the fact that the senior aide to the CEO, almost invariably the chief financial officer, is often viewed by the investment community as the firm's eminence grise.) Quoting from an op-ed essay in the *New York Times* by Jeffrey A. Sonnenfeld, head of the Yale School of Management's Chief Executive Leadership Institute, such companies are often "serial acquirers [whose] dazzling number of deals makes an absence of long-term management success easy to hide."[14] Tyco International, for example, acquired 700 companies before its day of reckoning came.

The final outcome of the strategy, as the *Times* essay explained, was almost preordained: "Their empires of [numbers] hype can be undone very quickly by market discipline." These firms, the article knowingly added, "base their strategies not on understanding the businesses they go into, but assume that by scavenging about for good deals, they can better allocate their financial resources than can existing financial markets."[15] (I would add that one of the motivations for the wave of mergers in the recent era was the ability to take huge write-offs—largely ignored by market participants—and create "cookie jar" reserves, available at the beck and call of management to inflate future earnings on demand.) As we observe the painful consequences of these strategies, it is clear that the reverse was true: the markets proved far wiser than the managements.

In the timeless children's game, we know that rock breaks scissors, scissors cut paper, and paper covers rock. In the recent stock market mania, as prices lost touch with values, paper indeed covered rock. "Paper" companies that *count* were able to acquire "rock" companies that *make,* and the results were devastating. When we consider, for example, the mergers of AOL and Time Warner, of Qwest and U.S. West, of WorldCom and MCI, and of Vivendi and Seagrams, it is crystal clear that the former firms were paper companies built on an illusory financial foundation, and the latter were rock companies, built on a real business foundation. Yet each of these mergers provided a poignant example of a tragic phenomenon, in whose aftermath hundreds of thousands of loyal long-term employees lost their jobs and watched as their retirement savings were unmercifully slashed.

Why Corporate America Went Astray

Corporate America went astray largely because the power of managers went virtually unchecked by our gatekeepers for far too long. Our corporate directors were primarily to blame. But our auditors, lawyers, regulators, legislators, and investors, those other traditional guardians of sound governance, share the responsibility. They failed to "keep an eye on these geniuses" to whom they had entrusted the responsibility of the management of America's great corporations.

There is little doubt that the modern corporation has been instrumental in the achievement of our society in obtaining a standard of living that is unprecedented in human history. But the system of management that has evolved over the past hundred years has proven to be badly flawed, and its shortfalls have been far from innocent and harmless. Without fixing the governance system, winning the battle to have our corporations run in the interests of their long-term owners is unlikely to have even a fighting chance. If the corporation's directors don't lead the charge, then the owners must do so. It *is* as simple as that.

CHAPTER 3

How to Return Corporate America to Its Owners

"Owners of the World, Unite!"

The previous two chapters represent my efforts to make it clear, first, that something fundamental has gone wrong in corporate America, and second, that its root cause lies in the ascendancy of capitalism that benefits managers at the expense of the owners. The consequences of this mutation in our system have substantially weakened our nation's system of capital formation, and what is wrong must be remedied. Before turning to some policy recommendations designed to right these wrongs, however, I want to discuss the progress that has already been made.

Surprisingly, it was not the profound problems of aggressive earnings management, faulty accounting, hyped expectations, imperial chief executives, loose governance, excessive speculation, and even the Great Bear Market itself that were the catalysts for reform. Rather, the catalyst was the disgraceful actions of the relative handful of notorious, brazen scoundrels—including the bad apples that I earlier identified—that galvanized the public's attention and generated the powerful reaction that at last initiated some much-needed reforms.

The corporate scandals involving shady behavior by those CEOs revealed widespread failure among those we had trusted to be our corporate stewards, the gatekeepers of our system, notably the corporate directors who had the direct and legal responsibility for oversight. There was an immediate public reaction, and the U.S. Congress, the New York Stock Exchange, and private institutions like the Conference Board all promptly went to work. Major steps have been taken toward improving corporate governance standards.

In July 2002, only eight months after the Enron scandal gained national attention, Congress passed the Sarbanes-Oxley Act, requiring senior corporate managers to attest to the validity of their companies' financial statements, providing for disgorgement of profits by executives who sell stocks of companies that later restate their earnings, and replacing self-regulation of accountants with a new federal Public Company Accounting Oversight Board (PCAOB), as well as other salutary provisions. The legislation includes substantial penalties for violators, including heavy fines and criminal prosecution.

There has been considerable complaint from business—especially smaller firms—about the cost of compliance and the utility of section 404 of "Sarbox," requiring the verification of internal control systems. Perhaps certain portions of the law should be reconsidered, particularly as they apply to small firms. But with the powerful, ethical, and even feisty leadership of the PCAOB's first chairman, William J. McDonough, the widely respected former president of the Federal Reserve Bank of New York, audit standards and the validity of financial reporting, already greatly improved, are virtually certain be improved even further.

In August 2002, the New York Stock Exchange approved a powerful set of corporate governance rules for its listed companies—including most of America's major corporations—calling for substantially greater director independence and new standards for audit committees and compensation committees. They even suggested a "lead director" independent of corporate management. (Later, the regulatory arm of the National Association of Securities Dealers—NASD—approved roughly comparable corporate standards for the companies listed on the NASDAQ exchange.) Collectively, these changes at least begin the process of separating the powers of *governance* from the powers of *management,* ensuring greater responsiveness to the interests of owners.

The Conference Board Commission

In September 2002, after a summer of intense study, the Conference Board Blue-Ribbon Commission on Public Trust and Private Enterprise completed its findings and made recommendations on executive compensation, followed three months later by similar reports on corporate governance and on audit and accounting. I was privileged to serve on that commission, led by co-chairmen Peter G. Peterson, former secretary of commerce, and John W. Snow, chairman of CSX Corporation (later named secretary of the treasury). The commission's examination covered considerable ground, and yielded some seventy-five specific recommendations designed to restore the public trust. Among the major recommendations were these:

- On executive compensation: performance-based compensation should be more broadly used, long-term accomplishment should take precedence over the short term, and *all* types of stock options should be treated as corporate expense, making it clear that fixed-price options are not "free."
- On corporate governance: the nominating/governance committee should be independent of management; codes of ethics should be established and enforced; and the roles of management (the CEO) and ownership (either an independent chair or a separate "lead director") should be separated.
- On accounting standards: audit committees and auditor rotation standards should be further strengthened. The remaining Big Four accounting firms (now known as the "Final Four") should focus on audit quality, consider a change to "principles-based" rather than "rules-based" audit standards, and eliminate *all* consulting and tax services that involve advocacy positions, notably those that provide executives with grotesque tax shelters designed to circumvent the law.[1]

All of these suggestions are sensible. None of them, in my opinion, is too much to demand. A sideline: as the commission's only member with a career in the management of other people's money, I helped my fellow commissioners focus on the unfortunate role played by institutional investors in the breakdown in the public trust of our private enterprise system. The commissioners all agreed to the strong recommendations of the report, directed at refocusing both corporate management and investment policy on long-term investing rather than the short-term speculation of the day.

Seven Policy Recommendations

Federal legislation, stock exchange rules, and even the recommendations of public commissions, however distinguished, can do only so much to bring about the needed reform. Changes in governance *process,* while absolutely necessary, are not sufficient to get us where we need to go. We need to change the behavior of *people,* specifically our corporate managers, our corporate directors, and our corporate owners, who, finally, must join forces to bring about the needed reform. These seven policy recommendations are designed to help reach that goal.

1. *Encourage corporate citizenship.* For managers and directors to become more responsive to the needs of owners, the owners of stocks must behave as responsible corporate citizens, thoughtfully voting their proxies and constructively communicating their views to corporate management. The SEC's 2003 requirement that mutual funds disclose to their owners how the funds vote their owners' proxies—proxies, to be clear, that should always be voted in the interests of the *owners* rather than in the interests of *managers*—is a long overdue first step in increasing the motivation of financial intermediaries to participate in governance matters.

The fund industry was dragged, kicking and screaming, into providing this disclosure. Indeed, deeply concerned about the industry's opposition to the SEC proposal in December 2002, I wrote an op-ed essay in the *New York Times,* arguing in its favor: "Fund managers are the agents; fund shareholders are the principals. . . . Shareholders are owners of the stocks; to deny them information [about how funds voted their proxies] would stand on its head the common understanding of the principal-agency relationship. . . . By their long forbearance and lassitude on governance issues, funds bear no small share of the responsibility for the failures in corporate governance and accounting oversight that were among the major forces creating the recent market bubble. . . . If the owners of our corporations don't care about governance, who else is there to assume that responsibility?"[2]

As logical as those words might seem, two industry leaders fired back a month later, in January 2003. In their own op-ed in the *Wall Street Journal,* Edward C. Johnson 3rd, head of Fidelity, and John Brennan, my successor as head of Vanguard, made no effort to rebut the obvious principle I had expressed. (When two directly competitive firms join to fight back regulation, it reaffirms the adage that "politics make strange bedfellows.") Rather, they argued that disclosure of votes "would politicize proxy voting . . . opening mutual fund voting decisions to thinly veiled intimidation from activist groups." Instead, surprisingly, they suggested SEC oversight of fund voting, recommending that regulators assume the responsibility for examining fund managers' votes to ensure that they were "consistent with company guidelines."[3]

Three months later, the commission ordered that its proposal become effective as of August 31, 2004. We have already seen a sharp increase in the participation of funds in the proxy process without, at least so far, any significant "politicization." Indeed, an AFL-CIO report in the autumn of 2004 found that seven of the ten largest fund managers voted for most shareholder proposals to limit excessive executive compensation.[4] (I'm pleased to note that Vanguard received the second highest score in the ratings.) Funds have clearly become more active, now often voting against excessive option issuance, withholding votes for directors with business conflicts, and voicing their views on other corporate policy issues.

But *motive* is only half the battle. Our financial intermediaries also need the *opportunity* to act. They need access to corporate proxy statements so that they can place, directly in proxies, both nominations for directors and proposals on corporate conduct, including compensation policy. While in recent years the SEC has granted greater access to shareholders wishing to make such proposals,* one can only be troubled by the commission's 2004 decision to allow corporations to reject the proposals by the shareholders of a number of companies to present proxy resolutions that would allow shareholders to nominate their own board candidates. (The SEC had earlier actually denied Walt Disney the right to *exclude* such a proposal, only to reverse its position later.) It remains virtually impossible for shareholders to nominate their own candidates for director, and even the weak proxy access proposal made by the SEC in late 2003 now seems unlikely to be approved. Yet it must be obvious that the insulation of directors from shareholders lies at the crux of the recent governance problems. I discuss the issue in greater depth at the end of this chapter.

2. *Clearly separate ownership from management.* We need to recognize the bright line between *directing*—the responsibility of the governing body of an institution—and *managing*—the responsibility of the executives who run the business. It's called *separation of powers.* It requires that boards be composed largely of truly independent directors who have no history of employment with the company, nor any business relationships, past or present. However difficult spirit is to measure, board members must be independent in spirit, concerned solely with placing the interests of the owners as the overriding priority.

---

*The commission allows corporations to exclude from the proxy any proposal that is deemed to relate to the "ordinary business" of the corporation.

Simply put, while the CEO should be the boss of the *business,* an independent chairman should be the boss of the *board.* In addition, directors should move toward greater reliance on outside advisers and consultants to provide them with independent information that is free of management bias, particularly on compensation and accounting matters, but also on major policy issues as well. This may involve the formation of a small board staff, strictly answerable to the board, that would assemble, distribute, and monitor relevant information. These further reforms in board governance would help to clarify that the role of senior officers is to manage the property of the owners, and the role of directors is to act as their stewards.*

3. *Fix the stock option mess.* To the extent that management holds a substantial and continuing ownership position, obviously, management and ownership are more closely aligned (for example, as in publicly held companies in which the original families continue to hold a substantial stake). Therefore, we should encourage managers to acquire and hold substantial stock positions. In the language of the economists, we must align the behavior of the agents with the interests of the principals.

While building stock ownership by executives is an appropriate objective, it must be done in a way that is fair to the other owners who assumed the risks of ownership when they purchased their shares at the market price. Directors, therefore, should carefully consider the dilution engendered by additional option issuance, as well as the cumulative dilution of previous options. Directors should make these decisions with reference to the particular circumstances of their own company. "Everybody else is doing it" is hardly a sound reason to award excessive portions of corporate ownership at bargain prices to managers.

And option expenses must at last be expensed. They have never been "free," and expensing will help compensation committees to consider the magnitude of the dilution in ownership interest that they entail. While business interests continue to mount a powerful lobbying effort in Congress, in the courts, and even at the SEC, to head off the Financial Accounting Standards Board's final approval of a requirement that the cost of fixed-price stock options must be accounted for as a corporate expense, it seems obvious that sound accounting principles demand that such op-

---

* *Put Investors First: Real Solutions for Better Corporate Governance,* by Scott C. Newquist, provides an excellent review of what is needed, especially in Chapters 6, 7, and 8. I wrote the foreword for this book.

tions receive the same tax treatment as other stock-based compensation, and taken into account as an expense of the corporation.

Directors and owners should not be tricked into, nor should owners ratify, the awarding of options in the traditional form. Even if expensed, fixed-price options remain fundamentally flawed as instruments that reflect the longer-term intrinsic value of the corporation. With the accounting playing field now expected to be leveled off by expensing all forms of options, it is time that we turn to other, better forms that are designed to reward executives for more substantial accomplishments than pushing stock prices momentarily higher; options whose prices take dividends into account, and whose prices are adjusted for the cost of capital; options that index a company's stock price to the prices of corporate peers and/or of the stock market itself; and options that reward executives for building enduring corporate value.

Further, options should be issued on a long-term basis, so as to further discourage management focus on short-term results, with provisions that require executives to hold a certain amount of their stock during their employment by the company, and perhaps even for a specific period thereafter, with "clawback" provisions for returning profits to the company if earnings are restated. (I once asked a CEO if his company had any requirement that the shares he acquired through options should be held for a certain period. He responded, "Why on earth would anyone want to do *that!*") Of course substantial stock ownership by executives would help align the interest of managers with those interests of owners, but the shares should be acquired on terms that are fair to owners as well as managers, and holdings that are largely sustained during the executive's tenure and even beyond. Boards that see their duty as placing the interest of the owners ahead of the interest of the managers will carefully consider these issues.

4. *Focus pay on performance, not peers.* Stock options have become the major avenue to the grossly excessive executive compensation of the recent era. But it is only by considering total compensation that we can work toward solutions. The compensation system has been built, not on "pay for performance," but on "pay versus peers," resulting in the year-after-year ratcheting up of pay. In a truly vicious circle, complaisant boards move their lower-ranking CEOs up the ladder, causing other CEOs to move down. In their presentations to compensation committees, compensation consultants have come to rely heavily on a ranking of executives vis-à-vis their peers in terms of their total compensation—salary, short-term incentives

(bonus), and long-term incentives (stock). But tabulations that focus on the compensation of peers to the exclusion of the corporate performance achieved by peers are at the heart of what went wrong in corporate America. At the very least, consultants should also rank the executives in a given firm in terms of the performance of the firm vis-à-vis a well-defined peer group. In this way, only top performers would receive the top incentive compensation. Average performers would receive average compensation. And if the word *incentive* is to have any substantive meaning, those who fall below average would receive no incentive pay whatsoever.

Of course the measurement of corporate performance is complex and to some extent arbitrary. But some sensible measurement is better than nothing. It should relate not to evanescent stock prices but to the creation of corporate value—cash flow, dividend generation, return on total capital compared to peer companies and to American industry in general, and so on. Setting standards and calling on employees to measure up to them is, after all, what CEOs *do*. (Indeed, dare I say that the CEO is also an employee of the corporation?) Is it asking too much to demand that directors do the same as they measure their CEOs in terms of their peers' accomplishments as well as their peers' compensation? Those measurement standards, more than incidentally, should be made available to stockholders in the corporations' proxy statements. The owners have a right to some assurance that "pay for performance" is not only the guiding principle but the operative reality.

5. *Return to a long-term focus.* Owners and managers must unite in the task of returning the focus of corporate strategy and corporate information alike to long-term financial goals, cash flows, intrinsic values, and progress in the development of strategic direction. Quarterly earnings guidance, pernicious yet still omnipresent, should be eliminated, replaced by quarterly reports that cover not only the operations and financial results for the firm but a discussion of significant changes to the long-term business plan; unexpected changes in costs, business volumes, and market share; status of competitive position; and so on.

While all of this information must be publicly disclosed, it is professional analysts and money managers who will most carefully analyze it. Thus, open video meetings of executives with these experts (with publicly available transcripts) should become common. Long-term shareholders who engage in candid communication with management and are cooperative rather than confrontational, describing what they expect from their investment—including what dividends they expect—will play a major role in the restoration of owners' capitalism. Management can help by abandoning "best foot forward" press releases and "pro forma" earnings reports that ignore the negative events of the period.

6. *Let the sunlight shine on accounting.* Given the enormous latitude accorded by the Generally Accepted Accounting Principles, owners must demand, and managers must provide, full disclosure of the impact of significant accounting policy decisions. Indeed, perhaps corporations ought to be required to report their earnings both on a "most aggressive" basis (presumably what they are reporting today) and on a "most conservative" basis as well. Seriously, why not report a range, along with reasons for the differences, and let investors decide if the differences are meaningful or not.

Although such a stark policy may be too much to expect, serious work already has begun to improve the reporting of financial results and increase their relevance. The book *It's Earnings That Count*,[5] for example, presents two supplemental income statements that Hewitt Heiserman dubs "enterprising" (showing the company's return relative to its total capital base) and "defensive" (showing the extent to which a company depends on outside sources of capital), in addition to the present GAAP statement. Do we really need three earnings reports? For those who recall the sensible rule of the ancient carpenter, "measure twice, cut once," measuring thrice is one more way to enhance the ability of shareholders to understand the corporation's financial statements.

Another improvement would be requiring corporations to make their federal tax returns available to the public, perhaps summarized in their annual reports. (Owners of more than 1 percent of a corporation's stock already have the right to examine its federal tax returns.) It is widely understood that the earnings that corporations report to the Internal Revenue Service are almost invariably lower than the earnings they report to shareholders, and an understanding of the differences is crucial to informed analysis. Interestingly, tax return information is the basis for the aggregated corporate earnings reported by the Department of Commerce, which found that corporations were consistently "misreporting on income tax returns." The Commerce data are adjusted for this "understatement of income," which totaled a stunning $772 billion in 1996–2001 alone (most recent data available).[6]

Over time, we must develop a set of common principles for reporting earnings and presenting balance sheets. We also must establish a rigorous standard of full financial disclosure that goes beyond simple compliance with accounting rules. Corporate books and records and corporate tax returns should be opened up to all interested parties, certainly including the millions of shareholders who together *own* the corporation, either directly or through mutual and pension funds, just as we would if the corporation had a single owner.

We also need to strengthen the backbones of our audit firms to stand up to managements that want to push the envelope in order to report the best possible results. Now that we are down to the so-called Final Four giant accounting firms, the power in the traditionally client-dominated relationship may in fact be slowly shifting from client to auditor.

One of the tragedies of recent years was the decision of the Department of Justice to indict the entire Arthur Andersen firm, the "fifth auditor," which had radically departed from its rich heritage of principled behavior. A group led by Paul Volcker (of which I was a member) was prepared to step in and provide truly independent directors for the firm and create a gold standard for accounting practice. But at the Justice Department claim, clients fled in droves, and Arthur Andersen—and the progressive idea—died.

Nonetheless, true independence is the direction in which the governance of accounting firms must move, with auditors providing solely audit services (and not consulting services) to a particular client. In an environment in which the stability of the relationship between auditor and client is vital to the confidence of investors, auditors need but a little gumption (and perhaps the omnipresent threat of shareholder litigation) to stand on principle. The PCAOB can help to foster this development.

7. *A new mindset for the board.* Every bit as important as establishing a more effective board structure is establishing a new mindset for corporate directors. Rules-based governance can all too easily lead to a counterproductive "checklist mentality," so we must go further by changing the governance climate. The mood of the boardroom must develop into one of true intellectual independence (even at the cost of some collegiality), with a corresponding diminution of groupthink and CEO dominance.

We need to recognize, as journalist James Surowiecki has pointed out, that dissent need not mean dissension, and that even when they may disagree, informed and enlightened individuals can reach an intelligent collective decision. He cites the wise and courageous words of Alfred Sloan, who ran General Motors from 1923 to 1956: When the GM board unanimously approved a resolution in favor of one of his proposals, he said, "Gentlemen, I take it that we are all in complete agreement on the decision here. Then, I propose that we postpone further discussion . . . to give ourselves time to develop disagreement and perhaps gain some understanding of what the decision is all about."[7] In that anecdote lies a marvelous insight into how truly effective corporate governance should work.

No Easy Answers

No one would argue either that these steps will come easily, or that they will in themselves put to rest the pervasive conflicts that presently exist between managers and owners. A recent article by Mark J. Roe of Harvard Law School got to the heart of the matter: "One of the core instabilities of America's corporate governance is the separation of ownership from control—distant and diffuse stockholders own, while concentrated management controls—[which] creates big recurring breakdowns. . . . One structural response would be to facilitate gatekeeping in strong boards that check managers, via strong stockholders with the motivation toward profitability, and via powerfully independent accountants who verify managers' 'report cards.' . . . We can resolve the immediate problem, and move on, [but] new problems will arise. We muddle through; we don't solve them because we can't."[8]

But as we muddle through, an earnest search for the best means to reconcile the interests of management with the interests of owners must go on for capitalism to thrive. Moving strongly in the direction suggested by the seven foregoing recommendations will help. Although the owners of America's corporations have traditionally relied on corporate directors to ensure that ownership interest will be honored, true governance reform would be accelerated if our stockholders—especially our large institutional investors—recognized that *a direct relationship exists between sound corporate governance and corporate performance,* and conducted their ownership responsibilities accordingly.

Common sense suggests that such a linkage exists, and a 2003 study was done on the subject. While its findings have been confirmed by some studies and contradicted by others, the research demonstrates that it is at least a credible thesis. The findings of the study are summarized in Box 3.1.

Box 3.1 Dictatorship, Democracy, and Corporate Performance

Using the same analogy as I used in chapter two, a recent Harvard University/Wharton School paper on "Corporate Governance and Equity Prices" studied governance and the performance of corporate "dictatorships" versus corporate "democracies":

> Corporations are republics. The ultimate authority rests with the voters (shareholders). These voters elect representatives (directors) who delegate most decisions to bureaucrats (managers). . . . One extreme tilts toward democracy, reserves little power for management, and allows shareholders to quickly and easily replace directors. The other extreme tilts toward dictatorship, reserves extensive power for management, and places strong restrictions on shareholders' ability to replace directors.[9]

The paper examined the relationship between the financial performance of corporations that were relatively rigorous in restricting shareholder rights during the 1990s, and corporations that were relatively liberal in their defenses. It reviewed twenty-eight governance provisions, including classified boards, compensation plans, golden parachutes, indemnification, cumulative voting, supermajority, anti-greenmail, pension parachutes, and, of course, poison pills, ranking 1,500 companies in terms of management power and shareholder rights and then creating a governance index with ten deciles.

The 10 percent of firms with the lowest management power and strongest shareholder rights were designated as the Democracy Portfolio, and the bottom 10 percent were designated as the Dictatorship Portfolio. The largest companies in the Democracy Portfolio included IBM, Wal-Mart, DuPont, American International Group, and Berkshire Hathaway, with governance scores ranging from 2 to 5. (Low scores mean less management power and more shareholder rights, and vice versa.) The largest companies in the Dictatorship Portfolio included GTE, Waste Management, Limited, Kmart, and Time Warner, all with scores running in the 14 to 16 range.

It's difficult to do justice to this complex landmark study in brief, and in layman's terms. Although the absolute numeric differences appear small, the implications are large and important. First, a lower score meant a high Tobin Q ratio—a technical measure of the relationship of a company's market capitalization to the book value of its capital that is widely used by financial analysts. In fact, each one-point reduction in the index was associated with an 11.4 percentage point improvement in the Q ratio.

Second, and even more important, especially in an era in which human capital is often considered more important than book capital, the total returns of the stocks in the Democracy Portfolio outperformed those in the Dictatorship Portfolio by 8.5 percentage points *per year* during the 1990s—a truly staggering margin that, compounded over the decade, spelled the difference between extraordinary investment achievement and abysmal failure.

The largest firms in the extreme portfolios

Democracy portfolio		Dictatorship portfolio	
Firm	*Score*	*Firm*	*Score*
IBM	5	GTE	14
Wal-Mart	5	Waste Management	15
DuPont	5	General Re	14
Pepsico	4	Limited Inc.	14
AIG	5	NCR	14
Southern Co.	5	Kmart	14
Hewlett Packard	5	United Telecom.	14
Berkshire Hathaway	3	Time Warner	14
Comm. Edison	4	Rorer	16
Texas Utilities	2	Woolworth	14

Source: "Corporate Governance and Equity Prices," The Quarterly Journal of Economics, *February 2003.*

There was a clear link between superior returns on the one hand and, on the other, corporate cultures that both respected shareholder rights and were led by managements self-reliant enough to believe that the best defense against takeover was good operating results. Also, inferior returns were associated with poor performing companies that may be more inclined to shelter themselves from earnest, independent opinion; that is, companies that have something to hide may try to do exactly that. While the authors of the study do not argue that the relationship they found between governance and performance was necessarily causal, they conclude, "the long-run benefit of eliminating [restrictive] provisions would be enormous." While some academics have found fault with this study, other equally comprehensive and independent academic studies, as well as other analyses, have supported the paper's conclusions. Investors would be well served if they focus on the elimination of provisions that impinge on the traditional rights of shareholders.*

*I use the term *investors* referring to all long-term shareholders. But I recognize that it is major institutional investors who hold the ultimate power.

A Call for Corporate Democracy

The problem with corporate America, it seems increasingly clear, lies not only in the fact that far too many corporate executives and directors have been placed in positions of great power and authority without an adequate understanding of their fiduciary duties. At the same time, far too many institutional intermediaries have failed to take them to task by insisting that their interests as shareowners must be served. Our nation's shareholders seem not to care very much about assuring that their ownership claims are honored, although they have the power to do exactly that. As the next chapter points out, our one hundred largest financial institutions—managers of mutual funds, pension funds, and endowment funds—alone hold some 52 percent of all U.S. stocks outstanding, absolute control over corporate America. It's a scary thought. But, in the vernacular of the day, "not to worry." By and large, all we have heard from these owners is the sound of silence. If the owners don't give a damn about the triumph of managers' capitalism, it is fair to ask, who on earth should?

Stock owners must demand that directors and managers alike honor the primacy of their interests. The corporation, after all, is their property. Put me squarely in the camp of those who believe in corporate democracy. If the elected directors of the republics that govern corporate America are not responsive to the interests of their constituency—even worse, if dictatorships come to hold sway—then the voters ought to have the power to throw the rascals out. It's not very complicated: *Owners should be allowed to behave as owners.* If ownership rights are not placed front and center, where should they be placed? Who would dare to suggest that barriers be placed in the way of the right of shareholders to elect as a director whomever they wish to serve as their agent? To compel management to function in a fashion that serves them? To assume responsibility for how the executives of their company are compensated? Aren't these among the essential rights of ownership?

Clearly, these are among the rights of the 100 percent owner, who brooks no interference with his will. And any manager who flatly refused to consider the views of a 50 percent owner, or even a 20 percent owner, soon would be looking for another line of work. What about a dozen institutions, each holding a 3 percent interest and sharing a particular viewpoint, or wishing to nominate a director? Where does the proverbial shovel break? And does the argument that it *might* break when shareholders are deprived of the same rights in cases in which no single shareholder owns more than, say, one-tenth of 1 percent of the corporation's shares justify rejecting the idea of democracy in corporate governance? Not for me it doesn't. For I believe, paraphrasing Churchill, that corporate democracy is the worst form of government . . . except for all those others that have been tried from time to time.

The Opposition to Corporate Democracy

Logical or not, the idea of a democratic agenda for most corporations has met with little favor among some commentators. Top securities attorney Martin Lipton argues that enhancing shareholder ownership rights to nominate directors and to make proxy proposals could "disrupt the proper functioning of the board and limit the ability of the directors to fulfill their fiduciary duties."[10] In an op-ed essay in the *Wall Street Journal*, Henry G. Manne, dean emeritus of the George Mason University School of Law, argues that "the theory of corporate democracy . . . has long been a standing joke among sophisticated finance economists." (He named no names.) "A corporation is not a small republic . . . and the board is not a legislature . . . a vote attached to a share is totally different from a political vote . . . the essence of individual shareholder participation is 'exit,' not 'voice' . . . and they can exit their corporate 'citizenship' for the cost of a stockbroker's commission."[11] In other words, if you don't like the way your company is being run, sell to the first bidder. Whether or not the price reflects the corporation's intrinsic value, and regardless of the losses you may incur, just get out, and stay out. "Like it or dump it," however, doesn't seem like a particularly enlightened basis for public policy.

There are legitimate issues regarding corporate democracy, and Dean Manne points them out. Of course, among those who are interested in embracing ownership rights are, as he writes, "special pleaders with no real stake, activists [whose] primary interest . . . is to facilitate publicity for their own special-interest programs . . . and to interfere with the property and contractual rights of others in order to achieve their own ends."[12]

To be fair, such activists with their own agendas do exist among America's investors. Although I'm confident that at least some corporate activists have agendas that do not comport with the public weal, I'm not prepared to accept a sweeping diatribe that broadly describes corporate democracy as a "form of corporate fraud" as a basis for excluding all investors from exercising their rights. Of course, some proposals are made by special-interest groups with small holdings of stock. Religious orders, for example, often make principles-based or morality-based proposals. Other proposals, such as those made by labor unions and even state and local government pension plans, are too often politically based. Public policy ought to focus on ways to limit the actions of activist investors so as to preclude special-interest proposals that have at most a tenuous relationship to the betterment of the company's shareholders as a group. But it's hard to see what harm is done by protecting their shareholder rights.

Exercising the Rights of Citizenship

Fulfillment of the promise of responsible corporate citizenship —shareholder democracy, if you will*—does not require a radical change in the existing institutional *structure*. What we need to change are the *policy* constraints that unreasonably limit stockholder rights. We must summon the courage to address two principal issues, each of which pertains to "shareholder access" to the company's proxy statement. The ability of owners, one, to elect or reject management's board nominees and to nominate other candidates for board membership, and two, to place governance and other appropriate proposals in the proxy that, if approved, require compliance by management.

The first issue is the ability of owners to mount electoral challenges to independent directors.[†] As the Chancery Court of Delaware noted in its 1985 *Unocal* decision, "If the stockholders are displeased with the action of their elected representatives, the powers of corporate democracy are at their disposal to turn the board out."[13] In a later case (*Blasius Industries,* 1988), chancellor William T. Allen added, "the shareholder franchise is the ideological underpinning upon which the legitimacy of directorial power rests."[14]

Yet in the proxy process, the cards are heavily stacked against the ability of owners to exercise their franchise. Even when there is a theoretically independent nominating committee, the CEO is apt to control the slate, and challenges to management-nominated directors have been rare. Among the thousands of publicly traded firms, there was an average of just eleven challenges per year during 1996–2002, and only one per year for compa-

---

* Here, I'm using the term *corporate democracy* to comprehend the right of shareholders both to elect their representatives on the board as well as to vote directly on proxy proposals on governance, executive compensation, etc.

† My ideas have been informed by the fine analysis prepared by Lucian Bebchuk, professor at Harvard University School of Law.

nies with a market capitalization exceeding a mere $200 million. In Harvard professor Lucian Bebchuk's words, "the incidence [of challenges to incumbent directors] is practically zero."[15]

Not surprisingly, corporate managers strongly object to changing the system to facilitate challenges to their slate. The Business Roundtable warns that shareholder participation in the nominating process "has the potential to turn every director election into a divisive proxy contest,"[16] involving heavy cost and the diversion of management effort. But even if that could happen, there is no reason that a well-designed access proposal— one that required a substantial block of long-term owners, for example, along with SEC oversight—couldn't resolve most of the difficulties. Managers also argue that potential directors would be deterred from serving, although we have yet to be given any evidence whatsoever that would justify this claim. The fact is that all we have so far are specious, even self-serving, reasons for allowing those at the top of the business pyramid to have virtually complete protection from challenge and possible removal from office—exactly what dictatorship is all about.

While a board constantly engaged in civil war would hardly serve the owners' interests, however, those interests may be equally ill served when harmony is so embedded that no dissent can be brooked. Surely we can all think of individual cases in which shareholders have paid a high price for collegiality so deep-seated that major management decisions are approved almost uncritically, with limited discussion or debate. The entrenched business interests also allege that even limited access to the slate would open the door to "special interest" directors, less well qualified directors, and dysfunctional boards. But there is no reason to assume that a majority of shares would be voted for unqualified or irresponsible directors. *Importantly, these adverse developments cannot occur without the consent of the owners themselves.*

What is more, all directors, no matter how they are nominated, have a fiduciary duty to act solely in the interests of the shareholders of the corporation. It's up to the owners, not the managers, to weigh the pros and cons of the issues surrounding electoral challenges and board composition and, by exercising their franchise, decide them. If the owners have the unfettered power to select the directors, subject only to reasonable constraints, then it follows that the board will be far more responsive to their interests. Since treating owners as second-class citizens and insulating the board from serious challenge clearly played a major role in the triumph of managers' capitalism over owners' capitalism, today's status quo is no longer acceptable.

Shareholder Proposals

Shareholder access to the corporate ballot not only involves the right, even if limited, of owners to nominate directors but also affords owners with the ability to make proposals regarding certain corporate activities. In an earlier era, the Securities and Exchange Commission allowed management to exclude the overwhelming majority of such shareholder proposals from the proxy because they were related to the "ordinary business" of the corporation. In recent years, however, the SEC has permitted a variety of proposals to be included in proxies, including some proposals designed to limit executive compensation. It would not be unreasonable for the owners to insist that executive compensation to senior management be directly related to the real business achievements of executives in building long-term corporate value.

The short-term price of a stock, as we must have learned by now, is a flawed basis for compensation. Investors ought to be demanding such benchmarks as, say, a company's five-year return on total capital relative to peers and to American industry in total, and growth in cash flow. How much extra return on capital should be required for the CEO to earn box-car bonuses? How much cash-flow growth? Those decisions are up to each individual board. I wonder how many companies would dare to follow the threshold set in 2004 by General Electric for the compensation of CEO Jeffrey Immelt: 10 percent cash-flow growth each year, for five consecutive years. That strikes me as a shareholder-friendly approach!

The executive compensation issue only begins the list of where owners should get involved. As a group, owners and their fiduciaries also ought to have the right to make other critical decisions, including:

- The approval of large mergers and acquisitions;
- The elimination of anti-takeover provisions, staggered boards, and poison pills;
- The right to say grace over dividend policy; and
- The right to vote on any reasonable proposal that is designed to ensure that a company is managed in the interests of its shareowners.

If we think of these kinds of proposals relating to governance and strategy as distinctly different from those relating to the operation of the corporation's ordinary business (that is, to eliminate a product line, or not to close a plant), there is no justification for their exclusion from the proxy.

Changing the System

The changes that I am urging will require SEC initiatives, and I confess to being disappointed in the commission's 2003 proposal to give shareholder access to nominating directors. Given the pressure from the Business Roundtable, it is easy to understand why the proposal is so limited and restrictive: In year one, a "triggering event"—a 35 percent vote to withhold support from one of the directors, or a majority vote in favor of a proposal for shareholder access to the ballot—must take place. Then, in year two, shareholders who have held at least 5 percent of the company's stock for at least two years could nominate up to three candidates, and bear the costs of trying to persuade other owners to vote for their candidates. If a majority of shares approved, likely some years after the company first got into trouble, there would be a small change in the board.

While well intentioned, the SEC proposal is far too torturous and severe. Given that nearly all institutional investors have demonstrated far more willingness to vote for a reform proposed by other owners than to propose a reform on their own, access to the proxy statement should require only some reasonable dollar holding, say, $25 million to $100 million. Further, any group of institutions that has held more than, say, 10 percent of a company's shares for at least two years should be exempt from the limitations, and have the right to propose new directors, or even an entire slate, in the proxy without delay, and with costs reimbursed by the company.

To return capitalism to its owners, we not only need to open up the director nomination process to qualified long-term owners. We also need the SEC to establish standards that clarify, broaden, and liberalize the issues that may be raised by owners in corporate proxies without running afoul of the "ordinary business" exclusion. But as we provide stock owners with those *rights* of corporate citizenship, we also need to demand the observance of their *responsibilities* of corporate citizenship, with some guidelines that limit shareholder ability to make proposals that are designed to serve the interest of particular constituencies, rather than the interest of shareowners as a class.

Shareholder Power

Shareholders have a right to a fair process in which they can demand that the corporation honor their ownership position. Let me be crystal clear, however, that shareholders—even large institutions—aren't there to tell the management of the corporation how to run its business. (My own observation is that these giant institutions would be better served by removing the motes from their eyes that blind them to the flaws in their own operations.) But if enough shareholders believe that their elected representatives—the directors—are not observing their duty of stewardship, they ought to be able to elect those who will do so. And they ought to have the ability to do so without onerous restrictions. If this sounds like a call for anarchy, I remind you: *Action would be taken only if a majority of shares were voted in favor of any proposed change.*

Even today, if a proxy proposal is made and an overwhelmingly favorable vote is obtained—no mean parlay!—companies can, and often do, ignore it. For typically, under the laws of most states, shareholder votes are nonbinding, in legal terms, "precatory," a word that I have come to detest. We need firm rules that require management to honor shareholder decisions. The whole underpinning of our capitalistic system depends upon the notion that the will of shareholders shall be done.

Even before these reforms are put into place, however, there is no need for shareholders to remain asleep at the governance switch. Today, owners can make their will felt in other, more subtle ways. If they're not satisfied with a company's leadership, they can withhold votes from directors who are CEOs. In March 2004, for example, 43 percent of shares were voted against director Michael Eisner, CEO of the Disney Company, a vote that expressed widespread dissatisfaction with the combination of the company's unimpressive earnings growth; with his aggregate compensation of nearly $1 billion, a shocking raid on the company's treasury; and with the $140 million severance contract that he awarded, seemingly without adequate board consideration, to a president who lasted, uneasily at that, for barely a year. The lack of confidence demonstrated by the vote resulted in Eisner's relinquishment of his position as chairman of the board, and his agreement to step down as CEO in 2005.

In addition, owners already have the power to withhold votes for individual directors. A good place to begin is with directors who have failed to measure up to their responsibilities on compensation, nominating, and audit committees, and directors with conflicts of interest, or directors deemed otherwise unqualified. Owners who carefully and thoughtfully exercise their right to abstain can make an important difference.

Owners also can use their franchise to vote against auditors who also are providing consulting services, or at least against those whose fees for consulting services constitute a disproportionate relationship to audit fees. And of course owners can be, and I believe should be, more aggressive in rejecting option plans that involve cumulative dilution that is excessive. Even today owners have vast untapped powers, and they ought to put them to use before another proxy season passes into history. While such votes in and of themselves may not directly result in change, if enough owners use the ballot box to express their disapproval, directors will have to pay heed.

When shareholders decide to exercise willingly and forcefully the rights of ownership, and to assume the responsibilities of ownership, then a repeat of the debacle we have witnessed in so much of corporate America is much less likely to recur. No, I don't believe that shareholders of our giant financial institutions have the talent and ability to manage the businesses they effectively own. But they do have both the ability and the power to demand that directors act, always and above all, in the interest of the company's owners.

Such a return to owner's capitalism may seem like a novel, even revolutionary, idea. It is hardly that. Owners' capitalism is the concept under which privately held companies, as well as publicly held companies with powerful family ownership, such as Wal-Mart and Microsoft, are managed. It is the best way—indeed, the only predictable way—to minimize the possibility of recurrence of the outrageous excessive compensation, the financial misrepresentations, the corporate mismanagement, and the speculative excesses of the recent era.

"Owners of the World, Unite"

The road ahead is well marked. It leads to restoring owners' capitalism by taking it back to its proud roots: "trusting and being trusted," as I said at the outset, no more than what St. Paul told us (1 Corinthians 4.2): "It is required of stewards that they be found trustworthy." The reforms that point in the direction of stewardship, director responsibility, corporate democracy, enhanced disclosure, and cooperation between owners and managers need not await long study followed by gradual, if grudging, acceptance. They will happen quickly and expeditiously if the owners of corporate America join together and honor their responsibilities of corporate citizenship.

At the start of the twentieth century, the rise of our nation's labor movement was inspired by the radical slogan "Workers of the World, Unite!" As the twenty-first century begins, the return of owners' capitalism will inspire a new and equally compelling, if far less radical, motto: "Owners of the World, Unite." Institutional investors have the ability to make that happen, and they must take the lead. What they need is the willpower and determination to do so. In the last analysis, it is up to the owners to bring back true corporate democracy, to demand republican government of our corporations, governance that is entrusted to directors who, rather than serving the interests of the management, dedicate themselves to serving as stewards for the interests of the owners, just as our traditional system of capitalism did so successfully, for so long.

TWO

Investment America

The first chapter in this section reiterates the "what went wrong?" theme, but here the focus is on investment America. Today, the earlier diffusion of stock ownership by many individual investors described in chapter two has almost vanished, replaced by the concentrated ownership of a relative handful of powerful financial institutions. The one hundred largest of these firms own 52 percent of all corporate shares, constituting majority control of corporate America. Yet the change in focus of these institutions from long-term investment to short-term speculation—along with the serious conflicts of interest these institutions face by collectively owning huge amounts of the shares of the very corporate managers that are paying them enormous fees for investment advice—has made them reluctant dragons in the exercise of their responsibilities of corporate citizenship.

Why did our investment system go wrong? The main reason, described in the following chapter, is that financial institutions came to focus their investment strategies not on the intrinsic value of the corporation, but on the momentary precision of the price of its stock. They seemed to ignore the essential truth that the value of a corporation is neither more nor less than the discounted value of its future cash flow, not only a point endorsed by wise oracles but a mathematical certainty.

The final chapter in this section takes on the difficult task of suggesting how to fix what has gone so badly awry, urging institutional investors to move away from their counterproductive foray into speculation and return to the proven wisdom of long-term investing, at last taking up the cudgels of responsible ownership. I call for a return to corporate democracy, with open access by owners to proxy participation. Recognizing that the original notion of direct stock ownership has been displaced by a new form of indirect, or agency, ownership, the chapter closes with a warning that "capitalism without owners will fail."

4

What Went Wrong in Investment America?

King Kong, or Mighty Joe Young?

Having "investors of the world unite" is far easier said than done. So as we turn our attention from corporate America to investment America—the shareholders who are the owners of our corporations—let's begin by examining, first, the ownership of our nation's publicly held firms, and second, the relationship between ownership and control.

When Berle and Means first examined this issue all those years ago in *The Modern Corporation and Private Property,* individual investors owned substantially all shares of U.S. stocks outstanding.[1] Unimaginable as it may seem today, the world of the early 1930s that they described was a world without institutional investors. With corporate ownership widely diffused among those legions of individuals, only a relative handful of whom held anything resembling a controlling interest in a given corporation, the door that allowed senior managers to operate in their own self-interest was wide open. Nonetheless, in that stringent economic era, there was little evidence of a pervasive "agency problem" in which boards of directors (agents) had failed to keep an eye on the interests of shareholders (principals). Corporations were run, or so it seemed, for the benefit of owners rather than for the benefit of managers.

As the 1950s began, financial institutions started to replace individuals as owners of equities. General Motors was the first major corporate pension plan to make broad use of stocks in its investment portfolio, and other pension plans quickly followed. By 1960, private retirement plans owned $16 billion of stocks, 4 percent of all shares outstanding. By 1970, they owned $67 billion (8 percent of shares). By 1990, $631 billion (20 percent). Today, private retirement plans hold $2.4 trillion in stocks, equal to 17 percent of all U.S. equities, and state and local government retirement plans own another $1.2 trillion, 8 percent of the total. All told, public and private retirement plans now hold a solid $3.7 trillion of U.S. stocks, representing the ownership of 26 percent of all U.S. equities.

Two decades ago, the structure of private retirement plans began to change. Corporations moved away from defined-*benefit* plans and toward defined-*contribution* plans. The traditional defined-benefit pension plan— a company-managed plan in which retirees are promised a pension based on their past earnings and years of service—gradually surrendered its dominance to the defined-contribution investment plan—in which employees regularly put away savings in profit-sharing and 401(k) thrift accounts in which they control their own investments. This shift represented a massive transfer of investment return, investment risk, and investment cost from corporations to individuals, who became increasingly responsible for their own retirement benefits.

By 1996, the assets of corporate defined-contribution saving plans exceeded those of defined-benefit pension plans, and the gap continues to grow. In 2004, private pension plan assets totaled $1.8 trillion and savings plan assets totaled $2.6 trillion, some $1.6 trillion of which represents the ownership of stocks, including company stock and equity mutual funds. Like the assets of their pension plan cousins, aggregate assets of thrift plans are broadly diversified among stocks and bonds. Table 4.1 shows the growth of the stock holdings of various kinds of retirement plans over the past fifteen years, as well as the holdings of other institutional investors.

The rise of the defined contribution plan played a major role in the growth of the mutual fund industry, a reflection of the particular suitability of the mutual fund structure for such plans. Funds offer a range of stock and bond fund choices, flexibility to change investments, transparency, daily valuation, and other conveniences. With the impetus of corporate thrift plans, mutual fund assets have grown exponentially, from a mere $2

Table 4.1. **Institutional ownership of equities.**

	Total assets (billion)		Total equities (billion)		Share of total equities outstanding (%)	
Retirement plans	1990	2004	1990	2004	1990	2004
Private defined benefit	$900	$1,811	$346*	$848*	11%	6%
Defined contribution	727	2,639	285*	1,570*	9	11
State and local government	800	2,072	285	1,205	9	8
Federal government	340	1,024	0.3	99	0	1
Total ret. plans	$2,767	$7,541	$916	$3,722	28%	26%
Mutual funds	$1,155	$8,107	$249	$3,996	8%	28%
Insurance companies	1,885	5,343	162	1,300	5	9
Endowments	712	2,132†	197	593†	6	4
Personal trusts and estates	522	925	190	223	6	2
Other	2,605	5,560	24	243	1	2
Total	$9,646	$27,481	$1,712	$9,349	53%	66%

Source: Federal Reserve Flow of Funds Accounts of the United States.

*Includes estimated equity mutual fund holdings for 1990 and 2004, respectively, of $4 billion and $128 billion in defined benefit plans and $21 billion and $600 billion in defined contribution plans. Total excludes this duplication. "Other" includes brokers, state and local governments, and savings institutions.
†Estimated based upon 2000 data, which is the most recent year reported by the Federal Reserve.

billion in 1950, to $1 trillion-plus in 1990, to more than $8 trillion currently. Retirement plans have been a dominant force in this growth, now constituting nearly $3 trillion of fund assets, or about 40 percent. (Employer-sponsored plans total $1.4 trillion, and individual retirement accounts represent $1.3 trillion.) Assets of equity funds alone have soared from $1.5 billion in 1950 to $250 billion in 1990, to $4 trillion currently, and mutual funds, owners of but 3 percent of all U.S. common stocks fifty-five years ago, now hold 28 percent.

Amidst all these changes—the shift in the structure of private retirement plans, the rapid growth of public retirement plans, and the rise of the mutual fund industry—the overriding theme continued unabated: We have witnessed the institutionalization of corporate America. Institutional investors of all types—public and private retirement funds, mutual funds, endowment funds, and bank trust departments—now own 66 percent of all U.S. equities.

The Institutional 100

Once scattered among masses of individual owners, then, the ownership of our corporations now is held overwhelmingly by institutional owners. Unlike the dominant but inchoate individual ownership that Berle and Means described in 1932, a remarkably small group of institutional managers now dominate the ownership scene. The largest three hundred managers hold $7.5 trillion of stocks, 56 percent of the U.S. stock market's total capitalization of $13.2 trillion. This ownership is highly concentrated: the largest one hundred managers alone hold $6.8 trillion in U.S. equities, 52 percent of all shares. These giant investors have the real—not merely the theoretical—power to exercise dominion over the corporations they own. The holdings of the largest of these institutions are awesome in and of themselves. Eighteen managers each supervise more than $100 billion of U.S. equities, including four managers that each hold some $400 billion or more.

A half-century ago, when the surge of institutional investing began, there were two fairly separate and distinct investment cohorts: pension managers and mutual fund managers. Today, however, virtually all of the institutions that I describe as the Institutional 100 now manage both pension accounts and mutual funds. In some cases (for example, Vanguard and Fidelity), mutual fund activities predominate; in others (for example, State Street Global, Barclays Global) it is pension management that predominates.

Among these giants, every one of the top twenty-five firms is engaged in both activities, as shown in Box 4.1. The thirteen state and local government retirement plans included in the Institutional 100 are considerably smaller, with the largest such plan (the California Public Employees' Retirement System) holding $56 billion of equities, ranking fifty-fourth. In total, these public plans, all engaged exclusively in pension management, own $390 billion of equities (5.7 percent of the top one hundred total). With this melding of pension plan and mutual fund interests, institutional investing is now a virtual totality, with the power to be the dominant force in investment America.

Box 4.1 King Kong: America's Largest Money Managers

The table below lists the equity assets managed by America's twenty-five largest money managers, and also includes the total equities held by the remaining seventy-five managers—together, the "Institutional 100." With 36 percent of the total equities held by the Institutional 100 represented in mutual fund portfolios and 64 percent held directly by retirement plans, and with the continuing shift of investments toward defined-contribution plans, there are no longer significant distinctions between the once-separate fields of managing mutual funds and managing pension funds.

The 25 largest holders of U.S. equities as of January 1, 2004

Rank	Firm	Total holdings (mil)	Holdings in mutual funds
1.	Fidelity Investments	$527,267	83%
2.	Barclays Global Investors	473,500	7
3.	Vanguard Group	415,173	97
4.	State Street Global Advisors	399,216	10
5.	Capital Group Companies	321,665	66
6.	AXA Group	237,431	10
7.	Mellon Financial Corp.	179,058	15
8.	Northern Trust Global Investments	176,356	3
9.	Wellington Management Co.	169,046	45
10.	Citigroup	151,587	27
11.	Amvescap	132,597	48
12.	Prudential Financial	120,442	18
13.	Putnam Investments	118,162	61
14.	T. Rowe Price Group	113,960	65
15.	Bank of America Corp.	111,317	21
16.	TIAA-CREF	110,486	4
17.	Merrill Lynch Investment Managers	104,887	23
18.	J. P. Morgan Fleming Asset Management	103,407	5
19.	Legg Mason	97,934	34
20.	Morgan Stanley Investment Management	95,652	48
21.	Janus Capital Group	92,569	67
22.	Sun Life Financial	89,259	59
23.	Franklin Resources	86,500	62
24.	American Express Company	81,290	32
25.	Allianz Dresdner Asset Management (U.S.)	74,846	25
Top 25 holders		$4,583,607	39%
% of all public stocks		35%	
Top 100 holders		$6,853,430	36%
% of all public stocks		52%	
Top 300 holders		$7,448,593	34%
% of all public stocks		56%	

Source: Institutional Investor *magazine, July 2004.*

The Sound of Silence

With its 52 percent ownership position in corporate America, the Institutional 100 is the King Kong of investment America. Standing, metaphorically speaking, at the top of the Empire State Building and shaking their fists, these giant firms, with the voting power to work their will among the nation's corporations, hold absolute control over corporate America. In effect, the Institutional 100 is the 800-pound gorilla that can use its heft and latent power to sit wherever it wants, whenever it wants, as often as it wants, at the table of virtually any board of directors in the nation. The societal implications of the collective power of this concentrated ownership of American business, in fact, could be easily described as elitist, anti-democratic, potentially menacing, and even frightening.

Yet so far there is no evidence that our society has reason to fear that power. To the contrary, our giant institutions have behaved less like King Kong than like Mighty Joe Young, the fierce gorilla who was the protagonist of the eponymous 1949 movie. Like King Kong, Mighty Joe Young could easily demolish almost any object in his path. But, when he heard the strains of "Beautiful Dreamer," he became serene and compliant. Without pushing this analogy too far, it could accurately be said that most of today's large institutional fund managers seem to be placidly listening to "Beautiful Dreamer." To the extent that they even consider their responsibilities to act as good corporate citizens, they seem to be lulled by the song's soft music into a deep and tranquil slumber.

Investment America could hardly have been ignorant of what went wrong in corporate America. Even before Enron dominated the news, week after week we would learn of another accounting problem, another corporate compensation excess, another company stock whose demise devastated a thrift plan, another earnings report that "pro-formaed" heaven and earth to produce earnings that met expectations, in a drumbeat that continues to this day. But with very few exceptions, the only sound we've heard from our investment institutions in response to these ethical and financial aberrations is the sound of silence. Even the investment banking scandals that came to light in early 2002 drew little public comment from money managers, who ought to have been leading the charge for remedial action.

School for Scandal

Investment America includes not only those institutions and individuals who share the ownership of corporate America but all of the participants in our financial system, including investment managers, stock brokerage firms, investment bankers, and stock exchanges. Reminiscent of the scandals in corporate America that revealed the flaws in the system in late 2001, the scandals that took place in investment America first called unwelcome attention to how rotten our investment banking system had become.

In April 2002, New York Attorney General Eliot Spitzer brought an enforcement action involving serious conflicts of interest in investment banking. Most of the large firms in the field had called on their "research" analysts to make investment recommendations to customers, not on the basis of an unbiased evaluation, but in order to enhance the firm's ability to support the initial public offerings they underwrote, and to attract new underwriting clients. In the words of the complaint, the attorney general found "fraudulent research reports . . . exaggerated or unwarranted claims . . . receiving payments for [favorable] research . . . [and] inappropriate 'spinning' of 'hot' initial public offerings [essentially, awarding shares to win potential underwriting clients]."[2]

Within a year, the actions had been settled, with the investment banking firms agreeing to cough up a stunning $1.4 billion, including penalties of $488 million, disgorgement of $388 million of profits, and payments of $512 million into a fund to sponsor independent research and investor education. The settlement also called for a variety of structural reforms designed to sever the links between investment banking and research, and to restore the integrity of investment research.

Obviously the Wall Street scandals could not be blamed on a few bad apples, for the firms involved represented the backbone of American investment banking, as shown in Box 4.2. But this is not to say that there were not some particularly bad apples in the investment banking barrel. Among them:

- *Henry Blodget.* The former Merrill Lynch analyst of Internet stocks first gained fame by predicting that the price of Amazon.com shares would reach $400 (which it did, albeit only for a brief moment). As one of the New Era's "gurus," his favorable opinion could send the price of a technology stock skyrocketing. However, while he was publicly touting these stocks (often underwritten by Merrill Lynch), his real opinion seemed to be quite the opposite. In private e-mails, he described these same stocks as "junk" or "crap" or worse.[3] Blodget was fined $4 million and barred from the securities industry for life.

Box 4.2 Bad Apples or Bad Barrel? Phase II

Unlike the case of corporate America, after the Wall Street scandals came to light the usual cry of only a few "bad apples" was conspicuous by its absence. Why? Because the firms involved represented the very backbone of the investment banking field. As shown in the table below, eight of the nation's ten largest banking firms, including Merrill Lynch, Goldman Sachs, Citigroup (Smith Barney), and J. P. Morgan Securities, were involved in the complaint and agreed to the subsequent settlement. Measured by the size and prominence of these firms, the investment banking barrel itself was chock full of bad apples. The heavy penalties levied on these firms represent the beginning of the serious repair that is required.

Investment banks implicated in the Wall Street scandals

			Payments related to Spitzer investigation			
Firm	Rank	Value of merger participation (billion)	Total (million)	Disgorgement (million)	Independent research and education (million)	Penalty (million)
Goldman Sachs	I	$400	$110	$25	$60	$25
Morgan Stanley	2	240	125	25	75	25
Citigroup*	3	220	400	150	100	150
Merrill Lynch	4	210	200	0	100	100
J. P. Morgan	5	210	80	25	30	25
Lazard	6	150	—	—	—	—
CSFB	7	150	200	75	50	75
UBS	8	150	80	25	30	25
Lehman Brothers	9	150	80	25	30	25
Deutsche Bank	10	130	—	—	—	—
Piper Jaffray	n/a	—	33	13	7	13
Bear Stearns	n/a	—	80	25	30	25
Total		$2,010	$1,388	$388	$512	$488

Source: Merger participation from Thomson Financial.
*Includes payments made by Smith Barney, a Citigroup subsidiary.

The bankers' settlement with Attorney General Spitzer and the SEC also envisioned a quasi-public organization to supervise an investor-education fund, funded by a $55 million endowment. The executive director and board initially appointed by the SEC, however, made little progress and later resigned; they have yet to be replaced. But the crying need remains for education of individual investors, not in picking stocks or mutual funds, but in sound investment fundamentals and asset allocation principles, as well as awareness of industry abuses.

- *Jack Grubman*. Described as the "ultimate power broker in the telecom industry," Grubman was paid more than any analyst in Wall
  Street's history, at his peak earning $20 million annually.[4] As the tele-
  com analyst for Salomon Smith Barney (SSB), he was a central figure
  in that sector's meteoric rise in the late 1990s, earning his firm
  $343 million in fees in 1998 alone. In his research reports, he was
  unstintingly bullish on the telecom industry, an apparent quid pro
  quo in which telecom firms would provide SSB (or its parent, Citigroup) with underwriting business. His favorite stock seemed to be
  WorldCom, almost until the day it collapsed into bankruptcy, the
  victim of a massive financial fraud. (In an infamous incident, too
  long to recount here, Grubman wrote a favorable report on AT&T,
  apparently at the request of then Citigroup chairman Sanford Weill,
  to enlist Weill's support in getting Grubman's children enrolled in a
  prestigious New York nursery school.[5]) In 2003, the SEC found that
  Grubman had issued fraudulent research reports. He was fined
  $15 million, and barred from the securities industry for life.
- *Frank Quattrone*. This former head of the technology banking group
  at Credit Suisse First Boston (CSFB) was responsible for some of the
  era's largest IPOs. Quattrone and CSFB got into trouble for accepting
  kickbacks from institutional managers eager to get an allocation of
  those hot IPOs. In return for significant allocations—which they
  expected to "flip" for a quick one-day profit—clients would agree
  to make another trade through CSFB in which they would pay a
  commission upwards of $1 per share, instead of the usual $0.05,
  a practice all too common on Wall Street. What tripped-up Quattrone
  was an e-mail he sent to his colleagues in late 2000, immediately after
  he learned of a coming federal investigation of CSFB's IPO practices.
  In it, he improperly urged them to "clean up" their files. In
  September 2004, Quattrone was found guilty of obstructing justice
  and witness tampering, and sentenced to eighteen months in prison.

Power Without Participation

It is easy to understand, albeit difficult to excuse, the overreaching by the sell-side of the powerful marketing machine that is Wall
Street. Puffery is its stock in trade, and participants in the system could
hardly have been unaware that Street research is far from objective. But it
is almost impossible to understand why the buy-side—largely the institu-

tional investors who purchased Wall Street's wares—seemed so willing to rely on its research reports and analysts, to put aside its deep-seated skepticism, and to accept, seemingly uncritically, that information as valid. An army of professional money managers and securities analysts nearly 100,000 strong was employed by our financial institutions.

Yet there is little, if any, evidence that these professional investors took with any seriousness the ownership responsibility of the institutions that employed them or understood the due diligence required of security analysts. These institutions were part of no scandal, except the scandal that they failed to do their homework on the stocks they were buying and selling each day, and the scandal that they failed to speak up for the interests of the last-line shareholders—the mutual fund owners and the pension beneficiaries—they were duty-bound to serve. The participation of our private financial institutions in corporate governance was close to nonexistent.

One reason for this forbearance of these institutions from the governance process is the clear conflict of interest they face in managing the retirement plan assets of the very corporations whose shares they own, and collectively control. While industry leaders regularly deny that such a conflict exists, it is easy to imagine that a private institutional manager would be reluctant to vote against an entrenched corporate management that has hired it to supervise its multi-billion-dollar pension plan or 401(k) thrift plan, and was paying the manager huge fees to do so. Even when a governance or proxy issue involves a corporation that is not a client, the reluctance to speak out persists, giving credence to this perhaps apocryphal comment by a pension fund manager: "There are only two types of clients we don't want to offend: actual and potential."

In the mutual fund arena, managers vote as a single unit the proxies of each of the corporations whose shares they hold directly in the names of individual shareholders as well as in the names of the pension and thrift plans. In the pension plan field, while the corporate shares are registered in the name of plan trustees, both the corporation that operates the plan and the money managers themselves are in a position to make their influence felt. In all cases, the beneficiaries' interests are supposed to be served, but the waters are muddied by potential conflicts.

An American *Keiretsu*?

While pension trustees are fiduciaries who are legally obliged to vote shares in the interest of plan beneficiaries, it doesn't take a lot of imagination to realize that corporations themselves are unlikely candidates to be governance activists, aggressively voting the shares their pension plans hold in other corporations. Why would a CEO want to be known as a trouble-maker among his colleagues at the Business Roundtable, where some one hundred of the nation's most prominent and powerful CEOs gather to discuss the state of American business? Whether tacit or explicit, the watchword of corporate behavior has become "let he who is without sin cast the first stone." Through their defined-benefit pension plans and defined-contribution thrift plans, trillions of dollars worth of shares of other corporations are in the hands of the corporations themselves, whose firms, at least tacitly, look after their own collective interests. Today, we have something that resembles an American *keiretsu*, the Japanese term for a group of businesses that share an ownership stake in one another as a means of mutual security.

Worse, with so many managers of mutual funds and retirement plans now owned by large financial conglomerates, the managements of these conglomerates themselves hold substantial weight in deciding how portfolio shares are voted. Almost without realizing it, we have developed a system of circularity in which the owners are the owned. For example, the accounts managed by Citigroup's money management arm now hold some 42 million shares of Citigroup itself. That holding, almost one percent of the bank's 5.1 billion shares, is large in and of itself. But when combined with Citigroup shares held by other managers who face the same conflicts, reinforced by the ownership of other managers controlled by these conglomerates, the aggregate is enormous. (Institutions own about 65 percent of Citigroup's shares.) Small wonder that we're never quite sure who is paying the piper and calling the governance tune, and with what motivation. This is not merely asking the fox to mind the henhouse. It's more like asking the fox to mind the foxes in the henhouse.

Practical voting issues are easy to imagine. Suppose there were a proxy proposal to separate the jobs of chairman and CEO of Citigroup, where a single individual now holds both positions. How would the Citigroup investment management officials vote the Citigroup shares they hold? What process would they use to decide? What if their money managers believed that the proposal to separate the roles was good governance policy, but the CEO of Citigroup wanted to keep both of his jobs?* While rarely discussed,

---

*At a 2005 conference sponsored by the Council of Institutional Investors, a representative of Citicorp informed me that such decisions were left solely to their investment managers.

the obvious conflicts that arise from this circularity of ownership and control raise important policy questions about the fiduciary duty that money managers and trustees owe to their ultimate owners and beneficiaries.

Bring Back Glass-Steagall?

The acquisition of investment management firms by financial conglomerates has been a major, if largely unrecognized, trend of the recent era. It poses compelling conflict-of-interest issues that demand public examination. Such cross-ownership has become more the rule than the exception among large management companies. Table 4.2 lists twenty of the giant conglomerates—banks and other financial firms, U.S. and foreign—that own mutual fund managers. From Citigroup to American Express to Goldman Sachs and Merrill Lynch, most of these firms are household names. Together, they control $2.3 trillion of mutual fund assets, including nearly $1 trillion of common stocks.

Much of the acquisition activity that led to this conglomeration depended on the gradual dilution of the provisions of the Glass-Steagall Act of 1933, culminating in its effective repeal. That act was designed to remedy the unsavory alliance of commercial banking and securities underwriting that had been deeply involved in the widespread financial manipulation and stock-rigging during the great bull market of the late 1920s, which contributed so heavily to the great bust that followed. But over time, legislative changes and lax regulation eroded the protections provided by Glass-Steagall, and the banking and securities fields again drew close together.

During recent times, the combination of banking and underwriting functions seemed to repeat the sins of the earlier era. It may not be coincidental that subsidiaries of most of the banks listed in Table 4.2 are not only managing and distributing mutual funds but also operating brokerage businesses, underwriting securities, and lending money and then syndicating loans to the very companies whose shares they hold in the portfolios of the mutual funds and pension accounts they manage. Indeed, in a suit brought on behalf of New York State Teachers Pension Fund, five of the firms listed in Table 4.2 paid $5.4 billion early in 2005 to settle claims that they failed to exercise due diligence in underwriting the bonds of WorldCom. Bank of America, also on the list, recently paid $69 million to settle claims against it for damages in selling the notes of Enron to institutional investors, while

Table 4.2. Total assets under management of largest mutual fund companies owned by conglomerates, January 2005.

Manager parent	Mutual fund unit	Total mutual fund assets (billion)
Allianz AG	PIMCO Funds	$182
American Express	American Express	63
AMVESCAP	AIM Investments	107
AXA	AllianceBernstein	90
Bank of America	Nations Funds	116
Barclays Bank	Barclays Global	114
Citigroup	Citi/Smith Barney Funds	143
Deutsche Bank	Scudder	103
Goldman Sachs	Goldman Sachs	100
J. P. Morgan Chase & Co	J. P. Morgan/American Century Funds	277
Marsh & McLennan	Putnam	119
MassMutual	Oppenheimer Funds	131
Mellon Financial	Dreyfus	141
Merrill Lynch	Merrill Lynch	190
Morgan Stanley	Morgan Stanley	92
PNC Financial	BlackRock	91
Prudential Financial	Prudential	35
State Street	State Street Global	38
Sun Life of Canada	MFS	78
Wachovia	Evergreen Investment	102
	Total	$2,314

Source: Strategic Insight.

another five have been named in that same lawsuit. "Oh what a tangled web we weave, when first we practice to deceive."

It is not clear that conglomeration is here to stay. Indeed, in the aftermath of the fines and settlements of recent years, the increasing regulation, and the new governance standards for mutual funds, there are some signs of its unwinding. In 2004, Merrill Lynch, Morgan Stanley, and Citigroup were reported to be considering the sale or restructuring of their asset management divisions; early in 2005, American Express announced its intention to spin off its giant investment management and fund marketing unit. Only time will tell, but if such a reversal comes to pass, mutual fund shareholders, as I show in chapter eight, should be the beneficiaries.

The Cost-Benefit Equation

Passivity in governance, furthermore, earns a high score on the cost-benefit scale. Let others undertake the hard work, the high profile, and, however moderate in the grand scheme of things, the costs of activism. If their efforts are successful, the passive investors who hold, say, the remaining 95 to 99 percent of the target company's shares spend nothing but reap substantial rewards. What is more, they also benefit by increasing their chances of luring away the pension and thrift plans managed by the activists. The decision to remain silent, then, becomes a sort of "win-win" decision for the do-nothing investor.

Given the existing conflicts of interest described above, most corporate activism has been left largely to independent institutional investors that are *not* in the business of serving private pension clients: state and local government pension funds and TIAA-CREF, the giant institution whose mission is to provide investment services for faculty and staff of schools, colleges, and universities.

Although the assets of their pension funds are relatively small, labor unions are also active in promoting reform. Union plans, and sometimes state and local government plans as well, however, often have allowed political agendas to shape their voting policies. Political pressure creates a different form of conflict of interest in the public arena than the business pressures of the private sector, but the conflict is no less real—the potential to serve investors with special interests rather than the stock owners as a group. But the public interest cries out for *all* agent institutions to serve as the faithful fiduciaries of their principals, the investors whose interests they are duty-bound to honor.

From Active Citizens to Passive

The rise of managers' capitalism has been greatly facilitated by broad changes that have led owners to be largely passive: the shift from individual to institutional ownership; the agency problem under which these institutional intermediaries often seem to place their own interests over the interests of those mutual fund owners and plan beneficiaries they are supposed to serve; the obvious conflicts of interest; the rise of financial conglomeration that characterizes contemporary investment America; and the cost-benefit ratio that favors passivity. Together, these developments have had the counterproductive effect of generating vastly reduced participation by investors in the governance of our nation's corporations.

But it wasn't supposed to be that way. In my 1951 Princeton thesis that examined the economic role of mutual funds, for example, I devoted a full chapter to their role "as an influence on corporate management," noting with approval the SEC's 1940 call for mutual funds to serve as "the useful role of representatives of the great number of inarticulate and ineffective individual investors in corporations in which funds are interested."[6]

The industry seemed prepared to accept that mandate. The 1949 *Fortune* article that inspired my thesis reported, "One of the pet ideas of [Merrill Griswold, longtime chairman of Massachusetts Investors Trust, the nation's original mutual fund, and for its first fifty years the industry's largest equity fund] is that the mutual fund is the ideal champion of . . . the small stockholder in conversations with corporate management, needling corporations on dividend policies, blocking mergers, and pitching in on proxy fights."[7] In my thesis I approvingly quoted a comment from an article by Griswold in *Harvard Business Review:* "Investment companies are . . . in a position to work intelligently with corporate managements on plans for mergers, recapitalizations, and other corporate changes. They can point out objections to such plans and suggest changes necessary to assure fair treatment of all stockholders. As intelligent and unbiased stockholders, investment companies can also come to the defense of business organizations and their managements against unwarranted attacks by others."[8]

A half-century ago then, institutional investors—personified by the mutual fund industry of yore, and, by implication, the embryonic pension plans that were just beginning to make their mark—seemed destined to play an active role in corporate governance, diligently observing their responsibilities of corporate citizenship.

It was not to be.

Benjamin Graham on Corporate Governance

Even then, the legendary Benjamin Graham was disappointed by the failure of corporate owners to act in their own interests. But, like Griswold, he had high hopes that shareholders would, when necessary, get involved in governance. In 1949, in the first edition of his classic *The Intelligent Investor,* Graham—the Columbia professor who was mentor to

investment icon Warren Buffett—devoted fully thirty-five of the book's
240 pages to the importance of shareholder-management relationships.*
An excerpt from that early message:

> The first level is that of legal rights and legal machinery. Here the stock-
> holders as a class are king. Acting as a majority they can hire and fire
> managements and bend them completely to their will. Though owner-
> ship may be widely scattered, there is no legal obstacle to many stock-
> holders' joining forces so as to create an effective majority voice on any
> issue that may arise.
>
> The second level is that of the assertion of stockholders' rights in
> practice. Here the stockholders are a complete washout. As a class they
> show neither intelligence nor alertness. They vote in sheep-like fashion
> for whatever the management recommends no matter how poor the
> management's record of accomplishment may be.
>
> The third level is that of the stockholders' actual treatment by man-
> agements. Here the picture is by no means a bad one. The typical man-
> agement is honest, competent, and fair-minded. It does the right thing,
> even though it could easily get away with the wrong thing. It might be
> seriously remarked here that our generally good managements have
> produced stupid stockholders. If inefficient or dishonest managements
> were the rule, it would not take long for the country's stockholders to
> wake up.[9]

Optimism Dashed

As managers' capitalism came to the fore in corporate America,
however, the country's investors—now dominated by the giant firms of
the Institutional 100—did not wake up. Benjamin Graham's first two
points remain valid today: one, stockholders remain the "kings" he described; two, they remain largely on the sidelines, washouts displaying
"neither intelligence nor alertness." But on the third point, his optimism
that owners would respond with alacrity to overreaching by managers,
proved ill founded. In 1949, long before the self-serving excesses of managers' capitalism that we have witnessed of late, he observed, "Conditions
are indeed good on the whole—but there are far too many exceptions. If

---

*Twenty-four years later, in the book's fourth and final edition, Mr. Graham devoted just 7½
pages to this subject.

in one company out of ten either the management is incompetent or the stockholders are not getting proper treatment, we have a situation that requires intelligent action by the owners of the nation's large businesses."

When Graham described the typical management of his day as doing "the right thing," he hardly could have imagined that in a later era so many managers would think that they "could easily get away with the wrong thing." Yet even in cases when incompetent, dishonest, and inefficient managements came to ride in the saddle of some of America's largest businesses, the country's institutional stockholders largely stood by in silence. If in Graham's era, "our generally good managements [had] produced stupid stockholders," there is little evidence that the recent era, with too many "bad managements"—inefficient, overcompensated, pushing the ethical envelope, engaged in financial engineering, and placing their own interest first—produced the smart stockholders that Graham would have expected to emerge. (More of Mr. Graham's thoughtful wisdom on owner-manager relationships is presented in Box 4.3.)

Clearly, the general level of management integrity that Graham described all those years ago has gradually deteriorated. Consider the contrast between the egregious management compensation and character failings described in my first chapter with the managements of corporate America in Graham's day, an earlier age that was accurately described by *New York Times* columnist Paul Krugman:

> In the 1960's, America's great corporations behaved more like socialist republics than like cutthroat capitalist enterprises, and top executives behaved more like public-spirited bureaucrats than like captains of industry. I'm not exaggerating. Consider the description of executive behavior offered by John Kenneth Galbraith in his 1967 book, *The New Industrial State*: "Management does not go out ruthlessly to reward itself—a sound management is expected to exercise restraint." Managerial self-dealing was a thing of the past: "With the power of decision goes opportunity for making money. . . . Were everyone to seek to do so . . . the corporation would be a chaos of competitive avarice. But these are not the sort of things that a good company man does; a remarkably effective code bans such behavior. Group decision-making insures, moreover, that almost everyone's actions and even thoughts are known to others. This acts to enforce the code and, more than incidentally, a high standard of personal honesty as well."[10]

Box 4.3 Benjamin Graham on Owner-Manager Relationships:

There are just two basic questions to which stockholders should turn their attention: (1) Is the management reasonably efficient? (2) Are the interests of the average *outside* stockholder receiving proper recognition? Strangely enough, neither of these questions has received proper presentation, even in stockholder-management disputes. Such disputes have turned mainly on matters of managerial compensation and of alleged improper dealings by those in control. Excessive compensation to officers is by no means a negligible matter. There are real abuses here, especially through the use of stock options at inadequate prices and sometimes through unduly liberal pension plans.

The attitude of the financial world toward good and bad management seems to this writer to be utterly childish. First, we have the solemn assurance that quality of management is the most important consideration in selecting an investment. Second, we have the complete absence of any serious effort to determine the quality of management by any rational tests. Third, we find no interest of any kind in the common-sense objective of improving or replacing weak managements—even though their existence is freely admitted. The first and last word of wisdom to the owners of American business is: "If you don't like the management, sell your stock."

One reason why stockholders have largely ignored the question of the role of boards of directors in the determination of managerial ability is their belief that the directors they elect are the ones who have both the duty and the opportunity to pass critical judgment on the executive staff. Since the stockholders are much farther removed from the scene than are the directors, their traditional inertia is reinforced by a certain logic, which limits their expression of ownership to voting for the directors whose names appear on the official proxy statement. The rest is then up to the directors.

The trouble with this idea is that directors are rarely independent of management. . . . Our observation is that the officers choose the directors more often than the directors choose the officers. [When executives] constitute a majority of the board . . . the notion that the directors serve as a check on the management is patently incorrect. But . . . even the non-officer directors are generally bound closely to the executives by ties of friendship and often of business dealings. When a president has outlived his usefulness or fails to measure up to the growing requirements of his job, he is not going to be removed by his personal friends.

Source: Benjamin Graham, The Intelligent Investor *(1949; New York: HarperCollins, 2005), 208–9, 212. Reprinted by permission of HarperCollins Publishers Inc.*

What Harvard professor Galbraith described in 1967 was the same world of corporate managers that Ben Graham had earlier described in *The Intelligent Investor,* managers who typically were "honest, competent, and fair-minded . . . doing the right thing." It was a world that was a far cry from the world of corporate America that was about to emerge. It proved to be a new and less attractive form of capitalism. Commenting on the change, Paul Krugman continued:

> Claims that we've entered a second Gilded Age aren't exaggerated. In America's middle-class era [the era described in the preceding citation], the mansion-building, yacht-owning classes had pretty much disappeared. . . . In 1970 the top 0.01 percent of taxpayers had 0.7 percent of total income—that is, they earned "only" 70 times as much as the average, not enough to buy or maintain a mega-residence. But in 1998 the top 0.01 percent received more than 3 percent of all income. That meant that the 13,000 richest families in America had almost as much income as the 20 million poorest households; those 13,000 families had incomes 300 times that of average families.[11]

While this relative handful of high-powered earners includes not only CEOs but entertainers, sports stars, and entrepreneurs, the obvious parallel between the compensation of the average CEO and that of the average worker described in chapter one—280 to 1—is both striking and ominous.* Yet the nation's stockholders still did not awaken.

Exploding the Firecracker

We cannot say that Ben Graham didn't warn us about what might lie ahead. The legendary investor concluded his analysis "with a dash of acerbity which may seem out of harmony with the sweet reasonableness of our earlier discussion. The change of tone is intentional. Years of experience has taught us that the only way to inspire the average American stockholder to take any *independently* intelligent action would be by exploding a firecracker under him."[12]

---

*It is said that soaring CEO compensation was in part a reflection of the enormous, and increasingly public, compensation paid to star athletes, entertainment personalities, and movie stars. Such comparisons are absurd. These celebrities are essentially paid by their fans or the owners of teams or networks out of their own pockets. CEOs are paid by directors, not out of their own pockets but with other people's money, a clear example of the "agency problem" in our investment system.

In the half-century following the publication of *The Intelligent Investor,* few, if any, firecrackers have exploded under our stockholders. Although the Institutional 100 of investment America has risen to power over corporate America that is theoretically beyond challenge, these owners have seemed to ignore the gross excesses of corporate America in the recent era and have been virtually absent, not only from the governance scene, but from legal and regulatory processes aimed at reforming the faltering system. Consider this astonishing lack of participation by managers of private (versus public) funds:

- No mutual fund firm, pension manager, bank, or insurance company has ever sponsored a proxy resolution that was opposed by the board of directors or management.
- Not a single institutional manager testified before Congress regarding the expensing of options, despite the fact that they must have had an opinion.
- No institutional investor testified before Congress about the most significant piece of legislation affecting public companies in the last fifty years, the Sarbanes-Oxley reform bill.[13]
- Among the some 17,000 responses to the SEC proposal to grant limited access to proxies to permit institutions to nominate corporate directors, no large shareholder demanded more substantial access, and most didn't even bother to comment. (A few even argued for more stringent limitations on access.)
- No large shareholder has urged the Financial Standards Accounting Board to get on with the job of requiring stock options to be expensed.
- No senior executive of a major mutual fund complex has spoken out on the subject of the rights and responsibilities of either corporate shareholders or mutual fund shareholders.*

It is high time we explode that firecracker under investment America. Indeed, in this new age of managers' capitalism that even Graham could not have imagined, we ought to explode a whole barrage of firecrackers under each corporation that places the managers' interest ahead of the

---

* I have looked carefully at the records, but I may have missed some participants in one of these final three points. If so, I apologize for the oversight.

owners' interest. Much of that failure of our corporations to look after their owners' interests can be attributed to what went wrong in investment America. Even as individual investors were largely supplanted by institutional investors, these powerful new owners seemed to attend only peripherally to the interests of those individuals in whose name they invested.

At the same time, the strategic ethos of investment America moved from the wisdom of long-term investing to the folly of short-term speculation. As otherwise intelligent institutional investors came to focus on stock prices rather than corporate values, stockowners were transmogrified into stockholders. Those who *rent* stocks hardly need care about their responsibilities of corporate citizenship, but those who *own* stocks *must* care about governance. Indeed, they can't afford *not* to care.

As investment America came to focus on momentary stock prices rather than intrinsic corporate values, it presided over an era of excessive executive compensation and financial engineering for which our society continues to pay substantial costs and bear heavy burdens. As yesteryear's *owners* of corporate America became today's *holders* of corporate America, they enabled, aided, and abetted the pathological mutation from owners' capitalism into managers' capitalism. I explore the issues of why investment America went wrong in the following chapter.

Why Did Investment America Go Wrong?

The Momentary Precision of Stock Prices
Versus the Eternal Importance
of Intrinsic Values

The failure of investment America to exercise its ownership rights over corporate America has been the major factor in the pathological mutation that has reshaped owners' capitalism into managers' capitalism. That mutation, in turn, has been importantly responsible for the gross excesses in executive compensation, as well as the flaws in the investment system itself that emerged in the late twentieth century, reaching their climax during the mania of the stock market bubble. One of the most important contributors to that transformation was the sea change in the philosophy of investment America that I mentioned in the previous chapter, from the wisdom of long-term investing to the folly of short-term speculation, turning the stock owners of an earlier era into the stock traders of our contemporary world.

An Eerie Silence

Institutional investment managers had to have been aware of what was happening in corporate America. Well before the stock market imploded, the industry's well-educated, highly trained, experienced professional analysts and portfolio managers *must* have been poring over company fiscal statements, evaluating corporate strategic plans, and measuring how cash flow compared with reported earnings, the degree to which those ever-fallacious "pro forma" earnings diverged from reality, and the extent to which long-term corporate goals were being achieved. Yet few, if any, voices were raised. Whatever the reasons for turning a blind eye, the record clearly shows that investment America largely ignored corporate governance issues. Using Pogo's formulation, "we have met the enemy of governance reform and he is us."

One searches the records in vain to find a seminar on corporate governance sponsored by the Investment Company Institute, the mutual fund industry's trade association, or even a breakout session at one of its general membership meetings on "Earnings Guidance—Blessing or Bane?" or "Do Stock Options *Really* Link Executive Compensation to Shareholder Value?" or a speech by an industry leader entitled "Serving Fund Shareholders by Eliminating Financial Engineering." Even the few truly activist fund managers of the past—one thinks of Mutual Shares' Michael Price and Windsor Fund's John Neff—have left the scene, replaced by a new generation of managers that includes far too few noble members such as Legg Mason's Bill Miller.

There were myriad factors that fostered the freewheeling environment of the stock market bubble. As always, seemingly compelling new ideas played a part: for example, the turn of the millennium, the coming of the information age, and the Internet "revolution," one more unhappy parallel to the expected boom in trade over the South Seas in the bubble of the early 1700s. But the major force, inadvertent or not, was the happy conspiracy between corporate managers and institutional managers. When our financial markets are driven by speculative trading, there is overwhelming pressure to cook the books in order to sustain artificial prices in the stock market, and, using Oscar Wilde's formulation cited earlier, managers seemed to know "the price of everything, but the value of nothing."

How money managers behave cannot be divorced from how corporate managers behave (and vice versa). If the money manager focuses almost exclusively on the price of the stock rather than on the intrinsic value of the corporation, we should not be surprised when the corporate manager, in an attempt to "game" the system, focuses on the stock price, too. By the same token, when the corporate manager plays games with earnings, we should not be surprised when money managers endeavor to capitalize on the market's callow acceptance of whatever earnings the corporation reports, accepting uncritically the illusory along with the real.

The Triumph of Short-Termism

When our stock owners—especially our giant institutions—focus so heavily on short-term investment horizons, responsible corporate citizenship is among the first victims. While corporate governance issues would seem to demand vital concern on the part of the long-term investor, they lose much, if not all, of their importance for the short-term speculator.

Far too large a portion of the investment management industry may be fairly characterized as having a bad case of short-termism. The temperature of the investment patient, as it were, can be measured by his portfolio turnover rate. In equity mutual fund portfolios, for example, the average turnover of stocks leaped from a remarkably stable annual rate of roughly 15 percent year after year for decades, up to and including the mid-1960s, to 100 percent or more since the late 1990s.* Interest in governance faded accordingly.

If that six-year holding period of yore for the average common stock in a fund portfolio marked mutual funds as an *own-a-stock* industry, surely today's one-year holding period marks the field as a *rent-a-stock* industry. Why spend money on evaluating a company's governance, for example, when you likely won't even be holding your shares when the next proxy season rolls around? Indeed, given the hyper-short-term trading activity that now characterizes most institutional investing, the apparent reluctance of portfolio managers to speak out on governance issues, however counterproductive, may actually reflect a sort of perverse common sense.

Keeping a Low Profile

But there's more than short-termism that accounts for the absence of most financial institutions from the governance scene. Consider that market index funds and other funds that follow essentially static buy-and-hold strategies now hold some 25 percent of the equities owned by the Institutional 100. Such funds typically purchase each stock in the stock

---

*Turnover is defined as the lesser of portfolio purchases or portfolio sales as a percentage of portfolio assets. Thus, a fund with $1 billion of assets and $1.2 billion of stock purchases and $0.9 billion of sales would report turnover of 90 percent, even though total transactions amounted to $2.1 billion, or 210 percent of assets. (The excess of $0.3 billion of purchases over sales was created by net cash flows into the fund.)

market (or in the Standard & Poor's 500 Composite Stock Price Index—the "S&P 500"), weighting the holdings on the basis of each company's market capitalization. They then hold these stocks, well, forever. Index funds are the quintessential long-term investors. They cannot—and they do not—follow the old Wall Street rule, "If you don't like the management, sell the stock." Their only recourse in responding to corporate problems is to press the company's directors to fix them. Yet even the voices of these consummate long-term investors have been, if not totally silent, at least reduced to a whisper.

What's more, even active managers engaging in what passes for low turnover in the current environment (say, less than 35 percent annually) have generally refrained from intrusion into the affairs of the corporations in which they invest. One obvious reason for this passivity is the desire to avoid controversy. In the asset-gathering business that money management has become, a high profile on a divisive issue is more curse than blessing. Managers with reputations as pesky gnats aren't likely to attract many corporate clients. "Let sleeping dogs lie" seems to be the operative rule among institutional managers. They seem to consider corporate governance issues to be peripheral, unrelated to their quest to generate the highest possible returns.

The Wisdom of Benjamin Graham and Warren Buffett

The short-termism that characterizes the behavior of institutional managers defies the wisdom of some of the sagest investors of the modern age, and the wisdom of an earlier age as well. In the present era, all too few investment managers buy and hold for the long term, and all too many rapidly trade their stocks based on the changing valuations that "Mr. Market"—the metaphorical character created by legendary investor and teacher Benjamin Graham, whom we met in the previous chapter—offers each day.

As Graham pointed out, "Mr. Market" knocks on each investor's door every business day and offers to buy each of his stocks—or to sell him more shares—at its current price. But succumbing to the wiles of Mr. Market allows the emotions of the moment to take precedence over the economics of the long term, as transitory shifts in prices get investors thinking about the wrong things. "In the short-run, the stock market is a *voting* machine," Graham pointed out, "in the long-run, it is a *weighing* machine."[1]

Graham's view was that corporations managed with a view toward enhancing their long-term intrinsic values—gaining extra *weight*, if you will— would prove to be better investments than those focused on building short-term stock prices by engineering quarterly earnings with a view toward gaining extra *votes*. His simple metaphor works out in practice. The record is clear that fund managers who hold *companies* for the long term and allow intrinsic value to build over time have provided higher returns to their clients than managers that hold *stocks* for the short term and trade them whenever Mr. Market offers a tempting but momentary price.

Over the past decade, for example, the low-turnover quartile of equity mutual funds provided a risk-adjusted annual return of 11.6 percent, outpacing the 8.8 percent return of the high-turnover quartile by an average of 2.8 percentage points per year, a 31 percent increase in annual return. Compounded over the decade, the return of the low turnover funds was +200 percent, compared to +132 percent for the high-turnover funds, a truly incredible 51 percent increase. That pattern also held true when funds were sorted by the market capitalizations of their portfolios, and by their investment objectives. (Many other studies have confirmed this inverse correlation between turnover and fund performance.)

Berkshire Hathaway's equally legendary investor Warren Buffett, Benjamin Graham's protégé, is among the most pristine of corporate managers. As an investor who runs Berkshire's $38 billion equity portfolio of publicly-traded stocks, he is attuned, not to the vote of the short term, but to the weight of the long term. He describes his favorite holding period as "forever." With long-term returns that have exceeded by a wide margin the returns achieved by even the most successful other major investment organizations, his results speak for themselves. What is more, his philosophy as a money manager is in lockstep with his philosophy as a corporate manager.

Buffett's firm is publicly held, and he regularly hammers home to his shareholders the message that he prefers Berkshire stock to trade at or around its intrinsic value—neither materially higher nor lower. He explains that "intrinsic value is the discounted value of the cash that can be taken out of the business during its remaining life. . . . When the stock temporarily over-performs or under-performs the business, a limited number of shareholders—either sellers or buyers—receive out-sized benefits at the expense of those they trade with. *[But] over time, the aggregate gains made by Berkshire shareholders must of necessity match the business gains of the company.*" [2] What a refreshing perspective from one who knows what's important in investing.

John Maynard Keynes Affirms the Wisdom

Graham and Buffett were not the only brilliant investors to be concerned about the growing role that speculation played in the behavior of professional investors. Even earlier, in the 1930s, the great British economist John Maynard Keynes worried about the implications of such short-term speculation for our society. "A conventional valuation [of stocks] which is established [by] the mass psychology of a large number of ignorant individuals," he wrote, "is liable to change violently as the result of a sudden fluctuation of opinion due to factors which do not really matter much to the prospective yield, since there will be no strong roots of conviction to hold it steady."[3] The resulting "waves of optimistic and pessimistic sentiment are unreasoning, and yet in a sense legitimate where no solid base exists for a reasonable calculation."

Then, prophetically, Lord Keynes added that this trend would intensify as even "expert professionals, possessing judgment and knowledge beyond that of the average private investor who, one might have supposed, would correct these vagaries . . . would be concerned, not with making superior long-term forecasts of the probable yield on an investment over its entire life, but with forecasting changes in the conventional valuation a short time ahead of the general public." As a result, Keynes warned, the stock market would become "a battle of wits to anticipate the basis of conventional valuation a few months hence rather than the prospective yield of an investment over a long term of years."

Keynes 1, Bogle 0

In 1951, I cited those very words in my Princeton thesis, and then had the temerity to disagree. Portfolio managers, in what I predicted would become a far larger mutual fund industry, would "supply the market with a demand for securities that is *steady, sophisticated, enlightened,* and *analytic* [italics added], a demand that is based essentially on the [intrinsic] performance of a corporation rather than the public appraisal of the value of a share, that is, its price."[4] Alas, the sophisticated, analytic demand I had predicted from our expert professional investors simply didn't happen. Fifty-four years after I wrote those words, I must reluctantly acknowledge that the worldly wise Keynes was right, and that the callowly idealistic Bogle was wrong. Call the score, Keynes 1, Bogle 0.

During the recent era, we have paid a high price for the shift that Keynes accurately predicted. As professional institutional investors moved their focus from the wisdom of long-term investment—what Keynes called "a steady stream of enterprise"—to the folly of short-term speculation, "the capital development of a country [became] a by-product of the activities of a casino." Just as he warned, "when enterprise becomes a mere bubble on a whirlpool of speculation, the job of capitalism is likely to be ill-done."[5]

The triumph of emotions over economics reflected in the casino mentality of so many institutional investors has harsh consequences. When perception—the precise but momentary price of the stock—vastly departs from reality—the hard-to-measure but enduring intrinsic value of the corporation—the gap can be reconciled only in favor of reality. It is virtually impossible to raise (or, for that matter, to lower) reality to perception in any short time frame, for the demanding task of building value in a corporation in a competitive world is a long-term proposition. As our institutions lost their bearings during the recent great bubble, capitalism's job was indeed ill done.

Ignoring the Wisdom

Yet investment America not only ignored the sage investment foundation laid by its greatest gurus, but also ignored how far the financial markets had sunk into the quagmire of speculation. This change in focus from the eternal importance of intrinsic corporate value to the momentary precision of stock price was the root cause of much of what went wrong in investment America. It took only common sense to see it coming.

In October 1999, only a few months before the Great Crash of 2000–2002 began, the exuberant mood of the stock market was almost universally shared. Only short-sellers, a small minority looking for overpriced stocks, were on the outside looking in. It was then that I expressed my concerns in a speech entitled "The Silence of the Funds" before the New York Society of Security Analysts. I described the pervasive bullishness of the moment as the result of the "happy conspiracy" among corporate managers, CEOs and CFOs, directors, auditors, lawyers, Wall Street investment bankers, sell-side security analysts, buy-side portfolio managers, and indeed investors themselves—individual and institutional alike.

"Earnings Guidance" and Misrepresentation

The euphoric era that was soon to end was built on high expectations of corporate earnings growth that defied both reason and historical precedent. Corporate management would project high earnings growth (say, 12 percent per year), offer regular guidance to the financial community as to the firm's short-term progress, and, quarter after quarter, *never* fall short of the expectations it had established. As these forecasts of future growth became reality—or at least were perceived as reality—the stock price rose accordingly, delighting the shareholders, raising the value of the firm's currency for acquisitions, enhancing the profits executives realized when they exercised their stock options, enticing employees to allocate large portions of their thrift plans to their employer's stock, and facilitating a rush of initial public offerings, many of dubious provenance. Price-to-earnings multiples ascended to ever-increasing levels, and in the new economy companies, where there were often no earnings, price-to-sales ratios filled the gap without missing a beat. Investment America demanded predictable, steady earnings growth and, by golly, corporate America would deliver it!

A study of 500,000 earnings forecasts from 1973 to 1996 found that the odds that a security analyst could forecast, with the help of company guidance, to within 5 percent of the actual earnings reported by the corporation for ten consecutive quarters were one in 200,000. Yet over the twenty consecutive quarters ended June 30, 1998, for example, the security analysts' consensus for General Electric's earnings was within 2.37 percent of the mark. "The odds of such a display of clairvoyance on Wall Street," according to an essay by James Grant, editor of *Grant's Interest Rate Observer,* "are one in 50 billion. Who says that bull markets make you stupid?"[6]

Given that business conditions change, that the economy fluctuates, that technology was advancing at exponential speed, and that dog-eat-dog price competition serves consumers at the expense of producers, it seems remarkable that investors would accept, then praise, and then ultimately rely on the notion that a corporation's earnings could march ever onward, ever upward, with such consistency. But it wasn't real. Rather than true stability and consistency, hanky-panky had come to characterize the financial reporting of corporate America.

As evidence, Grant cited a *Business Week* poll of 160 chief financial officers, asking financial officers for their response to the following statement: "As CFO, I fought off other executives' requests that I misrepresent corporate results." Fifty-five percent answered, "Yes, I fought them off." Twelve percent said, "I yielded to the requests." Only 33 percent said, "Have never received such a request." In other words, Grant concluded, two-thirds of the CFOs in the sample have been asked to lie about the numbers. More tactfully, such deceit was rationalized as merely aggressive accounting.

Quoting money manager James Chanos, Grant added, "Everyone has gotten used to the nudge and wink about the abilities of companies to massage the bottom line through a variety of subterfuges and artifices, so there is not even a slight disappointment. . . . I have a problem," Chanos adds, "when goodwill write-downs [are followed by] kitchen-sink restructuring charges that write down all sorts of things or set up reserves that aren't needed. For example, a company will write down accounts receivable as uncollectible at acquisition and then collect them, with no cost associated. Writing down perfectly good plant and equipment to zero, and then having no depreciation expense against it. And then my favorite, setting up accrued liabilities, sort of nebulous future charges, and reversing them as no such costs are incurred. . . . Mergers give you all sorts of opportunities for accounting chicanery."

Reality Returns

What's wrong with that? What's wrong, as I said in that 1999 speech to financial analysts mentioned earlier, is that when we "take for granted that fluctuating earnings are steady and ever growing . . . somewhere down the road there lies a day of reckoning that will not be pleasant."[7] Well, measured by the level of stock prices, the day of reckoning was indeed close at hand. On March 24, 2000, only a few short months after my talk, the stock market made its high, and then began to descend. When it reached its low on October 9, 2002, the NASDAQ Index largely reflecting the "new economy" had plummeted by 78 percent, with the NYSE Index that largely reflected the "old economy" off 33 percent. While both have since recovered some of the lost ground, the aggregate market capitalization of U.S. stocks remains some $4 trillion below its $17 trillion high.

As we have seen, when we repeatedly fool ourselves and others, and when the gap between perception and reality grows beyond reason, it is only a matter of time until reality returns, usually with a vengeance. Speculators and day traders experience financial duress, often severe. Overly opportunistic investors realize the error of their ways and pull in their horns. Slowly the idea of *value* returns to the stock market. The eternal truth reemerges: *The value of a corporation's stock is the discounted value of its future cash flow.* All over again, we learn that the purpose of the stock market is simply to provide liquidity for stocks in return for the promise of future cash flows, enabling sellers of stocks to realize the present value of a future stream of income at any time, and buyers of stocks to acquire the right to that future income stream. Corporations, we again come to realize, must earn *real* money.

It almost goes without saying that bubbles are inflated by unrealistic expectations. And our financial system seems to thrive on building expectations that are optimistic beyond the pale. Wall Street analysts are unremittingly bullish; of 1,028 stock recommendations made by the typical brokerage firm during the first quarter of 2001, only seven were "sell" recommendations. Even as late as October 2001, just before its collapse, seventeen out of eighteen analysts rated Enron a buy. Going back to 1981, consensus estimates for future five-year corporate earnings growth have *never* been less then 10.2 percent and have averaged 11.5 percent,* nearly *twice* the 6 percent *actual* annual growth for that two-decade-plus period.

What Were the Professionals Thinking?

Were professional security analysts and money managers probing deeply enough into the financial engineering that was going on behind the scenes? Let me relate a personal experience. In 1997, SEC chairman Arthur Levitt commissioned the U.S. Independence Standards Board to consider the state of financial reporting, focusing on whether auditors were in fact independent of the clients for whom they were providing attestation services. That now forgotten Board included four independent members and four members of the profession—CEOs from three of the then Big Five accounting firms and the president of the American Institute of Certified Public Accountants (AICPA). William T. Allen, the eminent jurist and former chancellor of the Delaware Court of Chancery, served as chairman, and I was privileged to serve with him.†

In the course of the ISB's work, we retained a respected consulting firm (Earnscliffe Research and Communications) to prepare a study assessing the perceptions of various constituencies regarding the concept of auditor independence and objectivity. The firm interviewed 133 senior executives,

---

*The highest five-year earnings forecast, for earnings growth of 14.6 percent per year, came at the end of 2000, just before earnings plunged 50 percent in 2001.

†The other two independent board members were Robert Denham and Manuel Johnson. We began our work in the summer of 1997, and during the ensuing three years issued a number of independence standards. Given the intractable issue regarding the functional separation of accounting and consulting, however, the SEC ultimately decided to issue its own independence rules, and the ISB was dissolved in July 2000.

from constituencies that included CEOs and CFOs of SEC registrants, audit committee chairs, audit partners, and research analysts from both the "sell side" and the "buy side."

A Clean Bill of Health for Financial Reporting?

Chairman Allen and I also met with a small group of experienced and financially astute securities analysts from eight major money management firms. In that meeting, these experts expressed comfort with the integrity of both accountants and financial statements, albeit with a general willingness to accept that the auditor, paid by the client, cannot be truly independent. They also expressed the belief that the auditor's "reputational capital" would prevent fraud. (No one noted that an auditor with a reputation for standing rigidly against the demands of management would likely not be in business for very long!) Only one analyst among the eight, Trevor Harris of Morgan Stanley, expressed a serious concern: "Auditors have stopped thinking for themselves and have become clerks who are hiding behind rules (for example, post-retirement health care benefits), and putting form ahead of substance." He expressed "serious concern with the integrity of financial statements, which are sure to be revealed when the stock market collapses."[8]

The survey itself clearly indicated that the concerns Harris expressed were not widely shared, and financial reporting and auditing were given a clean bill of health. In its November 1999 report, Earnscliffe reported a clear consensus among executives that "the standard of financial reporting in the U.S. was excellent . . . that the actual figures being reported were painting an accurate picture of the financial health of the company involved . . . [that] very few believe the auditors have much to do with aggressive earnings management . . . [and that] most financial reporting could be trusted." As to the provision of both audit and consulting services to the same client, "almost everyone favored disclosure over prohibition." While some of those surveyed expressed concern about earnings management, the consensus was that "the SEC had overstated the problem of auditor independence, and worried that over-regulation would drive good people out of the [auditing] profession."[9]

When the Earnscliffe report was published, the AICPA engaged in a bit of hyperbolic breast-beating: "We share the report's view," the AICPA proudly proclaimed, "that the state of financial reporting in the United States is *extremely strong* . . . and agree that the media have created a perception that there is a serious problem where *none* exists."[10] (Italics added.)

Do tell! Six years and one great bear market later, we now know that the sunny but naive conventional wisdom of that earlier era—shared not only by CEOs and CFOs and by audit committee chairmen and auditors, but by security analysts as well—turned out to be the platitudes of the self-interested. Most members of the investment community, broadly defined, were participants in the happy, ingenuous, and mutually advantageous, conspiracy, sometimes unwitting, sometimes clearly not. As the stock market soared to its hitherto unimaginable peak in early 2000, the madness of the crowds of investment America's knowledgeable, professional market participants finally encompassed almost all investors.

Investment Versus Speculation

Investment America went wrong, then, because in the contagious enthusiasm of the day, financial engineering and manufactured earnings became the coin of the valuation realm, accepted by corporate managers and investment managers alike. What is more, the emphasis on short-term price came to overwhelm the reality of long-term value, as investors failed to honor the distinction between investment and speculation drawn by John Maynard Keynes six decades earlier. Observing the predilection of investors to implicitly assume that the future will resemble the past, Keynes warned: "It is dangerous to apply to the future inductive arguments based on past experience unless one can distinguish the broad reasons for what it [the past] was."[11] Yet we all knew, deep down, why the past returns on stocks were what they were. For there are two eternal factors that explain equity returns: (1) economics, and (2) emotions.

Keynes described *economics* as "enterprise"*—"forecasting the prospective yield of an asset over its entire life"—and *emotions* as speculation—"forecasting the psychology of the market."[12] Making the same distinction, I use the terms *investment return*—the initial dividend yield on stocks plus the subsequent earnings growth—and *speculative return*—the change in the price investors are willing to pay for each dollar of earnings

---

* From *The General Theory of Employment, Interest and Money*, chapter 12. This chapter makes as good reading today as when I first read it as a Princeton student in 1950. Interestingly, in the light of the thesis that I present in this book, Keynes introduced these concepts with no quantification whatsoever, so I have taken the liberty of casting them into arithmetic form.

(essentially the return that is generated by changes in the valuation or dis-count rate that investors place on future investment return).*

For example, if stocks begin a decade with a dividend yield of 4 percent and experience subsequent earnings growth of 5 percent, the *investment* return would be 9 percent. If the price-earnings ratio rises from fifteen times to twenty times, that 33 percent increase, spread over a decade, would translate into an additional *speculative* return of about 3 percent annually. Simply adding the two returns together, the total return on stocks would come to 12 percent. It's not very complicated!†

The Mathematics of the Markets

During the Great Bull Market of the 1980s, and then again during the 1990s, the sources of the absurdly generous 17 percent annual return on stocks that each decade generated were very similar. Dividend yields contributed about 4 percent to each decade's return and earnings growth was about 6 percent—a 10 percent investment return. But the price-earnings ratio increased by 110 percent in the 1980s and another 100 percent in the 1990s, in each case adding a remarkable and unprece-dented speculative return of 7 percent per year. Those stock returns, aver-aging 17 percent annually, reached the highest levels, for the longest pe-riod, in the entire two-hundred-year history of the U.S. stock market.

Who, you may wonder, would be so foolish as to project future returns at past historical rates that were so heavily influenced by speculation? Al-most everyone! The vast majority of individuals, including even those who considered themselves expert in investing, did exactly that. So did sophis-ticated corporate financial officers and their pension consultants. Indeed, a typical corporate annual report, describing the basis for the returns pro-jected for its pension fund, expressly stated, "Our asset return assumption is derived from a detailed study conducted by our actuaries and our asset management group, and *is based on long-term historical data*."[13] (Empha-sis added.)

---

*The reciprocal of the price-earnings ratio is the earnings yield on stocks. It is influenced by the risk-free bond yield. But because that relationship is so erratic, I have ignored it. For the record, the correlation between the earnings yield on stocks and the U.S. Treasury inter-mediate-term bond since 1926 has been 0.42. However, for the past twenty-five years it was 0.69, and for the past ten years 0.53.

†I recognize that one should actually multiply the two (i.e., 1.09 × 1.03 = 1.123), obviously making only a small difference. But such precision is hardly necessary in the uncertain world of investing. When addressing the lay investor, simplicity is a priceless virtue.

With each increase in past returns, then, astonishingly but naturally, corporations raised their future expectations. At the outset of the bull market in the early 1980s, for example, major corporations assumed a future annual return on pension assets of 7 percent. By the end of 2000, just before the Great Bear Market took hold, most firms had sharply raised their assumptions to an average of 10 percent per year or more. And since pension portfolios are balanced between equities and bonds, they had implicitly raised the expected annual return on the stocks in the portfolio to as much as 15 percent. (Box 5.1 discusses this issue in greater depth.)

Looking Ahead from the Bull Market Peak

As a new decade began on January 1, 2000, two things should have been obvious:

1. With dividend yields having tumbled to about 1 percent, even if that earlier 6 percent earnings growth were to be sustained in the years ahead, the annual investment return in the next ten years would be not the 10 percent investment return of the 1980s and 1990s but just 7 percent.
2. As for speculative return, however hazardous to predict, we knew that the price-earnings ratio of thirty-two times as the market reached what proved to be its peak was more than double its long-term average of fifteen times. If the p/e ratio were simply to remain in that stratosphere and go no higher, we were looking to a decade in which the total return on stocks would be 7 percent, composed entirely of investment return. But if the p/e ratio were to return to its long-term mean of fifteen times, that total 7 percent investment return on stocks over the coming decade would be *reduced* by 7 percentage points of speculative return per year, to a total return of exactly zero.

Whatever the precise case, when 2000 began, rational expectations suggested that we were facing a decade of greatly subdued returns on stocks.

If we had simply paused and considered Keynes's formulation that described the broad reasons that explained why the returns on stocks were so high during the previous two decades—a combination of investment return made up of a high dividend yield and solid earnings growth, and an enormous speculative return engendered by the soaring of p/e multiples to unprecedented heights—we could hardly have failed to recognize what

Box 5.1 The Scandal of Pension Fund Return Assumptions

In 1981, the average U.S. corporation projected an assumed return of 7 percent on its pension plan assets. It was a remarkably conservative figure. The yield on the ten-year U.S. Treasury bond was then 13.9 percent, and the prospective investment return on stocks was in the 10 percent range (5 percent yield plus assumed earnings growth of perhaps 5 percent), suggesting a return on a typical policy portfolio (60 percent stocks, 40 percent bonds) of 11.5 percent, some 40 percent higher than the assumption.

By the end of 1999, the assumed pension return had leaped to 9 percent. By then, however, the investment realities had radically deteriorated. The yield on bonds had tumbled to 5 percent, and the prospective return on stocks had fallen to about 6 percent (yield of 1.1 percent, plus assumed 5 percent earnings growth). Result: a comparable balanced portfolio would be earning a future gross return of about 5.5 percent per year, or 40 percent below the 9 percent assumption carried on the typical corporation's books.

Even that humble reality, however, is overstated, for those expected market returns ignore the costs of investing. If we assume a cost of as little as 1 percent for a large pension plan (smaller plans would incur higher costs) reasonable expectations would have suggested a net return of just 4.5 percent for the 1999–2009 decade, or 50 percent below the assumption.

Today's Outlook

As 2005 begins, the yield on the ten-year Treasury bond is 4.2 percent, and the expected stock return (with the dividend yield now at 2 percent) is perhaps 7 percent. Thus the expected return on the policy portfolio would be about 6 percent before costs, and 5 percent after costs, a figure that remains some 40 percent below the 8 to 8.5 percent return currently assumed by the average corporation.

In articles, in speeches, even in a televised give-and-take with a major corporate CEO, I've been challenging corporations on their pension return assumptions for years. Whether my analysis has helped change their thinking or not, firms seem to be less likely to base their assumptions on past market returns (perhaps for obvious reasons). But they defend their high projections on their growing use of real estate, venture capital, and "absolute return" strategies (usually hedge funds). But they rarely disclose the composition of their portfolios and the returns they expect from each segment, and simply ignore the costs of investing.

The steady upward march of assumed returns on pension funds by the corporations that operate them—even as prospective returns tumbled—

was one of the important facilitators of the "managed earnings" foolishness of the recent era. But while the flaws in pension accounting standards that allowed such manipulation could alter both the perception of investment success and pension plan solvency, simply assuming that future returns would be high couldn't alter the underlying reality. Assumptions, after all, are only assumptions.

Sooner or later, reality strikes, and the deficit between pension plan assets and plan liabilities to pensioners can reach boxcar proportions. Sooner in the case of some airlines (Delta's deficit is $5.7 billion); later in the case of automobile companies (General Motors' deficit is $8.6 billion). Largely as a result of excessive return assumptions and the inadequate plan contributions that follow, more major pension funds are bound to fail.

Three decades ago, in order to assure continuing pension benefits to beneficiaries of failed plans, Congress created the Pension Benefit Guaranty Corporation. While the PBGC has so far measured up to that mandate, today its own solvency is at risk. Its deficit at the end of 2004 was estimated at a record $23 billion, and it faces an additional potential liability of $31 billion from the beleaguered airline industry alone.

Clearly, we need far better ways to account for pension returns and pension liabilities, and better disclosure as well—disclosure of investment strategy, asset classes, expected returns for each segment, and reporting of the returns actually achieved. We also need to think long and hard about how pension fund assets should be invested, and how liabilities should be secured. But the handwriting on the wall warns us that it is the taxpaying U.S. citizen that will be left holding the bag for the irresponsibility demonstrated by corporate managers in their outlandish, indeed seemingly indefensible, projections of future pension fund returns.

Corporate Values and Pension Assets
This is not a trivial issue. Pension fund assets have come to constitute huge portions of corporate wealth. In fact, the pension plan assets of many large corporations are now often as large as—or even larger than—the business assets of the corporation itself. For example, the pension assets of the thirty corporations in the Dow Jones Industrial Average recently totaled $400 billion, compared to the collective book value of $700 billion for the businesses themselves. In some cases, the pension fund is relatively small compared to assets (Citigroup, Intel), and in some cases more or less normal (IBM, with pension assets of $74 billion and corporate assets of $159 billion). But GM, Ford, and Delta, for example, have pension assets (nearly $200 billion for the three firms combined) many times their corporate assets (just $60 billion).

was going to happen. The bubble created by all of those emotions—optimism, exuberance, greed, all wrapped in the excitement of the turn of the millennium, the fantastic promise of the information age, and the "new economy"—had to burst.

Unfortunately, rational expectations can tell us *what* will happen, but they cannot tell us *when*. As it happened, the day of reckoning came quickly. In early March 2000, less than three months after the year began, the Great Bull Market ended and a Great Bear Market began. When stock prices lost touch with corporate values, too many market participants seemed to anticipate that intrinsic values would soon rise to justify the prices of the moment. It was too much to ask. By the time investors learned this harsh lesson, the damage had been done.

Those who had been taken in by the emotions of the day were unwisely relying on the future investment return to be enhanced by a healthy dollop of speculative return that was virtually impossible to recur. Investors would have been wise to set their expectations for future returns with a clear understanding of the reasons for past stock market returns rather than falling into the trap of expecting history to repeat itself. But when they failed to do so, the bull market continued upward.

But the late stock market bubble was not only built on a rampant and pervasive bullishness. It was impacted by the willingness—nay, eagerness—of corporate America, abetted, as noted earlier, by the gatekeepers that were traditionally responsible for reining in the freewheeling corporate managers, but ultimately seemed only eager to please them. Too many managers focused not on building the intrinsic value of their corporations but on hyping the momentary prices of their stocks. Those prices, in turn, were driven by short-term earnings that were too often enhanced by financial engineering and leveraged by wildly unrealistic expectations. Seemingly uncritically, investment America embraced the speculative binge.

Values, Prices, and "Earnings"

As we now know, Wall Street's conflicted sell-side analysts, conscripted into being flacks for new public offerings, lost their objectivity and ignored the signs of trouble. Even the buy-side analysts of our large financial institutions engaged in their own search for stocks that could provide glowing investment performance, put aside their training, their experience, and their skepticism, and joined in the mania. After all, funds with outsized performance gains draw in assets to manage, and large assets generate large fees. So the professionals themselves share much of the responsibility for the bubble in stock prices.

In a trend that has attracted too little notice, investors quickly accepted a fundamental change in the very definition of earnings that make expensive stock valuations seem far more reasonable. As I noted earlier, while *reported* earnings had been the standard since Standard & Poor's first began to collect the numbers many years ago, during the 1990s the standard changed to *operating* earnings. Operating earnings are essentially reported earnings bereft of all those messy charges like capital write-offs, often the result of unwise or unfortunate investments and mergers of earlier years. Such charges are considered "non-recurring," though for corporations as a group they have recurred year after year, with remarkable regularity.

By focusing so single-mindedly on earnings per share, we failed to recognize that, in the words of *The Economist,* operating earnings are "an accounting fiction: Firms consistently overstate reported profitability. They tend to punctuate periods of oddly rapid growth with occasionally awful years of massive write-offs; admissions that most portfolio profits were overstated. In 2002, for example, write-offs soared to an astonishing 140 percent of earnings per share."[14]

The GAAP gap—the difference between earnings reported under generally accepted accounting principles and so-called operating earnings, or, even worse, so-called pro forma earnings in which even bad operating results are ignored—is widely accepted by both Wall Street sell-side analysts and money management buy-side professionals. But we ought to be careful when we accept the financial community's near universal willingness—nay, eagerness—to persuade us that the calculation of the stock market's price-earnings ratio on the basis of anticipated operating earnings is valid.

The net result of using the higher (albeit less realistic) number is to make price-earnings ratios appear more reasonable; that is, to make stocks seem cheaper. Based on $68 of operating earnings for 2004, for example, the p/e ratio for the S&P 500 Index in early 2005 came to a perhaps mildly reassuring seventeen times. But based on $58 of reported earnings, it came to a more concerning twenty times. Investment America and corporate America alike, I fear, have far too much optimism embedded in the higher earnings figure—and the resultant lower p/e ratio—to countenance the acceptance of the lower, yet far more realistic, version of accounting earnings. In the words of money manager Clifford S. Asness of AQR Management, calculating price-earnings multiples based on operating earnings is "either unforgivable confusion or conscious trickery."[15]

Loose Accounting Standards

Loose accounting standards have made it possible to create, out of thin air, what passes for earnings. One popular method is making an acquisition and then taking giant charges described as "non-recurring," only to be reversed in later years when needed to bolster sagging operating results. But the breakdown in our accounting standards goes far beyond that:

- Cavalierly classifying large items as "immaterial";
- Hyping the assumed future returns of pension plans;
- Counting as valid sales those made by companies that loan their customers the money to make the purchases;
- Making special deals to accelerate future sales at quarter's end; and so on.

What we loosely describe as creative accounting is only a small step removed from dishonest accounting, a boundary that in the recent era was crossed far too often.

Over time, this unwise, even lunatic, distinction between the reality of reported earnings and the illusion of operating earnings makes a staggering difference in corporate values. During 1993–2003, for example, cumulative operating earnings of the companies in the S&P 500 Index totaled $479 per share. Deducting $166 paid in dividends, the net earnings retention of $313 per share implied a commensurate increase in the book value, raising the Index's $177 book value in 1992 to $490 as 2004 began. But the final book value came to just $367 per share, or 25 percent less. Why? Largely because of the huge "non-recurring" write-offs of the era.

These per-share numbers vastly understate the problem. To understand their magnitude requires considering the aggregate earnings that vanished into thin air. When 1993 began, the total book value of the S&P 500 companies was $1.2 trillion. Over the next eleven years, retained earnings from operations totaled $2.6 trillion—operating earnings of $4.0 trillion less dividends of $1.4 trillion—suggesting a 2003 book value of $3.8 trillion. But, *mirable dictu,* the actual book value was only $3.4 trillion. For the 500 large companies in the Standard & Poor's Index, some $400 billion of book value had disappeared, the loss largely represented by those pesky "non-recurring" charges for write-offs that actually recurred in every single year of the period. While their impact on short-term operating earnings may have seemed unimportant, over the longer term they carved out a massive hunk of intrinsic value.

Loose accounting standards, furthermore, often come back to haunt companies that pushed to maximize earnings and meet the goals set forth in the guidance that they had provided to Wall Street. Result: later restatements of their financial reporting. During the recent era, the number of restatements reached unfathomable levels. The 1,570 public companies that restated their earnings from 2000 to 2004 (often for multiple previous years) were seven times the 218 companies that were forced to restate their earnings from 1990 to 1994. Reasons given for restatement included improper bookings of revenues and accounting for stock options, and errors in accounting for accounts receivable, inventories, and restructuring. It is fair to say that scores of additional restatements are in the wings today.[16]

Making the Numbers through Mergers

It is folly to rely on the higher earnings figure (and resultant lower p/e) without recognizing the reality that in the long run corporate value is determined not only by the results of the firm's current operations but also by the entire amalgam of investment decisions it has made, including all those mergers and corporate combinations. Since they don't usually work very well, investors should take a tough, skeptical stance when companies propose mergers and acquisitions, and be wary of claims that "value will be unlocked" or "substantial synergies will result." A *Business Week* study maintains that 61 percent of all mergers have been destructive of corporate value, a conclusion that comports with the consensus of investment professionals as well as with a detailed study of mergers by Bernstein Research.[17]

The Bernstein study revealed that companies that acquired other companies during the past decade turned in cumulative returns of 22.2 percent less than the stock market during the first three years subsequent to the acquisition. The greatest negative returns from mergers and acquisitions accrued to companies financing them with stock. Acquisitions by growth companies were most destructive to shareholder value, likely because the acquiring companies were happy to use as currency their stocks that were wildly inflated in the market bubble.[18]

Similar patterns were found in a study of 12,023 acquisitions since 1980, showing that public companies that paid cash for other public companies produced returns of 5 percent more than the S&P Index. When they paid stock for public companies, their cumulative returns lagged by 9.6 percent. And when they bought private companies they did even worse, lagging the S&P by 17.8 percent if they paid cash, and by 34.8 percent when they used stock, a difference that presumably arises because they are careful spending real money, and cavalier in spending shares that the insiders likely knew were overvalued. Corporate managers using stock for acquisitions, it seems, aren't stupid. But as Benjamin Graham suggested, perhaps owners are.

Suffice it to say that when mergers and acquisitions are proposed, attentive long-term investors should think about the lessons of history before they decide how to vote, and whether or not to use their powers of moral suasion to influence the management and directors. It's high time to recognize the fallacy that corporate acquisitions, when driven by dreams of empire by imperial CEOs or by their desire to artificially improve the earnings they report, automatically can be expected to improve business results.

The Search for Truth

Our financial market system is a vital part of the process of investing, and of the task of raising the capital to fund the nation's economic growth. We require active, liquid markets and we demand that they provide liquidity for stocks in return for the promise of future cash flows. In this way, investors can realize the present value of a future stream of income at any time. But in return for that advantage comes the disadvantage of the moment-by-moment valuation of corporate shares. We demand hard numbers to measure investment accomplishments. *And we want them now!* Markets being what they are, of course, we get them.

The consequences of ready marketability of shares are not entirely good. Keynes recognized both the favorable and unfavorable elements of public ownership of stocks, warning that "the organization of the capital markets required for the holders of *quoted* equities requires much more nerve, patience, and fortitude than for the holders of wealth in other forms. . . . Some [investors] will buy without a tremor unmarketable investments . . . which, if they had [continuous] quotations available, would turn their hair gray."[19] Translation: It's easier on the psyche to own investments that don't trade back and forth each day in public markets.

The Fallacy of Short-Term Earnings—However Calculated

The laser-like focus of investment America on corporate operating earnings clearly has to change. We can no longer ignore the seemingly unavoidable reality of smoothing—putting, as it were, the management's best foot forward—nor can we ignore the departure of pension-plan accounting from any vestige of reality, nor the invisibility of failed ventures and mergers that destroy value. But a focus on earnings reported under GAAP ignores the fact that even rigorously calculated earnings per share are a fallible measure of corporate performance. We don't give adequate thought to the differences between *accounting earnings*—however consistent with GAAP—and *economic earnings* that relate to the long-term health of a company's balance sheet.

This is not a new issue. Writing in the *Wall Street Journal* in the 1970s, management legend Peter Drucker entitled the first of a series of essays "The Delusion of 'Profits.'" "There is no such thing as profit," he thundered. "There are only costs. . . . The key figure is return on all assets (or capital employed) related to cash needs, to cost of capital, to risks." He hammered home the distinction between economic profit—what really matters—and mere accounting profit—an illusion. This argument made great sense to the late Robert Bartley, longtime editor of the *Journal*, who noted that "true profits are represented by cash—a fact—rather than reported profit—an opinion."[20]

What is generally lacking, according to G. Bennett Stewart III of Stern Stewart and Company, promoter of the EVA (Economic Value Added) concept, is the failure to recognize that it takes capital to produce cash flow. (EVA is essentially the return a corporation earns on its equity capital, related to the return an investor could earn simply by owning the entire stock market.) Stewart would require a charge against income for the use of equity capital. Why? Because, as Bartley attests, "unless a corporation earns more than the going rate of interest, it is destroying value."

Alfred Rappaport, professor emeritus at the Kellogg Graduate School of Management at Northwestern University, puts real meat on the bones of the ideas bruited about by Bartley, Drucker, and Stewart. In a 2004 article, he called for "a three-pronged attack on short-term performance obsession," calling for:

1. "*A Corporate Performance Statement,* focused on separating cash flows from accruals, dividing flows into those from operating activities

and those from financing activities, excluding non-recurring gains and losses, defining accruals in terms of levels of uncertainty—low, medium and high." (The estimated future costs of pension and stock option plans would fall into the latter category.) Result: meaningful help to analysts in forecasting future cash flows by understanding how much of company performance comes from realized cash flows and how much from accrual estimates, and by recognizing the risk that the most-likely accruals will prove to be understated.

2. "*Incentives for Corporate Executives,* using discounted index-options plans with extended time horizons, based on peer group indexes, extended vesting periods, and the requirement that executives hold meaningful equity stakes." He especially favors "discounted equity risk options (DEROs), in which the exercise prices rises by the yield on the ten-year Treasury note plus a fraction of the expected equity risk premium." Result: real pay for real performance that recognizes the opportunity cost of equity (the risk-free rate plus the equity premium).

3. "*Incentives for Investment Managers,* focused on rolling three-to-five year performance, deferring some payments in anticipation of future performance, and requiring managers to make a meaningful investment in the fund [that they manage]." Result: encouraging a focus on long-term investment rather than short-term speculation. He suggests that pension trustees rely heavily on index funds with a seasoning of funds that bear little resemblance to today's "benchmark huggers."[21]

Rappaport concludes: "there is no greater impediment to good corporate governance and long-term value creation than earnings obsession." He sums up his argument with the essential point: "Earnings-per-share-growth does not necessarily create shareholder value." It is not enough to demand performance, he concludes, but to demand the "right performance." In other words, economic earnings, not accounting earnings, are what's important.

Corporate America and investment America alike should heed Rappaport's constructive suggestions. In the competition for ideas to improve our financial reporting system, there may well be other, perhaps even better, changes that could be made. But the changes should encourage institutional investors to move away from their present obsession with short-term earnings of dubious validity, and toward a new obsession focused on the creation of intrinsic value over the long term.

Where Does Value Come From?

Benjamin Graham, as usual, expressed the eternal truth:

> Common stocks have an important investment characteristic and an important speculative characteristic. Their investment value and average market price tend to increase irregularly but persistently over the decades, as their net worth builds up through the reinvestment of undistributed earnings. However, most of the time common stocks are subject to irrational price fluctuations in both directions, as the consequences of the ingrained tendency of most people to speculate or gamble—i.e., to give way to hope, fear, and greed.[22]

> There is no truth more fundamental in investment than the simple statement that dividends and market value are the only concrete returns which a public stockholder ever gets for the money he puts into a company. Earnings, financial strength, increased asset values—all these may be of vital importance to him, but only because they will immediately or ultimately affect his dividend and his market price.[23]

Graham would have been stunned to observe the decline in influence of his philosophy of focusing on long-term investing and corporate value and the rise in the attention given to corporate stock prices and their sensitivity to changes in quarterly earnings. He would have been even more stunned to observe how much manipulation has gone into the financial reporting of some of America's greatest corporations, as evidenced by the remarkable gap between the reported earnings and the operating earnings of the giant corporations that compose the Standard & Poor's 500 Stock Index.

Looking Ahead

Why did investment America go so wrong? Because it focused on the momentary precision of stock prices rather than the eternal importance of intrinsic corporate value, however difficult to measure. Because it ignored the critical importance of future cash flow, however difficult to predict with accuracy. Because it forgot that long-run stock values are created by the enduring economics of investment return rather than the transitory emotions of speculative return. Because it valued operating earnings over reported GAAP earnings, both ignoring and accepting the manipulation of the numbers. The community of professional institutional investors must bear a heavy share of responsibility for what went wrong in corporate America.

It's up to investment America—particularly professional money managers who take seriously the profession of investing—to learn from the mistakes of the past, and to work toward building a better market system as well as a better society. The mission to return capitalism to its proud roots begins with having the owners of our corporations stand up and be counted—not only in what they say, but also in what they do. If institutional investors work to favor enterprise over speculation as the highest priority in making their investment decisions, they will improve the returns of the investors that they are duty-bound to serve and also their own standing as investment professionals and responsible corporate citizens. As investors work to restore owners' capitalism, they will serve not only others but themselves, working simultaneously as a positive force for both economic and social progress. Here's how Lord Keynes expressed it:

> The social object of skilled investment should be—not "to beat the gun," to outwit the crowd, to pass the bad, or depreciating, half-crown to the other fellow—but to defeat the dark forces of time and ignorance which envelop our future.[24]

It will be no mean challenge to turn investment America away from today's deeply imbedded practices of short-term trading, aiming not merely to outwit the crowd but to build a sounder and more rational system. If investment America focuses the allocation of the capital at its command on the companies best positioned to build cash flow and intrinsic value, our economy and our society will benefit. The struggle to defeat the dark forces of time and ignorance can indeed be won, and corporate America can at last return to serving its owners.

How to Fix Investment America

"Capitalism Without Owners Will Fail"

Investment America needs to be more like King Kong. Not to threaten to destroy everything in its path, but to ensure that our citizens, who put up the capital and assume the risks of ownership, realize the rewards of ownership to which they are entitled. Only investment America has the power to bend corporate America to its will, and with that power, the ability to reverse the present ethos of managers' capitalism and return to the system of owners' capitalism that has been critical to the building of our nation's economic prosperity and global power. But demanding that owners again act like owners—working through corporate directors to ensure that their ownership interests are honored—is a multilevel challenge that is not for the fainthearted.

To do so, the principal focus of our financial system must shift from the counterproductive short-term speculation of the recent era toward the type of long-term investment that produces an optimal return on capital and creates wealth for investors. In addition, we must give stockholders both the will and the ability to act as owners. In a time in which most of corporate America is owned not by individual investors but by financial intermediaries entrusted with the responsibility for the prudent investment of the assets entrusted to their care, we must also address the dramatically changed nature of the very concept of ownership.

Turning Speculators into Investors

The first of these tasks is the most critical: moving institutional investors from short-term speculation toward long-term investing. For only then can we expect stock*holders* to behave like stock*owners,* exercising both the rights and responsibilities of corporate citizenship. In today's volatile stock market environment, bringing about such a change will be no easy task. To accomplish it at all will take considerable time. To be sure, speculation plays an important role in the markets, and will continue to do so, as professional investors seek to exploit inefficiencies in market prices in the search to earn an extra return on the capital that their investors have entrusted to them. The problem is that speculation, which should rightfully play only a supporting role in the drama that is the stock market, has become the star.

Where should we begin? Understanding the heavy cost burden of portfolio turnover is a good place. Focusing on the dividend component of long-term return is another fruitful area. And focusing public policy on the societal cost of speculation is yet another.

It is not only that the traditional community of professional investors—largely mutual fund managers and pension fund managers—has increasingly focused on "forecasting changes in the conventional valuation a short time ahead of the general public" rather than "making superior long-term forecasts of the probable yield of an investment over its entire life."[1] (As described in the previous chapter, this change is precisely what Lord Keynes predicted.) In addition, a whole new community of frankly free-swinging speculative investors has come into being, part of a hedge fund industry that is now the fastest growing sector of American finance. (See Box 6.1.)

The extraordinary growth of hedge fund assets is a powerful indication of the increasing tendency of investors generally to focus on speculation rather than on investment. But it is long-term investors who will be required if stockholders are to bring their influence to bear on corporate America to recognize the primacy of the rights of owners over the rights of managers.

Turnover Costs

Our success in turning a gambler's market into an investor's market will be measured by our ability to lower portfolio turnover and its costs. Bringing portfolio turnover down to traditional modest levels (say, 15 to 20 percent per year) depends in part on the willingness of investment managers to move toward the prudent investment of other people's money, acknowledging the drag of portfolio turnover costs on their returns. All-in transaction costs (not merely brokerage commissions, but spreads and market impact costs) are often insufficiently quantified, and our fiduciary institutions have an obligation to measure these costs with care, especially in this age in which "algorithmic trading" computer programs measure just about *everything* that it is possible to express in quantitative terms. One eye-opening test is comparing the portfolio's actual return with the return of a static portfolio at the start of the year, assuming that no changes were made. The clear inverse correlation between turnover and performance in mutual funds, described earlier, sends an unambiguous message about the counterproductivity of transaction costs. (As soon to be discussed in chapter seven, aggregate turnover costs for the system represent a drag on the returns of investors as a group that is certain and inevitable.)

It is ironic that a combination of government intervention and modern information technology has contributed mightily to the rise of portfolio turnover. Only three decades ago, stock exchange commissions were fixed at a cost that averaged about 30 cents per share, irrespective of whether the trade was for 100 or 100,000 shares. The abuses perpetuated under the umbrella of fixed commissions were myriad, with enormous "give-ups" of huge portions of the excessive commissions to brokers who sold fund shares or provided other services to the fund managers (or even provided nothing at all), at direct and substantial cost to the funds' shareholders.* Eventually, after extensive hearings, the SEC forced the New York Stock Exchange to abandon its fixed rate schedule in 1975.

The era of negotiated commissions followed. Faced with price competition, NYSE commission rates plummeted—to fifteen cents per share, to ten cents, then to five cents, and now to about four cents per share. (Despite this near-90 percent reduction in per-share commission rates, the abuses have yet to be totally eliminated.) This era also saw the rise of electronic communication networks (ECNs) that gradually came to dominate the NASDAQ market, slashing the costs of trading. Their rates settled at dramatically lower levels, first three cents, then one cent, then even lower. Electronic trades in today's active markets now take place for as little as $\frac{1}{10}$ of one cent or less.

---

*One broker who was a grateful recipient of the largesse brazenly sailed his new yacht into a marina near a resort as a fund dealers' sales convention was in session. The yacht was named "Give-Up."

Box 6.1 The Rise of the Hedge Fund

One of the major developments of the past five years has been the rise of a new community of hedge fund managers, every bit as intelligent, well educated, and professionally competent as their less-flamboyant (at least from the standpoint of investment style) peers in the traditional investment community. Some present both brilliance and extraordinary integrity; others are accidents waiting to happen. For some the accident has already happened (for example, the 1998 failure of the $7 billion hedge fund known, not entirely appropriately, as Long-Term Capital Management).*

In 1949, Alfred Jones ran what was said to be the first "hedge" fund, essentially endeavoring to hedge long positions in undervalued stocks against short positions in overvalued stocks, which Jones is said to have done with considerable success. Today, a hedge fund is whatever one wants it to be, *any* combination of long positions and short, bonds and stocks, unleveraged and leveraged (often by ratios that would curl one's hair), relying upon sophisticated quantitative methodologies or basic security analysis, and in some cases following merger arbitrage strategies or "event-driven" strategies. As a result, risk levels vary from extremely low to truly awesome.

Strategies

However different their strategies, hedge funds share four common characteristics: (1) "Manager-driven" strategies that emphasize "absolute returns" that are largely independent of stock market returns, rather than "market-driven" strategies that emphasize the "relative returns" implicitly sought by equity mutual funds that seek to beat a benchmark. (2) High portfolio turnover that may run as high as 300–400 percent annually or more, dwarfing the turnover of even the most aggressive group of equity funds. (3) Confidentiality, with almost no public disclosure of their financial data, minimal regulation, and exemption from the Investment Company Act by reason of their limiting their participants to a small number of wealthy, presumably financially sophisticated, investors. (4) *Very* high prices, charging fees of as much as 2 percent of assets per year (or even more) plus 20 percent—up to 50 percent!—of total profits. (This large slice of return is called, a bit disingenuously, the "carry.") It has been said, with some truth, that the hedge fund is not an investment strategy; it's a compensation strategy.

Whatever the case, the steady growth of hedge fund assets over the past three decades, culminating in their explosive growth during the past five

---

*Contributing to its demise was the fund's extensive use of leverage; so extensive, in fact, that the $7 billion fund owned some $140 billion of assets.

years, has carried their aggregate assets to nearly $1 trillion currently, including perhaps $600 billion in stocks. Although this amount is not nearly as large as the $3.8 trillion invested in equity mutual funds, neither is it a trivial amount. Recent studies suggest that hedge funds now account for 40 percent of total share volume on the New York Stock Exchange and NASDAQ. The importance of hedge funds in investment America, then, is paradoxical. In trading volume, they account for an impressive 40 percent of the total; in share of equity ownership, a modest 4 percent.

The past returns achieved by hedge funds hardly justify this public adulation. From 1996 through 2003, for example, the annual return achieved by the average hedge fund was just 9.3 percent.[2] Investors would have been better served simply by owning a low-cost balanced (bond/stock) mutual fund. The conservative Vanguard Wellington Fund, for example, returned 10.1 percent during the same period, with risk that was lower (standard deviation of 9.9 percent for Wellington versus 10.4 percent for the average hedge fund) and with far greater tax efficiency.

The Past Is Not Prologue

What is more, many hedge funds (the SEC estimates that there were almost 400) have achieved their success by virtue, as it were, of illicit time-zone trading in mutual funds. In the aftermath of the fund scandals discussed in chapter seven, mutual funds have put substantial barriers in place to eliminate further timing schemes. In addition, as the hedge fund community grows, more and more smart investors will be seeking out smaller inefficiencies in a market made increasingly efficient by the brainpower and sophistication of the hedge fund managers themselves. Their very existence, paradoxically, will make the successful completion of their mission less and less likely in the future. As a result, much of the past hedge fund record can be characterized as non-recurring.

It is not the responsibility of government to stand in the way of free markets, nor to attempt to tame the growth of hedge funds. The recent decision of the Securities and Exchange Commission to require their registration, while a positive step, is unlikely to do so. The growth will slow only as investors themselves come to decide that hedge fund managers offer no panacea, and that many, if not most, of them are likely to be not only overrated but overcompensated as well.

As investors come to recognize the difficulty of selecting winning hedge funds in advance, the high risk of failure (over 1,800 hedge funds have folded their tents from 1995 to 2003), the high costs, the low tax efficiency, and that even past results of most hedge funds were average at best (albeit with huge variations above and below the average), hedge fund growth will slow and assets recede. As that happens, ownership of stocks will move into stronger hands.

Yet, while the commission rates on Wall Street tumbled, Wall Street prospered. Why? Because commission dollars soared! The reductions were accompanied by, and helped to engender, a staggering increase in the level of transaction activity. Combined NYSE/NASDAQ volume leaped from 15 million shares a day in 1970, to 80 million in 1980, to 300 million in 1990, to nearly 3 *billion* in 2000. Even in the wake of the 50 percent stock market crash in 2000–2002, daily volume reached an all-time high of 3.3 billion shares in 2004, an average turnover rate of 150 percent. According to SEC reports, the revenues of the croupiers of Wall Street increased accordingly, with the revenues of broker-dealers rising from $20 billion in 1980, to $76 billion in 1990, to $325 billion in 2000, declining to an estimated $270 billion in 2004.[3] The soaring revenues reaped by these security dealers, of course, simply mirror the soaring costs paid by investors. These costs, in turn, result in a direct dollar-for-dollar reduction in the returns that the investors would otherwise earn.

Dividends Matter

Another major factor in the rise of speculation was the gradual diminution of dividends as an important part of the investment-return equation. Even during the 1930s, with portfolio turnover at but a fraction of today's level, Lord Keynes observed from his vantage point in London that, "in one of the greatest investment markets in the world, namely, New York, the influence of speculation is enormous. . . . It is rare for an American to 'invest for income,' and he will not readily purchase an investment except in the hope of capital appreciation. This is only another way of saying that he is attaching his hopes to a favorable change in the conventional basis of valuation, i.e., that he is a speculator."[4] While that same influence of speculation prevails today, Keynes could not have imagined either the soaring turnover or tumbling dividend yields in the United States.

Historically, dividends have accounted for almost one-half of the market's return—about 5 percent of the stock market's 10½ percent long-term annual return—with the remainder accounted for almost entirely by earnings growth averaging about 5 percent annually. Yet the dividend yield on U.S. stocks dropped to 1 percent in early 2000, a reflection of the counterproductive investor attitude. During an era in which stocks were held for growth; income didn't seem to matter. Even in early 2005, the dividend yield remains at an astonishingly low 1.8 percent. (Speculative return—measured by changes in the price investors are willing to pay for each $1 of earnings—varied enormously from year to year over the past century, but the additions and subtractions balanced out rather evenly, and have had a negligible impact on long-term investment return.)

It is argued that U.S. tax policy makes dividends a less-efficient way to distribute corporate profits than buying stock back in corporate repurchase programs, and there is some truth to that. Nonetheless, it is ironic that the steady decline in the dividend payout rate occurred during an era in which pension funds and mutual funds became the dominant owners of stock. Dividends received by pension funds are completely exempt from taxes; in equity mutual funds, management fees and expenses consume about 80 percent of dividends, leaving only 20 percent remaining for fund owners, some one-half of whom, in any event, hold their share in tax-deferred retirement plans. (Fund portfolio managers, paid on the basis of pretax returns, are notoriously unconcerned about the tax costs borne by their fund shareholders on dividends and capital gains alike.)

Dividend Policy

A distinct advantage of dividends is that the income-oriented investor is less likely to be seduced by Mr. Market's daily siren song. In theory, by relying on dividends that are steady and, over time, growing, the income-oriented investor ought to be inclined to hold on to his shares. Experience confirms this theory: The owners of dividend-paying stocks have twice the staying power of holders of non-dividend-paying stocks. Turnover in stocks that pay no dividends now runs at an average rate of 175 percent per year; turnover in stocks that pay dividends runs about 85 percent per year—only half as much, albeit quite high enough. So if stockowners demand that corporations place much more focus on dividend payouts, the market's emphasis on the speculative element of stock returns should begin to abate. Investing for income is a *long-term* strategy; investing for capital gains is all too often a *short-term* strategy.

Such an outcome, however unlikely it may seem today, is by no means impossible. Indeed, the sharp reduction of the tax rate applicable to dividends (essentially, to a maximum of 15 percent) in 2003 already seems to have given some impetus to increased dividends. Investor-owners ought to foster that embryonic trend, pushing corporations, as appropriate, to step up their dividend payouts, and work to restore dividends to their traditional importance in the investment equation. Despite the absence of evidence that earnings retention leads to sound capital allocations, the dividend payout rate has been in a declining trend for decades, tumbling from a norm of about 50 percent during 1974–94 to only about 30 percent during the past ten years. Yet history tells us that higher dividend payouts are actually associated with *higher* future returns on stocks.

In 2003, Robert D. Arnott and Clifford S. Asness wrote, "The historical evidence strongly suggests that expected future earnings growth is fastest when current dividend payouts are high and slowest when dividend payouts are low . . . [which] contradicts the view that substantial reinvestment of retained earnings will fuel faster future earnings growth. [This conclusion] is consistent with anecdotal tales about managers signaling their earning expectations through dividends or engaging, at times, in inefficient empire building. Our findings offer a challenge to market observers who see the low dividend payouts of recent times as a sign of strong future earnings to come."[5] Typically, the future earnings growth of the lowest payout firms—about 3 percent annually—lagged the growth of the highest payout firms—7.5 percent—by an astonishing 4.5 percent per year.

Earnings Are Conjecture, Cash Is Fact

Further, as dividends return to their deserved place in the sun, reliance on earnings as the key measure of stock valuations should recede. Lest we forget, dividends—at least dividends well covered by prospective earnings—are "real," in contrast to those illusory earnings per share that are manufactured each quarter, whether under the rubric of generally accepted accounting principles or not. Even in those cases in which earnings are honestly administered, the calculations depend on myriad estimates and assumptions of future events unknown.

The focus on corporate earnings above all else has led us down the primrose path to unwise capital commitments, to mergers done solely for financial reasons and without business rationale, and to that misbegotten financial engineering that was, as we now know, a triumph of form over substance. Dividends, on the other hand, remind us that "cash is king" and plays a major part in the creation of long-term returns. A return of dividends to their formerly high standing would do much to reduce today's high turnover and excessive speculation. Earnings are conjecture; cash is fact.

Curbing Speculative Excesses

The price paid by investors for the speculative ethos of our financial markets is sufficiently high that, as a matter of public import, policy makers should consider developing differential tax strategies aimed at stemming excessive speculation. Way back in 1986, Warren Buffett suggested a 100 percent tax on short-term capital gains, paid by all investors—not only by taxable individuals, *but also by tax-exempt pension funds*. Although a tax at that rate *might* seem a tad extreme, perhaps a 50 percent tax on very short-term gains on trading stocks, scaled down as the holding period lengthens, would help to bring investors to their senses. (Buffett says that idea was put forth tongue-in-cheek. But with stock market turnover having risen from a mere 25 percent when he expressed his opinion to 150 percent in 2004, perhaps he'd be serious about it now.) And why not consider the creation of a special class of stock that rewards investors with a premium dividend on the shares they have held for longer than, say, one year? If we have the will to foster a long-term focus by investors, we can find the way.

Changing the speculative mindset of investment managers also would be abetted by the development of new forms of investment advisory contracts, for example, contracts that remain effective for much longer periods than today's typical one-year duration (subject to cancellation on shorter notice), to perhaps three to five years, albeit with immediate termination clauses for extraordinary events; contracts that clearly define manager mandates; and contracts that reward managers for longer-term achievement in which premium fees are paid for returns that exceed appropriate benchmarks and penalty fees imposed for returns that fall short. While such "incentive" contracts are virtually anathema in the mutual fund field as shown in chapter nine, they are widely used in public pension funds. But because smart managers prefer to be paid generously whether their performance is good or bad, corporations and fund directors will have to demand "pay for performance" if they are to get it.

Finally, the financial community ought to make a major effort to enhance the understanding of our citizen-investors that enormous long-term penalties are engendered by short-term trading. The toll taken by the costs of our system of financial intermediation include not only those onerous turnover costs but the taxes extracted by our system of federal, state, and even local taxation. For taxable investors, taxes imposed on the huge short-term and long-term capital gains realized during the late bull market had a devastating impact on their pre-tax returns, taxes that were willingly, indeed almost callously, incurred on their behalf by their money managers. Over an investment lifetime, this drain of unnecessary taxes may easily spell the difference between triumph and disaster in the accumulation of wealth.

If there is a single principle that individual investors should understand, it is this eternal reality of investing: *The returns earned by investors as a group will inevitably lag whatever returns our financial markets are generous enough to provide.* That lag is precisely equal to the amount of the costs they incur through our system of financial intermediation, and the taxes they incur on dividends and realized capital gains. Yet most investors seem oblivious to the actual toll that costs and taxes take over their investment lives, a state of ignorant bliss that our fund managers have been pleased to accommodate.

Investors *must* understand the simple mathematical reality: if the stock market delivers an 8 percent return over the next fifty years, $1 compounded will grow to $47. Even a minimal 2.5 percent deduction for costs and another 1.5 percent for taxes would result in a net return of only 4 percent. Compounded, that same $1 grows to $7—only 15 percent of the optimum return. Surely our society pays a price when, simply because of the costs of investing and the taxes on investment activity, the investor takes home less than one-third of the market's long-term return. Once investors realize that short-term speculation is costly folly and that long-term investing is priceless wisdom, and then select only those portfolio managers who shun the former and rely on the latter, the financial system will fall in line accordingly, and promptly.

Mobilizing Institutional Investors

As noted in chapter three, the requirement that mutual funds disclose their proxy votes to their owners has created a new and powerful motivation for funds to exercise their rights as corporate citizens. With 95 million fund owners, of course, that is equivalent to public disclosure, and we ought to require public disclosure on the part of all fiduciaries, including traditional pension funds and endowment funds. But with rights come responsibilities, and we need to develop standards so that *all* of those with trusteeship responsibilities—including those of state and local government funds and university funds, where political and economic judgments have been known to overshadow fiduciary requirements—will be held to high standards of fiduciary duty.

With the motivation to do what's right, institutional investors should also be given the ability to do what's right, with clear access to the proxy statement. As discussed earlier, however, such access is being allowed only grudgingly, and the SEC's recent proposal only leaves the door ajar to such access. The proposal allows large shareholders to nominate one to three directors (depending on the board's size), but only after certain triggering events take place. The commission must go further, and open that door wide enough to permit much greater freedom of collective investor action.

It is a sad situation that, when the SEC issued its original access proposal and asked for comments, I saw not a single response by an institutional manager demanding more open access. Indeed, rather than seeking greater access, institutional investors seemed to seek even less. Some commentators sought to make a weak access proposal even weaker, suggesting even higher ownership thresholds. Nowhere did I see a hue and cry to let fiduciaries behave as active owners, and as far as I could determine, most of the industry's biggest guns didn't even respond. Fidelity, Putnam, Janus, MFS, Vanguard, and Dreyfus made no comment. Neither did Citibank, Merrill Lynch, nor Morgan Stanley respond, although they too control giant fund empires. And other institutions actually opposed the SEC's modest thrust toward corporate democracy—Schwab, Prudential, Northern Trust, J. P. Morgan Chase, all with large institutional investment and mutual fund units. If we are to return to owners' capitalism, investment America apparently will have to be dragged kicking and screaming into the fray.

Planting the seeds of cooperation among long-term investors is essential to progress in governance reform. While I have repeatedly called on the ICI to sponsor an industrywide effort to foster the interest of fund shareholders by harnessing the voting power of mutual funds, I have yet to receive any response. Failing industry action, perhaps a small group of fund managers could act as a nucleus in taking up corporate governance issues, with other like-minded managers then climbing aboard the bandwagon. Index mutual funds, indexed pension accounts, and index-like investment pools operated under quantitative strategies would form the initial core. (Two of the three largest institutional equity managers and three of the largest six are primarily indexers.) And there are other notable long-term active managers (for example, Capital Group, Wellington, Dodge and Cox) that would be prime candidates for subsequent membership.

For at least five years, I've called, without success, for such a federation of long-term investors to discuss issues of corporate governance and corporate citizenship. But it is only a matter of time until the idea gains traction. In the wake of the precipitous drop in the stock market and the tremendous losses incurred by millions of investors who came late to their stock ownership, the time may be at hand. One way or another, institutional investors that own companies, as distinct from those that trade stocks, must cooperate to make their will felt for their own good, as well as for the good of all owners of corporate shares.

What *Is* Ownership?

The largest challenge we face in fixing what went wrong in corporate America is to ensure that the giant institutions of investment America—largely retirement funds and mutual funds—behave like owners. The trustees and managers of these plans are not true owners; they are intermediaries who act on behalf of the beneficiaries (corporate employees, pensioners, and fund shareholders) to whom they owe a fiduciary duty of loyalty and care. Part of the reason for their failure is that they face conflicting, often self-serving, diversions from that responsibility.

The massive substitution of fiduciary ownership for personal ownership is one of the major challenges of twenty-first-century capitalism. Remember that only fifty years ago, institutional ownership was inconsequential; today institutions hold 66 percent of all stock. Direct ownership, then, has tumbled from virtually 100 percent to 34 percent. True stockowners—investors who own stock directly in their own right and for their own benefit—are becoming an endangered species. The first task, then, is to demand that the financial intermediaries that dominate investment America put the interests of those they serve as their first and overriding priority. We must strengthen the traditional fiduciary law, now only loosely administered by the states in which corporations are chartered. We ought to consider whether federal chartering of corporations—something that, as it happens, was debated at the Constitutional Convention in 1787—would be wise.

All those years ago, James Madison argued that the new federal government should be authorized to charter corporations. But as author Roger Lowenstein describes it, "federal charters smacked of royal perquisites, [so] it was left to the states to write the rules. Delaware, through its utter permissiveness, became the corporate residence of choice, much as the Cayman Islands is a paper domicile for secrecy-minded bankers. To this day, more than half of America's largest companies are incorporated in its second-smallest state. Delaware laws are so lax they don't even require publishing an annual report."[6]

If federal chartering is an impossible dream, then we need far stronger state regulation of corporations, perhaps a uniform state code that will obviate the likelihood of corporate "venue selection" in which firms, in a sort of Gresham's law in which bad governance drives out good, seek the states that provide that safest harbors for managements. So perhaps we ought to consider giving shareholders the right to ratify the state of incorporation.* But make no mistake about it, any idea of a uniform code of fiduciary duty among the several states would require years of massive effort and cooperation that at least today seem hard to come by.

What is essential, finally, is that the last-line owners—the investors themselves—demand high standards of trusteeship from those who represent their ownership interests. In mutual funds, those 95 million direct owners have no individual power, but awesome collective power. These fund investors need to understand what investing and trusteeship are all about, and, by voting with their feet, gradually gravitate to fund organizations that are serious about putting their interest first. In retirement plans, while the contributors to the thrift plans and the beneficiaries of pension plans presently have no mechanism for bringing about the same result, they surely deserve some formal legal voice in establishing standards of conduct for the trustees of the assets that have been set aside to fund their retirements. The law is clear that retirement plan fiduciaries have duties of loyalty and prudence. We need further articulation of what exactly those words mean, and the standards by which their achievement will be measured.

Action Steps

It is time to begin the process of reform that will ultimately enable investment America to fulfill its responsibilities of corporate governance. Our institutional investors need more than the motivation to vote proxies, however. They need both the opportunity and the ability to take action. Public policy should move in the direction of facilitating investor access to corporate proxies—allowing submission of proposals to establish governance standards and to eliminate governance restrictions, to accept or reject mergers, to set standards for executive compensation and stock options, and, for that matter, to establish dividend policy—legitimate issues

---

*I believe that this idea was first put forth by The Corporate Library's Nell Minow.

for all substantial investors interested in enhancing the intrinsic value of the corporation. While opening access to large, long-term, and responsible owners would carry some costs—proxy solicitation costs, legal costs, management focus, and other frictional costs—these costs would consume only a tiny fraction of the resources of most corporations and be vastly outweighed by the benefits garnered by owners.

I would also add a federal preemption of state law on issues that concern shareholders' rights and directors' duties, and take steps to preclude the obvious kinds of troublemaking foolishness by limiting such access to groups of investors who have held, say, at least 10 percent of shares outstanding for at least two years. In addition, I would allow director nominations on a similar basis, albeit bereft of the overbearing limitations proposed by the SEC. "Power to the long-term owners!" is a reform whose time has come.

An editorial in *The Economist* entitled "American Corporate Governance: No Democracy Please, We're Shareholders" put it this way:

> In the face of hysterical opposition from corporate bosses, who can think of nothing worse than being humiliated in a genuine election . . . the Securities and Exchange Commission summoned up enough spirit to propose a small step in the direction of genuine shareholder democracy. Yet the proposal is, if anything, too timid. . . . The SEC should implement this modest rule-change forthwith. It might then consider adopting another quite modest proposal, a rule long observed in more shareholder-friendly places such as Britain: if, by withholding support, shareholders cast more votes against a candidate then in favor, he should not be elected to the board. How daringly democratic.[7]

In the United States, a similar rule that counted withheld votes as votes against a director would radically change the dynamics of our corporate governance, and for the better. But as even modest proposals for reform struggle for traction, such a sweeping proposal is a long way down the road. That said, I am most gratified by the SEC's recent willingness to allow shareholder proposals that would require a majority vote of shares for the election of any director. Some eighty-one such proposals have been submitted during the 2005 proxy season, garnering 41 percent approval at Citigroup and 48 percent at Gannett, with thirteen more companies agreeing to consider the issue.

But even with existing restrictions, as I discussed earlier, owners have the power to make their will felt in some areas. They don't need to remain asleep at the switch until broad access rights are at last permitted. While we clearly need important structural changes if we are to enhance corporate democracy, financial institutions should not underestimate their existing ability to effect change.

Today, if only we summon the courage to exercise the voting franchise we already have, institutional owners hold the power to be a major force for change. To recapitulate, investors already can, and should:

- Withhold votes for board chairmen who are also CEOs. (Remember the difference between "boss of the business" and "boss of the board"?)
- Vote against auditors who are also providing consulting services (or receiving consulting service fees that are disproportionate to their audit fees).
- Withhold votes for board members who serve on audit committees, compensation committees, and governance committees when their qualifications or their independence seem doubtful.
- Vote for proposals to reverse limits on open governance (for example, staggered boards).
- Vote against proposals that excessively protect companies from take-overs, such as poison pills. (Provisions that are designed to enable companies to negotiate a higher price in the face of hostile takeover attempts are quite another matter.)
- Perhaps most meaningful of all, vote against overly dilutive stock option plans.

As the most pronounced vestige of managers' capitalism, stock option plans are a vital battleground on which to fight for a return of owners' capitalism. Owners must demand severe limits, not only when management proposes excessive share dilution, but also when the cumulative share dilution—actual and potential—over time exceeds reasonable limits. Now that the costs of fixed-price stock options seem highly likely to be accounted for as an expense (of all things!), owners should also demand better forms of options with the kind of owner-oriented terms described in chapter three.

While my recommendations for enabling institutional shareholders to exercise the awesome power that lies, King Kong–like, at their fingertips may seem radical and idealistic, they pale by comparison with the recommendations made by Benjamin Graham in the first edition of *The Intelligent Investor* nearly half a century ago. For example, he suggested that when a company's results are well below average, an independent committee of stockholders retain outside business engineers to evaluate the policies and competence of management, paid for by the company; or the appointment of specialized, experienced directors to evaluate the company's results and report directly to stockholders. In all, Graham expected, and indeed assumed, that substantial stockholders would be well informed, diligent, and eager to act in their own self-interest.

One can only imagine the horror of the corporate managers if Graham's proposals were to be advanced today. Call in outside business engineers? An independent committee of stockholders? Cost paid by the company? Demand by existing agencies to investigate management efficiency? In today's version of managers' capitalism, these ideas seem almost quaint. But Graham's call for action is now more important than ever. Some excerpts on this subject from his book are included in Box 6.2.

It is not my contention that the Institutional 100 can manage American business. It cannot. Indeed, it could be rightly argued that our institutional investors are far from perfect in the way that they manages themselves. Nor do I believe that, once granted a level playing field that establishes ownership rights for qualified long-term investors, the present proxy process will become a quagmire of ill-meaning nominations and proposals by ill-informed owners. I reiterate two overriding principles: (1) that no changes can take place unless a majority of shares are voted in favor, and (2) that all changes approved by the majority must be implemented by the board. If we have mechanisms in place that clearly establish the rights of substantial owners to intervene in governance matters and matters of major policy—dividend payments, executive compensation, options plans, and the like—then the behavior of corporate directors will move in the direction of putting the interest of the shareholder first.

Real change will come, then, not in the form of continual confrontation with corporate managers and boards of directors, but in the form of the omnipresent reminder that there is a constituency of owners, and that it has a strong voice. Faced with the latent power of investment America, the key gatekeepers of corporate America—members of the nation's boards of directors—will again honor their traditional role as stewards of the shareholders' assets. Corporate democracy, if you will, will yield republican governance.

Box 6.2 A Call for Action in *The Intelligent Investor*

What, then, are the concrete and practical steps by which stockholders can obtain efficient managers in place of poor ones? First, we think, a few of the more substantial stockholders should become convinced that a change is needed and should be willing to work toward that end. Second, the rank and file of the stockholders should be open-minded enough to read the proxy material and to weigh the arguments on both sides. They must at least be able to know when their company has been unsuccessful and be ready to demand more than artful platitudes as a vindication of the incumbent management. Third, it would be most helpful, when the figures clearly show that the results are well below average, if it became the custom to call in outside business engineers to pass upon the policies and competence of the management. . . .

The engineering firm preferably should not be engaged by the existing board of directors, nor should the report be made to the board. The firm should be selected by an independent committee of stockholders soliciting proxies for this purpose, and the report should be submitted directly to the stockholders. The cost of the study should be borne by the company.

Financial Agencies That Can Help

There are many existing financial agencies which could contribute mightily to the improvement of corporate managements. They have experience in these matters, as well as great influence with stockholders. They include the leading investment funds, the Association of Stock Exchange Firms, the New York Society of Security Analysts, the financial services, and the important investment-counsel firms. All of these have shied away from that field of activity as troublesome and unrewarding. We think they are missing a great opportunity for rendering service to the investing public and for obtaining its goodwill.

It is by no means necessary that such agencies take the initiative in demanding an investigation of management efficiency even where this seems to be justified—although it would be entirely appropriate for an investing fund owning shares in such a concern to do so. What is needed from these agencies is a willingness to support a demand of this kind when it is put forward with persuasive evidence by substantial stockholders. . . . Without such support, public stockholders are likely to remain apathetic and swayed by the management's propaganda.

As an alternative to the outside engineering survey, there are advantages to be gained through the selection of one or more professional and independent directors. These should be men of wide business experi-

(continued)

Box 6.2 *Continued*

ence who can turn a fresh and expert eye on the problems of the enterprise. They should receive adequate compensation for their time and skill. They should submit a separate annual report, addressed directly to the stockholders and containing their views on the major question which concerns the owners of the enterprise: "Is the business showing the results for the outside stockholder which could be expected of it under proper management? If not, why—and what should be done about it?" . . . We should say something about our use of the term "outside stockholders." These are the owners who should not and do not consider themselves as participating directly in the control of corporate policies. Obviously, more than 99 per cent of the stockholders of every large publicly held enterprise are outsiders. The inside owners must be very few in number, yet in most cases—but not all—they hold a substantial stock interest.

Insiders Versus Outsiders

Although in some important respects the inside and outside stockholders have identical interests, in others their viewpoints may be different and even basically opposed. Both groups, of course, would like to see large earnings and a large underlying value for the shares. But the insiders will not ordinarily be willing to change the management to improve the earnings picture, for that would mean discharging themselves. Furthermore, the insiders often have a special view of their own on the two questions which touch the outside stockholder most directly—the dividend payments and the average market price of the stock. . . .

Why is it that insiders may have no interest of their own in following policies designed to provide an adequate dividend return and an adequate average market price? It is strange how little this point is understood. Insiders do not depend on dividends and market quotations to establish the practical value of their holdings. The value to them is measured by what they can do with the business when and if they want to do it. If they need a higher dividend to establish this value, they can raise the dividend. If the value is to be established by selling the business to some other company, or by recapitalizing it, or by withdrawing unneeded cash assets . . . they can do any of these things at a time appropriate to themselves. Insiders never suffer loss from an unduly low market price which it is in their power to correct.

Source: Benjamin Graham, The Intelligent Investor *(1949; New York: HarperCollins, 2005), 212–13, 215, 216. Reprinted by permission of HarperCollins Publishers Inc.*

"Capitalism Without Owners Will Fail"

Few individuals have been as deeply involved in corporate governance issues—and even fewer have played as constructive a leadership role—as Robert A. G. Monks, founder of Institutional Shareholder Services (ISS) as well as the corporate activist firms Lens Inc. and Lens Governance Advisors. He has put forth a number of important ideas about the radical reform that is required. His fact-filled 564-page tome *Corporate Governance* (with Nell Minow) is a must-read for those who seek to understand what went wrong in corporate America and what needs to be done by investment America to fix it.[8] More recently, in *Capitalism Without Owners Will Fail: A Policy Maker's Guide to Reform* (with Allan Sykes), he sets forth a sound framework for reforming the system. His wisdom offers valuable perspective:

> Government involvement is clearly needed in corporate governance to guarantee the nation's citizens the neglected rights of ownership of their stocks. What is needed is a clear and consistently enforced public policy that gives all owners' representatives, the intermediary investment institutions and their fund managers, the clear fiduciary requirement to be active with respect to companies held in their portfolio accounts, and the confidence that they will not be placed at a competitive or reputational disadvantage with their competitors by complying. Above all else, it must be unmistakable that government intends, and is capable of enforcing, the trustee and fiduciary laws for the *sole* purpose and *exclusive* benefit of their beneficiaries' interests—the great part of the funded pensions of most citizens—in an even-handed way.

> 1. In support of the fundamental principle that there should be no power without accountability, government should affirm that creating an effective shareholder presence in all companies is in the national interest and that it is the nation's policy to aid effective shareholder involvement in the governance of publicly owned corporations.
> 2. All pension fund trustees, mutual funds and other fiduciaries must act solely in the long-term interests of their beneficiaries and for the exclusive purpose of providing them with benefits, in order to ensure the functioning of an appropriate board of directors.
> 3. To give full effect to the first two proposals, institutional shareholders should be made accountable for exercising their votes

in an informed and sensible manner. Votes are an asset which should be used to further beneficiaries' interests on all occasions, and their voting should be virtually compulsory.

4. To complete and powerfully reinforce the other three proposals, such shareholders should have the exclusive right and obligation to nominate at least three non-executive directors in each company (held in their portfolios).[9]

Wrapping Up

The title of Monks's monograph—*Capitalism Without Owners Will Fail*—is no overstatement. Only if its *managers* are focused on creating long-term value for its *owners* can corporate America be the prime engine of the nation's growth and prosperity and a major source of innovation and experimentation. To the extent that managers sit unchecked in the driver's seat, feathering their own nests at the expense of their owners, capitalism cannot flourish.

But even after needed systemwide reforms are put into place, the need to create an ownership ethic will remain. When it described the ideal owner as a long-term stockholder, perhaps even a permanent owner, whose goals are closely aligned with the corporation, *The Economist* of London expressed it well: "Everything now depends on financial institutions pressing even harder for reforms to make boards of directors behave more like overseers, and less like the chief executive's collection of puppets. . . . Financial institutions must also fight to restore their rights as shareholders and use their clout to elect directors, who would be obliged to represent only their collective interest as owners. Chief executives would still run their firms; but, like any other employee, they would also have a boss."[10]

The giant institutions of investment America must take the lead in accomplishing these goals. Our money managers not only hold 66 percent of all shares, but they have the staff to pore over corporate financial statements and proxies; the professional expertise to evaluate CEO performance, pay, and perquisites; and, once full disclosure of all proxy votes (by pension funds as well as mutual funds) becomes mandatory, the incentive to vote in the manner that their beneficiaries have every right to expect. As they return to their traditional focus on long-term investing, these institutional owners must fight for the access to the levers of control over the corporations they own that are both appropriate for their ownership position and a reflection of their willingness to accept both the rights and responsibilities of corporate citizenship.

The task of returning capitalism to its owners will take time, true enough. But the new reality—increasingly visible with each passing day—is that proper corporate governance is not merely an ideal to be debated. It is a vital necessity to be practiced. The role of the owners, I underscore, is to do no more than ensure that the interests of directors and management are aligned with those of the shareholders in a substantive way. When there is a conflict of interest, it is the shareholders who should make the decision. It is in the national public interest and in the interest of investors that the owners—represented largely by investment America—come to realize that enlightened corporate governance is not merely a right of business ownership. It is a responsibility to the nation.

THREE

Mutual Fund America

The mutual fund industry played a major role in the failure of investment America to observe its ownership responsibilities. But given its massive assets, its ownership by nearly 100 million individual shareholders, and its unique governance structure that makes shareholder democracy virtually impossible, it demands a separate and extensive treatment in this book. In fact, the fund industry is the consummate example of owners' capitalism gone awry.

The first chapter in Part III, "What Went Wrong in Mutual Fund America?" describes the extraordinary happenings of the recent era. Ignoring both the principles and words of the Investment Company Act of 1940, and placing their interests as managers ahead of the interests of fund owners, fund operators allowed abusive market timing by favored investors, engendered a major increase both in fund expenses and costly portfolio turnover, and focused on fund proliferation and marketing. Together, these actions resulted in a staggering lag in the long-term returns earned by the average equity *fund* compared to the returns available in the stock market itself, and an even larger lag suffered by the average equity fund *shareholder*.

In the next chapter, I discuss why the industry lost its way. Dominated by the interests of its managers, fund organizations focused on salesmanship over stewardship; abandoned traditional investment committees in favor of flashy portfolio managers; engaged in ever more risky investment policies; and provided new funds to meet the fads of the day, only to quickly dispatch them when they had outlived their usefulness.

Fixing these wrongs, as the final chapter acknowledges, will be no small task. We need a new fund structure that will at last give fund owners strong representation on fund boards. We also need a federal standard of fiduciary duty for fund directors. Finally, I urge regulators to undertake a long-overdue economic study of the mutual fund industry. But the best hope for major reform lies in giving fund investors the information, knowledge, and wisdom that will enable them to look after their own economic interests.

7

What Went Wrong in Mutual Fund America?

The Triumph of Salesmanship
over Stewardship

As part of the broad community of large financial institutions, mutual fund America played a major role in the failure of investment America to observe the responsibilities of corporate citizenship that resulted in the triumph of managers' capitalism over owners' capitalism in corporate America. What is more, by virtue of its own perverse governance structure, the fund industry itself presents the most extreme version of managers' capitalism.

Using an organizational design that would amaze (and delight!) the oligarchs of corporate America, the managers of mutual funds have enjoyed virtually free rein to place their interests ahead of the interests of the owners of their funds. While the policy promulgated in the preamble of the Investment Company Act of 1940 clearly ordains that funds must be "organized, operated, and managed" in the interests of their shareholders, "rather than in the interests of their managers and distributors," that sound policy has been honored far more in its breach than in its observance.[1]

Given the power held by fund managers over the owners of the funds that they supervise, it would have been miraculous if the mutual fund industry had been immune to the kinds of scandals that have faced corporate America and Wall Street. For in no other line of business endeavor is the conflict between *owners'* capitalism and *managers'* capitalism more institutionalized by tradition, and therefore more widely accepted. The conflict arises from a structure in which the fund itself, typically a corporation with its own directors but with no employees, begins its existence as a creature of its management company, a separate corporation with its own separate financial objectives. It is that very structure that gives managers near-total dominion over fund shareowners. As a result, it was almost preordained that fund managers, for all of their proclamations about their dedication to Main Street investors, would abuse their power, resulting in the profound conflicts that ultimately came to light.

Rocked by Scandal

Industry leaders, of course, denied that significant conflicts existed. Indeed, in his remarks at the Investment Company Institute's General Membership Meeting in May 2003, Matthew Fink, the president of the fund industry's trade association, pointed with pride at the industry's rock-solid reputation, citing SEC commissioner Harvey Goldschmidt's glowing tribute just a few months earlier: "The mutual fund industry has been blessed—and blessed is the only word—by being relatively free of scandal."[2] As he read those words, giant images depicting the quotation were displayed on both sides of the dais. Fink then added: "The record is no accident. . . . We have succeeded because the interests of those who manage funds are well-aligned with the interests of those who invest in mutual funds."

Fink's comments echoed those of ICI chairman Paul G. Haaga Jr., the keynote speaker: "Our strong tradition of integrity continues to unite us. . . . The word integrity has been the theme of every recent general membership meeting for one simple reason: integrity and the trust it engenders on the part of our shareholders is the basic foundation of our business. Our shareholders trust that their mutual funds are being managed with their interests in mind." Then he took on the industry's detractors, "former SEC chairmen, members of Congress and their staffs, academics, Bards of Omaha, journalists, television talking heads, competitors—even a saint with his own statue*—have all weighed in about our perceived failings. . . . It makes me wonder what life would be like if we'd actually done something wrong."[3]

---

*A lightly veiled reference to the author.

He need not have wondered. Less than four months later, on September 3, 2003, the mutual fund scandals exploded, epitomized in an eerie reprise to the corporate scandals that first came to light with Enron in 2001 and the Wall Street scandals that came to light in 2002. Widespread wrongdoing was exposed when New York's crusading attorney general Eliot L. Spitzer brought civil actions against four major mutual fund management companies, charging that they had conspired with, and even aided and abetted, preferred investors (including hedge funds that identified their strategy as "mutual fund market timing") to undertake illegal acts. These investors would buy and sell fund shares at closing prices based on late-breaking events that had taken place well after the market had closed, and trade international funds in the United States at values set in foreign markets hours before the trades took place. Spitzer accurately compared these practices to allowing favored investors to bet on a horse race after the horses have crossed the finish line.

The attorney general's seemingly airtight case was built, not only on covert *practices*, but on readily discernable *motives*—the receipt of payola, for the want of a better word. The managers received that payola in the form of side banking deals, earning high interest rates on their loans to the traders, requiring as a quid pro quo large investments in other funds on which the manager earns high fees—"sticky assets" in the vernacular of the trade—and the like.

One manager's e-mail could hardly have made the motivation clearer. "I have no interest in building a business around market timers, but at the same time I do not want to turn away $10–$20m[illion]!"[4] (Yes, the exclamation point was there.) The writer emphasized that allowing the timing trades would be in the manager's "best interests." Lest his colleagues be complete nincompoops who failed to get the point, he explained in a parenthetical aside what that meant: "increased profitability to the firm." Another e-mail (God bless e-mail), discovered during Attorney General Spitzer's investigation and made public in his September 3, 2003, complaint against Canary Capital Partners, also told the truth: "Market timers are a big problem . . . it's very disruptive to the operation of the funds. [But] obviously, your call from the sales side."

The industry's response to the market timing scandals can be best characterized by paraphrasing the classic line spoken by police captain Louis Renault, played by Claude Rains in the film *Casablanca*, as he was confronted by the Nazis in a bar well known for the gambling that took place inside. "I am shocked, *shocked* to find timing [in the movie, gambling] going on here." The public was told that the misdeeds were akin to "parking at a meter and not paying. Nobody is being bankrupted by this."[5] We've also been told that these breaches of fiduciary duty are attributable to only a "few bad apples," although as these scandals continued to come to light the definition of "few" had to be liberalized.[6] (See Box 7.1.)

As the trading scandals grew, other scandals surfaced. Brokerage firms, it turned out, were often selling higher-priced "B shares" (with the sales load spread over five or six years) rather than less expensive (but still costly) A shares with front end loads, as well as selling their own proprietary funds without disclosing the conflict of interest. It also turned out that some fund managers were directing brokerage commissions and other payments to firms that sold the shares of their funds without disclosure, and often in violation of SEC rules. Taken together, the wide-ranging scandals were the starkest example of the triumph of managers' capitalism over owners' capitalism in mutual fund America, a dispiriting echo of the same baneful warning cited earlier about corporate America: "When we have strong managers, weak directors, and passive owners, it's only a matter of time until the looting begins."

The Emperor's Clothes

How can it be that the fund industry takes its bizarre governance structure as the natural order of things? How is it that its leaders couldn't see that this structure was an accident waiting to happen? It reminds me of the classic story *The Emperor's Clothes*, which Hans Christian Andersen wrote in 1837:

> Suddenly a child called out: "But the emperor has nothing on at all!" . . . Soon everyone was laughing at the emperor's new clothes. The emperor was very embarrassed, for he knew they were right. All I can do is carry on, he thought, and grimly continued strutting through the town. And his servants went on carrying the train that was not there.[7]

The ability to ignore the seemingly obvious conflicts goes back even further. Hear Descartes in 1650: "A man is incapable of comprehending any argument that interferes with his revenue." Or even Demosthenes in 350 B.C.: "Nothing is easier than self-deceit. For what each man wishes, that he also believes to be true." Or as Upton Sinclair put it, in contemporary terms, "it is difficult to get a man to understand something when his salary depends on his not understanding it." Truth told, the fund industry, in the vernacular of today, "just doesn't get it."

Even as the spotlight that shined on the specific acts that brought notoriety to corporate America's bad apples—the Ken Lays, the Dennis Kozlowskis, and the Sam Waksals, even the Jack Welches and the others described earlier—the spotlight that shined on the mutual fund industry brought notoriety to the bad apples of the industry. Even more important, the scandals illuminated all the nibbling around the edges of proper and ethical conduct that, absent that intrusive spotlight, could otherwise have persisted for another decade or more, and demonstrated the frequent willingness—nay, the eagerness—of fund managers to build their own profits at the expense of the fund owners whom they are honor-bound to serve.

Some Notable Examples

As in corporate America, and in investment America, there were some particularly bad apples in the giant barrel that represents the fund industry.

- *Gary Pilgrim and Harold Baxter.* These two fund executives not only allowed certain preferred hedge funds to engage in market-timing schemes, but, through a hedge fund in which they held personal interests, even did so themselves. Since the inception of the PBHG (Pilgrim Baxter Holding Group) funds in 1985, their funds had operated under frankly speculative policies. They engaged in aggressive short-term trading tactics, and provided volatile returns, both up and down. But however spasmodic were the eye-catching returns periodically achieved by their funds, the firm hyped them in opportunistic advertising and drew huge investor capital to their funds *after* their good performance had been achieved, and almost inevitably just *before* it turned sour. Result: investors in the PBHG funds incurred literally billions of dollars of losses, while Pilgrim and Baxter earned at least $1 billion of profits at their expense. In addition to some $457 million of management fees paid by the funds for the services of their firm during the 1990s alone, they capitalized on these profits by selling their management company to a publicly held company created for the sole purpose of reaping a share of the huge profits earned by fund managers. The extra profits the two managers earned through the trading schemes represented but a minor addition to the staggering financial wealth they had accumulated. Their settlement with the SEC and Attorney General Spitzer included fines and reimbursements to the funds totaling $160 million, a virtual drop in the bucket that was filled to the brim with their ill-gotten gains. (In settling the civil charges they neither admitted nor denied guilt.)

- *Richard Strong.* Strong, principal owner of the management company that countenanced and encouraged market timing in the Strong Funds, also did such timing for himself and his friends and family members. While criminal charges were considered but never brought against Strong, he was barred from the industry for life (without his admitting or denying guilt to the civil charges). His firm's monetary penalty of $175 million was among the largest assessed against any fund manager. He was well compensated for his efforts, however, including $217 million of fees paid to the manager by the funds during the 1992–2002 decade, and an additional reward estimated at $400 million when the management company was sold to Wells Fargo Bank a year after the scandal.[8]

- *James Connelly.* This former brokerage vice chairman and head of mutual fund sales and marketing for the Alger Funds apparently was an "early adopter" of the strategy of increasing the management company's revenues by allowing abusive trading in their mutual funds. Beginning in the mid-1990s, Connelly devised a system that permitted timing in Alger's mutual funds that, by 2003, had provided the firm more than $200 million in assets from more than a dozen investors. Once he became aware of Spitzer's investigation, Connelly compounded his troubles by tampering with the evidence. He was fined $400,000, barred from the investment business for life, and sentenced to one to three years in jail. Ironically, in 2002, an industry publication had named Connelly its "Fund Leader of the Year."[9]

- *Lawrence Lasser.* This long-time chief executive of Putnam Management Company, consistently ranked among the highest-paid executives in the fund industry, with compensation totaling $163 million during 1998–2002 alone. (Putnam is a subsidiary of giant financial conglomerate Marsh and McLennan, whose insurance brokerage subsidiary would be implicated in the scandals involving "bid-rigging" and "preferred service agreements" uncovered by Spitzer in 2004.) In 2004, Putnam reported that Lasser was made aware of improper trading by portfolio managers as early as 2000 (ultimately, 40 Putnam employees, including six portfolio managers, were implicated).[10] Upon learning of this breach of fiduciary duty, Lasser neither disciplined nor terminated them, nor did he inform the management company, or the fund directors, or the fund shareholders, or federal or state regulators, of the malfeasance. (Putnam later agreed to pay $193 million in fines and restitution to their funds' shareholders.) Although he was charged with neither civil nor criminal misconduct, he eventually was ousted by Marsh and McLennan, but awarded a termination bonus of $78 million. Of Lasser it might be said, "nothing succeeds like failure."

As in corporate America, the names of many other bad apples could easily be added to this list. Executives from more than a score of major mutual fund management companies—including some of the oldest, largest, and once-most-respected firms in the field—have been implicated in the scandals and disciplined, often severely, by regulators. Similarly, the fund misconduct went far beyond a few isolated incidents involving a handful of wrongdoers. The problems are far more systemic, for the barrel of mutual fund capitalism is itself riddled with conflicts, reflected not only in the scandals involving market timing, brokerage payments, and overcharging for sales loads (see Box 7.1), but in excessive management fees and fund expenses and over zealous marketing of speculative funds, where the financial losses inflicted on fund owners by fund managers were far greater.

From Stewardship to Salesmanship

Just as a pathological mutation had transformed corporate America from owners' capitalism to managers' capitalism, so a similar mutation had occurred in mutual fund America—a mutation from the industry's traditional focus on the stewardship of shareholder investments to salesmanship and asset gathering. Building a giant asset base is the easy way to produce higher fees and larger profits for the management company, who regularly collects its cut as a percentage of the asset pool. But high fees come at the direct expense of the investors who own the funds. Just as it took the scandals at Enron et al. to illustrate the broader problems of corporate America, so it took the whole series of timing, distribution, and brokerage commission scandals to call attention to the broader problems that afflicted mutual fund America.

Box 7.1 Bad Apples or Bad Barrel? Phase III

Mutual Fund Firms Implicated in the Market-Timing Scandals
Just as with the scandals in corporate America, the market-timing scandals
in mutual fund America were said to be the work of only a few "bad
apples." But the plain facts belie any attempt to minimize the dimen-
sion of the problem. So far, state and federal regulators have implicated
twenty-three fund managers in these illicit practices.

These firms are hardly small johnnies-come-lately to the field. In fact,
the miscreants include some of the oldest and largest firms in the industry, with assets aggregating more than $1.2 trillion, one-quarter of the
long-term assets managed by the mutual fund industry. Worse, the
record suggests that precious few of the managers who were offered
"hot money" from hedge funds and other substantial investors turned
down the opportunity to enrich their own coffers.

Since the bull market high in 2000, the long-term assets under management of these firms have declined by nearly $300 billion, more than
$100 billion of which resulted from outflows of capital following the
revelation of the scandalous conduct.

Manager	March 2000 total assets (millions)*	January 2005 total assets (millions)*	Net flow September 2003 – October 2004[†] (millions)
AIM Investments	$164,500	$69,000	$(19,400)
Alger	5,900	3,400	(200)
AllianceBernstein	78,700	61,300	(3,700)
Banc One	31,900	37,500	(4,800)
Columbia Mgmt Adv	50,800	55,400	(2,500)
Federated	40,700	42,900	(3,900)
Franklin Templeton	168,500	226,600	15,000
Fremont	2,200	2,000	(900)
Heartland	1,500	2,300	20
ING Investments	16,800	19,900	500
J. P. Morgan Funds	24,300	61,100	(5,000)
Janus	220,200	68,200	(29,300)
Liberty Ridge Cap (PBHG)	15,800	4,700	(2,300)
MFS	101,100	76,600	(9,900)
Merrill Lynch	94,100	79,200	(1,800)
Nations Funds	22,100	33,700	(1,400)
PIMCO Funds	65,100	181,100	20,200
Putnam	269,100	114,600	(50,900)
RS Investment Mgmt	8,700	6,300	1,000
Scudder	102,700	66,400	(8,200)
Seligman	29,300	11,400	(1,900)
Strong	27,300	18,500	(9,200)
U.S. Trust Company	6,000	9,900	1,600
Total	$1,547,400	$1,252,000	$(116,800)

*Long-term funds only.
[†]From announcement of timing scandals in September 2003 through January 2005.

It has been argued that the adverse turn in the cash flows for most of these companies provides a "market discipline" that will prevent violations of the public trust. But the fact that some of the firms listed above were hardly punished at all strongly suggests that the penalties handed out by regulators are a necessary deterrent.

The Other Scandals

Soon after the market timing scandal erupted, other scandals came to light. Already eleven firms (many also implicated in the market timing scandals) have been charged by the SEC and the NASD with improprieties largely related to sales commission abuses involving undisclosed agreements of fund managers to provide compensation to brokers for share sales through direct quid pro quo payments or steering trades to them, and with illicit sales practices, including sales of fund share classes that carried undisclosed higher sales loads. As one scandal followed another, the allegation that the abuses in the fund industry were limited to a few bad apples lost all credibility.

These fund scandals have been critically examined by investment legend David F. Swensen, who has managed the Yale Endowment Fund with remarkable success for two decades. In his new book, *Unconventional Success,* he bluntly states that those scandalous abuses of trust "unequivocally show an investor-friendly mask covering the true, venal face of the industry . . ."

> When mutual-fund investors buy shares from brokerage firms, hidden incentives often cause brokers to push particular families of funds. In a flagrantly investor-unfriendly practice, the brokerage community charges outside families of mutual funds (Capital Group, Fidelity, Federated, Dreyfus, et al.) for the privilege of being a preferred provider . . . using their shareholders' funds to grease the dirty palms of the brokerage industry. "Pay-to-play" represents a deadweight loss to investors.[11]

For example, even the widely-respected Capital Group's American Funds provide payoffs to 51 pay-to-play partners, including most of the financial services elite. The NASD has charged that the firm directed "target payments" of $100 million in trading commissions to brokerage firms based on their past sales of the shares of its funds, an alleged violation of NASD rules.[12] The California Securities Commission has accused the firm of fraud, and the SEC has also launched an investigation. While Capital acknowledges the practice, it denies that it violates existing rules.

When a veteran investor with Mr. Swensen's credibility and integrity speaks out, regulators should listen. So should fund investors. It is their money that has been lost in the wide-ranging scandals affecting the mutual fund industry, which is, in Mr. Swensen's unflinching words, "sitting at the center of a massive market failure."[13]

The market-timing scandals are estimated to have cost long-term fund investors something like $3 billion in the dilution of their returns. That dollar-for-dollar loss, of course, exactly matched the gains made by the short-term speculators in fund shares.* But the penalties paid by fund shareholders in the form of excessive expenses, and by the unwillingness of fund managers to share with fund shareowners the staggering economies of scale involved in fund operations as fund asset levels soared, can be counted in the tens of billions, year after year.

Even more damaging were the losses incurred by fund investors as a result of the overbearing interest by fund managers in marketing and promotion. In the recent market boom and bust alone, investor losses totaled in the hundreds of billions of dollars. Capitalizing on the stock market fads and fashions of the recent stock market bubble, fund managers sold fully a half-trillion dollars in "new economy" funds to investors. In short, it turns out that the scandals that were initially publicized in the press were but a small tip of the giant iceberg that represents the enormous price paid by investors as the industry moved away from stewardship and placing shareowner interests front and center, to salesmanship and placing manager interests first.

The truth: most mutual fund managers were far more alert to improving their own financial welfare than to improving the financial welfare of those who entrusted them with their hard-earned assets. Managers used far more energy, creativity, and intelligence—and infinitely more resources—in the development of clever and opportunistic marketing schemes than in the fulfillment of their duties as responsible corporate citizens. Gathering assets and maximizing advisory fees are the sine qua non of most management companies, and it is their quest for higher profits that must bear heavy responsibility for the illegal late-trading scandals, the unethical time-zone trading scandals, and (though it has received almost no attention) the heavy waste of investor resources engendered simply by creating opportunities for garden-variety market timing—too many investors moving too much money among too many funds at too fast a rate.

---

*To understand the arithmetic, an extreme example may help. Assume that a fund's long-term owners hold 1,000,000 shares in a $10 million fund, each with a value of $10.00. If a favored investor were to purchase 100,000 new shares at a bargain price of, say, $9.00, the asset value of each share held by those owners would be immediately diluted to $9.90, or by 1 percent.

Market Timing to the Fore

The market timing issue is but one obvious example of that conflict of interest, and, from a financial standpoint, probably the least important example. The most obvious timing problem was reflected in the "late trading" scandal, the brazenness of which deserves a place in the financial cronyism hall of fame. That ploy is simple and straightforward. While the closing prices of funds are established at the stock market's close each day, from time to time "market-moving" events often occur after the close. When some sort of good news comes and is anticipated to cause stock prices to rise the next day, for example, preferred investors were allowed to buy shares at the presumably lower value set earlier. They could then redeem the shares the next day, turning a profit, but only at the expense of their fellow shareholders whose profits, in turn, were diluted.

But late trading was only one form of timing abuse. "Time-zone trading" was likely even larger in its negative impact on fund shareholders. This tactic, too, is simple. Here a favored speculator is allowed to take advantage of a free (to the timer!) arbitrage between an international fund net asset value calculated at 4 p.m. in New York but based on closing prices across the Pacific fourteen hours earlier. The shocking truth about time-zone trading is that it went on for so long without significant defenses being erected by managers. It has hardly been a secret. Academics have been publishing papers about it at least since the late 1990s.

In 2002, well before the scandal struck, an article in the *Financial Analysts Journal* carefully described the time-zone trading strategy, quantified its effectiveness, presented specific examples of how easy it was to make money by gaming the system. It also berated the industry for its benign neglect of the market-timing issue: "When the gains from these strategies are matched by offsetting losses incurred by buy-and-hold investors in these funds . . . why haven't more funds taken stronger actions to restrict short term trading?"[14] What is more, the authors cited fourteen other academic studies on the same point. Especially prescient in light of Spitzer's later discovery of market timing by the Canary hedge fund, this article noted that thirty hedge funds had openly defined their investment strategy as "mutual fund timing."* If, however unlikely, industry participants had

---

*The authors underestimated the total. A later report by the SEC put the number of hedge funds engaged in mutual fund market timing at nearly four hundred.

been fast asleep before that article was published, surely its publication would set the alarms ringing.

But it didn't. The sole published response to the revelation was a letter to the editor from a senior executive of a manager whose funds were mentioned in the story. The letter lamented that a publication aimed solely at financial professionals should never have published such a piece. It described the article as a bad idea in the best of times, but abhorrent when investor confidence was already shaken by corporate greed.[15] Nonetheless, just nine months later, the very firm that employed the respondent initiated a 2 percent redemption fee on its international funds, seemingly belatedly acting on the advice of the article to "take stronger action to restrict short-term trading."[16] (The firm states that the action was not engendered by the article.)

Market Timing Is Omnipresent

The soaring use of market timing by the average fund owner— not only the illegal late trader nor the unethical time-zone trader—indicated that ordinary investors, using the finest vehicle for long-term investing ever designed, were engaging in excessive short-term speculation in fund shares. *There's a lot of money sloshing around the mutual fund system.* How much market timing is there? We simply don't know. But we do know a great deal about what *is* going on.

First, there is much more timing activity than the industry acknowledges. One indication of how long fund owners hold their shares is the redemption rate—the annual amount of redemptions by shareholders as a percentage of a fund's average assets. By failing to acknowledge that redemptions whose proceeds are invested in another fund within the same family—"exchanges out"—are actually, well, redemptions, the ICI substantially understated the fund redemption rates it regularly published. Such intra-family redemptions are the clearest—though hardly the only— example of a market timing investment strategy; for example, frequent moves back and forth between a stock fund and a money market fund in the same family. While the ICI reported an equity fund redemption rate equal to 29 percent of assets in 2002, the actual rate, including exchanges out, was 41 percent, almost half again higher. The average fund investor, who during the 1950–75 era held his fund shares for an average of about twelve years (proxy for an 8 percent redemption rate), was holding shares for only about two and a half years (proxy for a 41 percent re-demption rate).*

What is more, the annual report of each mutual fund is required to re-port total redemptions, including these exchanges. For the funds involved in one aspect or another of the timing scandals, the numbers approached the brazen. The Alger equity funds, with total assets of $2.3 billion in 2002, reported redemptions for the year totaling $9.3 *billion*—a 400 percent re-demption rate, suggesting a three-*month* average holding period. Bank of America's Emerging Markets Fund experienced annual redemptions equal to 295 percent of assets, and Janus Adviser International Growth fund ex-perienced redemptions equal to 372 percent of assets.

With the dollar amount of redemptions clearly set out in each fund's fi-nancial statements and reported to shareholders without comment, we must assume that the figures were read by fund directors as well. The ob-vious market-timing activity, then, was happening not only with the tacit knowledge of the managers, directors, and regulators, but right under the noses of the shareholders, the press, and the public, fully disclosed for any-one who cared to look. Yet the record is virtually devoid of questions or challenges regarding the soaring market timing of fund owners.

Further, even if it doesn't entail market timing as such, nor reach the threshold for illegality, long-term fund investors pay a heavy penalty for in-vestor activity by short-term owners. When equity funds hold extra cash as a redemption reserve, long-term returns are diluted. When such a reserve is not held, fund investors incur the cost of portfolio purchases on inflows of money, and the cost of portfolio sales all over again when the cash flows out, and perhaps tax costs as well.

In Mutual Funds, You Get What You *Don't* Pay For

Nowhere in mutual fund America is the conflict between own-ers' capitalism and managers' capitalism more severe than in the costs as-sessed against fund shareholders. This general rule puts it bluntly: The more the manager *takes*, the less the owner *makes*. Yet despite the obvious and documented inverse relationship that clearly links mutual fund costs

---

*Following the timing scandals that were revealed late in 2003, fund managers tightened the controls designed to preclude excessive trading in fund shares, and the shareholder re-demption rate has tumbled to about 25 percent; nonetheless, the resulting average holding period is just four years, only slightly above the previous 2½-year average.

and mutual fund returns, costs have risen all through the industry's modern history. In the fifty-four years that I have been part of this industry, for example, the costs directly incurred by equity fund investors alone—largely management fees and operating expenses—have increased from a mere $15 million in 1950 to $37 *billion* in 2004.* (Including direct costs of bond and money market funds last year, the total was $58 billion.) That 2,400-fold increase far surpassed the near-1,600-fold growth in equity fund assets, from $2.5 billion to $4.0 *trillion*. (See Box 7.2.)

Thus, equity fund direct costs rose one and a half times as fast as assets, an astonishing result in an industry in which the economies of scale in investment management are little short of staggering. (There is no evidence, for example, that it takes any more security analysts and portfolio managers to run a fund with, say, $5 billion of assets than a fund with $1 billion of assets.) Reflecting this increase, the expense ratio of the average equity fund (unweighted by assets) actually rose from 0.77 percent to 1.56 percent during that long half-century—an increase of more than 100 percent.†

The Investment Company Institute of course strongly objects to measuring fund costs in dollars. (They're enormous.) It prefers ratios. (They're tiny.) When measured against aggregate fund assets, the largest possible denominator, almost any numerator looks small. Using asset-weighted data, incorporating sales charges, and basing its ratio on the cash flows of funds rather than their assets, the ICI concludes that the costs of equity fund ownership came to 1.25 percent of assets in 2003, compared to the 1.56 percent expense ratio for the average fund shown above.

It is difficult to take seriously the fund industry's allegation that the costs of fund ownership have steadily declined. Any decline, if such it be, arises only from the fact that investors are increasingly choosing funds with lower expense ratios, and *not* from substantial management fee reductions. When the ICI alleges that these lower costs are the result of vigorous price competition in the fund industry, it fails to recognize that price competition is measured, not by the decisions made by fund buyers, but by the pricing decisions made by fund sellers. Major fee cuts, however, have been conspicuous by their absence.

---

*A study released by Morningstar in April 2005 estimated that direct equity fund expenses totaled some $40 billion in 2004. I'm using the lower, more conservative, figure, which is based upon Lipper data.

†Yet such an increase was not universal. Since its formation in 1974, the expense ratio of the Vanguard Group's funds, which are operated on an "at-cost" basis, declined more than 60 percent, from 0.66 percent to 0.23 percent.

Box 7.2 Where Are the Old Economies of Scale?

Equity Fund Expenses up 2,400-fold since 1950

In my 1951 Princeton senior thesis, I envisioned substantial future growth for the mutual fund industry, fostered by a "reduction in sales charges and management fees." Alas, that happy scenario was not to be. Indeed, after appropriately moving lower as the industry grew over the next decade, fund expense ratios (expenses as a percentage of fund assets) began a relentless upward rise.

Table A below shows that although equity fund assets grew 1,600-fold during this period, from $2.5 billion to $4.0 trillion, expenses rose at an even faster 2,400-fold rate, from $15 million in 1950 to $37.1 billion in 2004. Fund managers not only failed to deliver to their investors the huge economies of scale that were available, they arrogated those economies largely to themselves.

For the average equity fund, the picture was even bleaker. While the average asset-weighted expense ratio rose more than 50 percent from 1959 to 2004, the expense ratio of the average equity fund (unweighted by assets) rose more than 100 percent, from 0.77 percent to 1.56 percent. Rather than sharing in the truly staggering economies of scale available in mutual fund management, fund investors have been victimized by far higher costs.

Table A. Equity fund expenses, 1950–2004.

Year	Total equity fund assets (million)	Expenses (million)	Un-weighted expense ratio	Asset-weighted expense ratio	Aggregate increase from 1950		
					assets	expenses	ratio*
1950	$2,530	$15.2	0.77%	0.60%	—	—	—
1960	9,914	53.5	0.71	0.54	3.9 ×	3.5 ×	0.90
1970	35,897	208.2	1.23	0.58	14.2 ×	13.7 ×	0.97
1980	44,957	287.7	0.94	0.64	17.8 ×	19.0 ×	1.07
1990	238,754	2,124.9	1.38	0.89	94.4 ×	140.0 ×	1.48
2004	4,034,500	37,117.4	1.56	0.92	1594.7 ×	2,445.2 ×	1.53

Sources: for 1950 and 1960 data, Wiesenberger Investment Companies Yearbook (1951 and 1961 editions, respectively); for 1970 data, the University of Chicago's CRSP database; for 1980, 1990, and 2004 data, Lipper.
*Cumulative ratio of expense increase to asset increase.

The Micro View

The micro view often surpasses the macro view in clarifying what is actually happening beneath those broad industry aggregates. Consider the expense ratios of each of the seven largest funds of that earlier era when

(*continued*)

Box 7.2 *Continued*

sharing the economies of scale resulting from asset growth with investors was an article of faith. As shown in Table B, when the total assets of these funds grew from $1.2 billion in 1950 to $6.2 billion in 1960, the total expenses paid by their shareholders increased from $6.6 million to $27 million. Nonetheless, their average expense ratio dropped 20 percent, from 0.60 percent to 0.48 percent.

But while the economies of scale were shared with fund owners during the 1950s, the tide then turned. Ever since, driven by fee increases, by the industry's focus on marketing and by the transfer of some earlier front-end sales charges directly to fund expenses through "asset based" 12b-1 distribution fees, the average annual expense ratio of these seven industry leaders rose by 144 percent, to 1.02 percent.

There was a single exception to this trend. While its peers were raising their expense ratios by an astonishing average of 167 percent since 1960, Vanguard Wellington Fund defied the trend. Its expense ratio tumbled by an additional 22 percent, and is now 47 percent below the 1950 level. (A significant part of this reduction arose from Vanguard's "at-cost" organizational structure, adopted in 1974.) This pattern clearly suggests that huge economies of scale exist, although most managers have used the lion's share of those economies for their own benefit rather than sharing them with the shareholders of the funds that they manage.

Table B. Expense ratios of 1950's largest equity funds.

	Expense ratio			Change	
	1950	*1960*	*2003*	*1950–60*	*1960–2003*
MIT	0.33%	0.19%	1.22%	−42%	+540%
Investors Mutual*	0.58	0.53	1.05	−9	+99
Wellington*	0.60	0.41	0.32	−32	−22
Affiliated Fund*	0.72	0.43	0.93	−40	+116
Incorporated Investors*	0.55	0.60	1.20	+9	+101
Dividend Shares*	0.74	0.53	1.53	−28	+189
State Street Investment	0.62	0.56	1.19	−10	+113
Fundamental Investors	0.69	0.62	0.71	−10	+15
Average	0.60%	0.48%	1.02%	−20%	+144%

Sources: 1950 and 1960 data, Wiesenberger Investment Companies Yearbook (1951 and 1961 editions, respectively); 2003 data, Lipper.

*Now, respectively, American Express Mutual, Vanguard Wellington, Lord Abbett Affiliated, Putnam Investors, and Alliance Growth and Income.

A Stunning Example

A single stark example illustrates the point about how much mutual fund costs have risen, and how much they matter. In December 1949, when

I first read "Big Money in Boston" in *Fortune* while researching my Princeton thesis, Massachusetts Investors Trust was not only the oldest and largest mutual fund, but it also operated at the lowest expense ratio in the field. *Fortune* reported that the annual fee the fund paid to its trustees for management and operations had just been reduced from 5 percent of its investment income (the traditional basis for trustee fees) to just 3.2 percent. With MIT's assets at $300 million, the new fee amounted to $827,000 for the year.

By 1951, its expenses came to just 0.29 percent of its assets, dropping to a low of 0.19 percent by 1960. But by 2003, despite an increase in MIT's assets to $7 billion, its expense ratio had risen sixfold to 1.22 percent; its total expenses had risen one hundredfold to $83 million. The portion of the shareholders' dividend income consumed by those expenses had risen a truly shocking twenty-five-fold, eating up 87 percent of the total, compared to just 3.2 percent a half-century earlier. One can only wonder what those prudent MIT trustees of yore would have thought.

Measuring the Impact of Expenses

Fund investors and the public have been educated to measure fund management fees and operating expenses as an annualized percentage of fund assets. So the resulting expense ratios, as shown in Tables A and B, inevitably take on a *de minimus* cast. Tiny numbers like 0.92 percent, or even 1.56 percent, seem almost trivial. Yet when we examine expenses as a percentage of a fund's dividend income (as shown in the preceding MIT example), the numbers take on a more ominous cast. Indeed, as noted in chapter six, with today's dividend yield on stocks at about 1.8 percent, a typical 1.5 percent equity fund expense ratio consumes fully 80 percent of a fund's income.

It could be said that expense ratio data conceal more than they reveal. First, because expense ratios represent only about one-half of the true cost of owning mutual funds; hidden portfolio transaction costs and sales loads likely double the typical cost of equity fund ownership, raising it from 1.5 percent to as much as 3 percent of assets. Second, because that total expense numerator is compared with the largest possible denominator—the total assets of the mutual fund. But if we compare it with fund returns, the cost is enormous. Even at 2.5 percent, costs consumed about 20 percent of the 13 percent annual return on stocks over the past two decades, 35 percent if the future return were in the 7 percent range. Even more starkly, if the future annual return of bonds were 5 percent, costs would consume 125 percent of the resulting equity premium of 2 percent. The return on bonds, then, would actually exceed the net return earned by the average equity fund, eliminating the risk premium that investors have a right to expect.

But the management fees and operating costs included in expense ratios are by no means the only cost entailed in the ownership of fund shares. Mutual funds have become active—indeed, hyperactive—traders of the securities in their portfolios. The annual impact of these costs can be fairly estimated to come to another 0.8 percent to 1 percent of equity fund assets. On that basis, the costs of portfolio transactions may have grown by more than a thousandfold from 1950 to 2004—from an aggregate of, say, $25 million to perhaps $25 billion.

And that's only part—if the largest part—of the fund expense picture. In addition to operating costs ($37 billion) and transaction costs ($25 billion) incurred by equity funds, at least another $10 billion comes in the form of front-end sales charges, penalties on early redemptions of shares, out-of-pocket costs, fees paid by investors to independent investment advisers who provide asset allocation and fund selection services, and opportunity costs.* Equity fund investors paid costs estimated at $72 billion in 2004 alone, and as much as $300 billion over the past five years. That is what investors paid for, and it is therefore what they didn't get in terms of the net returns that were available in the stock market. When we add these costs up, it's fair to estimate that the all-in annual costs of equity fund ownership now run in the range of 2½ percent to 3 percent of assets.

The Arithmetic of Investing

To understand the impact of all of these costs on mutual fund investors, it is necessary only to understand the eternal arithmetic of the investment equation. *Gross return in the financial markets, minus all of the costs of financial intermediation, equals the net return actually delivered to investors.*

Whatever returns the financial markets are generous enough to deliver, please don't make the mistake of thinking that investors as a group actually earn those returns. To explain why this is the case we need only to understand the simple mathematics of investing: All investors *as a group* must necessarily earn *precisely* the market return, but only before the costs

---

*"Opportunity cost" is how we describe the long-term returns lost to shareholders by the fact that equity funds now hold a fairly constant position in cash reserves equal to about 5 percent of assets. So if the long-term return on stocks exceeds the return on U.S. Treasury bills by, say, 6 percent per year (assume that stocks return eight percent and Treasury bills 2 percent), the opportunity cost would be that 6 percent equity premium multiplied by 5 percent of assets, or 0.3 of assets percent per year.

of investing are deducted. *After* all the costs of financial intermediation are deducted—the management fees, the transaction costs, the distribution costs, the advertising and marketing costs, the operating costs, and the hidden costs of financial intermediation—the returns of investors must, and will, and do, fall short of the market return by an amount precisely equal to the aggregate amount of those costs.

For all investors as a group, then, beating the market *before* costs is a zero-sum game; beating the market *after* costs is a loser's game.* It is inevitable that the returns earned by investors in the aggregate will fall well short of the returns that are realized in our financial markets. The great paradox of investing is that you don't get what you pay for. The fact is quite the opposite: *You get what you don't pay for.*

Of course it's possible that our professional mutual fund managers and pension fund managers as a group could somehow beat the market, but only at the dollar-for-dollar detriment of amateur individual investors. But there is not a scintilla of evidence that such is the case. (Most studies of the returns of both institutional and individual investors show that their average returns equal the market return before costs but in the aggregate fall short of the market by the amount of their trading costs and any advisory fees, an unsurprising finding.) The average mutual fund manager has proven to be, well, average before costs are deducted, and below average thereafter, by approximately the costs of fund ownership. In the recent era, as we will soon see, equity funds lagged the market by an amount roughly equal to the level of their all-in costs of some 2½ percent to 3 percent per year. So yes, *costs matter.*

How *Much* Do Costs Matter?

How *much* do costs matter? A ton! Indeed, the record is crystal clear that fund costs have played the determinative role in explaining why funds lag the market's return. During the 1985–2004 period, for example, the annual return on the average mutual fund averaged 10.4 percent when the return on the stock market itself averaged 13.2 percent. That 2.8 percentage-point differential is almost exactly just what one might expect, given our rough estimate of fund costs. (Never forget: *Market return minus cost equals investor return.*) Simply put, fund managers

---

* I first came across this phrase thirty years ago in a prophetic article by Charles D. Ellis in the July/August 1975 issue of the *Financial Analysts Journal.*

have arrogated to themselves an excessive share of the financial markets' returns, and left fund owners with a commensurately inferior share.

There is little doubt that, in nearly all cases, a fund's independent directors and its management company share a common interest in providing good returns to the fund shareholders. But when it comes to *how* good, their interests diverge. Why? Simply because the higher the management fees and other fund expenses incurred by the fund, the lower the fund's return.

In some types of funds, this relationship exists on a virtual dollar-for-dollar basis. For example, the correlation coefficient between the yields that money market funds deliver to their shareholders and the expense ratios of these funds is minus 0.98, perilously close to a perfect negative correlation of -1.00. Each percentage point of increase in cost results in a reduction in return of almost exactly one percentage point. When money market yields are 3 percent, for example, a high-cost fund will deliver as little as 1¾ percent to its owners; a low-cost fund will deliver as much as 2¾ percent, or 50 percent more. Indeed, whenever fund gross returns are commodity-like (for example, in stock index funds and bond index funds), the same kind of locked-in relationship prevails in which each extra dollar of costs entails a reduction of almost exactly the same dollar in returns.

Costs, Returns, and Risks

While in the short term the relationship between the costs and the returns of managed equity funds is more tenuous than over the long run, costs clearly differentiate the superior performers from the inferior performers. An examination of the total costs and gross and net returns of all 942 diversified U.S. equity funds in the Morningstar database showed that for the decade ended February 28, 2005, the total costs for this select group of funds that were in existence over the full ten-year period came to 1.9 percent per year. (Average expense ratio of 1.2 percent plus average portfolio transaction costs estimated at 0.7 percent. The study conservatively assumed that transaction costs totaled 1 percent of turnover, equal to only ½ percent on each side of the trade. It did not take sales charges or other out-of-pocket costs into account.)

Conclusion: the high-cost quartile of funds, with all-in expenses of 3.0

percent, provided an average annual return of 9.0 percent.* The low-cost quartile, with expenses of 0.9 percent, provided an average annual return of 11.7 percent, an advantage of 2.7 percentage points per year, even larger than its average cost advantage of 2.1 percentage points. (On a fund-by-fund basis, the inverse correlation between cost and return was remarkable: *minus* 0.42 percent.) The low-cost funds enjoyed a premium of 30 percent *per year* in annual return over the high-cost funds, confirming the thesis that the higher the cost, the lower the total return. Notice in Table 7.1 how closely the gross returns cluster around 12.5 percent, a further confirmation of the thesis that the average mutual fund manager, before costs, is, well, average.

What's more, the funds with the highest costs also assumed the highest risks. The high-cost quartile carried a risk that was an amazing 34 percent *higher* than the risk carried by the lowest-cost quartile. (The standard deviation of their returns—a widely accepted norm—was used to measure volatility, the customary measure of the amount of risk assumed by a fund.) The high-cost funds also generated vastly higher annual portfolio turnover versus the lowest-cost group, 152 percent versus 19 percent. In all, the low-cost funds had an even greater advantage—3.8 percentage points per year—in risk-adjusted return. The investor who simply sought out low-cost funds, then, enjoyed an amazing increase on annual risk-adjusted return from 8.1 percent to 11.9 percent, an enhancement of nearly 50 percent per year.

Compounding these returns made a good situation better for the low-cost funds. For their high-cost cousins, compounding costs made a bad situation worse. Each dollar initially invested in the low-cost group would have grown by $2.07—to $3.07—during that ten-year period, compared to the growth of only $1.18—to $2.18—for the high-cost group. Investing on the basis of relative costs alone, then, fund investors would have improved their ten-year profit by 75 percent, simply by doing their fishing in the low-cost pond and avoiding like the plague the high-cost pond. It's hard to imagine a more persuasive case regarding the relation between fund costs and fund returns.

---

*Because we used the fund classes without 12b-1 fees, and omitted the impact of initial sales charges, the expense ratios of these 942 funds were understated relative to industry norms. Further, since we made no adjustment for survivor bias, the average return was also overstated.

Table 7.1. Equity mutual funds—returns versus costs. Annual returns for ten years ended February 28, 2005.

Cost quartile	Gross return*	Costs†	Net return	Risk‡	Risk-adj. return	Growth of $1
One (lowest)	12.6%	0.9%	11.7%	16.0%	11.9%	$2.07
Two	12.5	1.5	11.0	17.0	10.9	1.81
Three	12.8	2.0	10.8	18.5	10.1	1.63
Four (highest)	12.0	3.0	9.0	21.4	8.1	1.18
Average fund	12.5%	1.9%	10.6%	18.2%	9.8%	$1.55
Lowest vs. highest	+0.6%	−2.1%	+2.7%	−5.4%	+3.8%	$0.89
Low-cost enhancement	+5%	−70%	+30%	−25%	+47%	+75%

*Gross return is calculated by adding costs to the funds' reported net returns.
†Includes expense ratio and estimated portfolio turnover costs as a percentage of assets.
‡Standard deviation of returns.

The Real-World Consequences of High Costs

These conclusions on the impact of fund costs on fund returns may seem like an interesting theory, no more, no less. But a comparison of the long-term returns achieved by mutual funds with the returns earned in the stock market itself confirms the reality that the returns actually earned by mutual funds have lagged stock market returns by the amount of costs incurred. When you think about it, how could it be otherwise? When a mutual fund manager buys a stock, he is usually buying it from another manager of a mutual fund or pension fund. When he sells a stock, he is also usually selling it to another professional. On each trade, one manager is right; one is wrong. That might look like a zero-sum game, but it isn't. After an intermediary broker takes his commission, it becomes a loser's game on balance. So the return of the average fund ought to equal the return of the market before costs, and ought to lag the market by the amount of fees paid to its manager plus the aggregate costs of portfolio trading.

And it does. During the period 1985–2004, as noted earlier, the U.S. stock market, as measured by the Standard & Poor's 500 Stock Index, provided an annual rate of return of 13.2 percent. The return on the average equity mutual fund was 10.4 percent. The reason for that 2.8 percentage-point lag is not very complicated: As the trained, experienced investment professionals employed by the industry's managers competed with one another to pick the best stocks, their results averaged out. Before costs are deducted, the average mutual fund should earn the market's return. Since all-in fund costs can be estimated at something like 2.5 percent to 3 percent per year, the annual lag of 2.8 percent in after-cost return simply validates our eminently reasonable hypothesis.

When these returns are compounded over the years, the gap between the return earned by the stock market and the return earned by the average mutual fund reaches staggering proportions, as shown in Table 7.2.

The table shows that even over as short a period as twenty years—the expected investment lifetime of a new investor today is at least sixty years—fund costs consumed more than 40 percent of the return provided by the stock market itself. Put another way, an initial investment of $10,000, simply invested in the stock market in 1985, would have produced a profit of $109,800. The profit on the same investment in the average mutual fund would have come to $62,900.

Looked at from yet another perspective, the investor put up 100 percent of the capital and assumed 100 percent of the risk, but collected only 57 percent of the profit. The mutual fund management and distribution system put up zero percent of the capital and assumed zero percent of the risk, but collected 43 percent of the return. If this example does not represent the paradigm of the triumph of managers' capitalism over owners' capitalism in mutual fund America, it is hard to imagine what would. Almost half of the fund owners' money was siphoned away by those who quite literally had everything to gain and nothing to lose.

Table 7.2. The stock market and the average equity fund. Total return on initial investment of $10,000: 1985–2004.

	Annual return	Final value	Profit
Stock market*	13.2%	$119,800	$109,800
Average fund†	10.4	72,900	62,900
Fund shortfall	2.8%	$46,900	$46,900
Share of market return earned by average fund	79%	61%	57%

*S&P 500 Stock Index.
† Source: Lipper: Annual reported return of 11.3 percent for average equity fund, net of fund expenses. Adjusted for estimated survivor bias (0.5 percent per year), annualized front-end sales charges (0.3 percent), and other indirect costs (0.1 percent), a total reduction of 0.9 percent.

A Marketing Business—We Make What Will Sell

It gets worse. While the conflict of interest between fund managers and fund owners explains the large cost-driven gap in long-term performance between the average fund and the stock market itself, there is another major conflict that has cost fund investors even *more*. Fund managers have moved away from being prudent guardians of their shareholders' resources and toward being imprudent promoters of their own wares. They have learned to pander to the public taste by capitalizing on each new market fad, promoting existing funds and forming new funds, and then magnifying the problem by heavily advertising the returns earned by their "hottest" funds, usually highly speculative funds that have delivered eye-catching past returns. This focus on marketing has had a profoundly negative impact on fund investors, who have paid a huge penalty both in the timing of their fund purchases and in the selection of funds they purchased. As a result, mutual fund shareowners have fared far worse than have the funds themselves.

The fund industry has become a business-school case study in marketing—packaging new ancillary products in order to increase its penetration of existing markets and to expand into new markets. Modern marketing has played a major role in the exponential growth in mutual fund assets. But while it has enriched fund managers, it has cut deeply into the returns earned by fund owners.

In this ever-market-sensitive industry, firms are content to hide their light under a bushel in bearish times when stocks are depressed and unsought. But when stocks suddenly burst into the spotlight in bullish times, the managers create hundreds of funds—described as "new products"—focused on the hottest sectors of the market, seeking attention, wallowing in press coverage, identifying their managers as "star" performers, and engaging in vigorous advertising campaigns.

Rather than focusing on the sound investment choices that were once the industry's hallmark, fund managers worshiped at the altar of the Great God Market Share, creating funds that the investing public would be willing, if not eager, to buy. In the late bull market, what the public wanted to buy was the hottest idea of the day—"new economy" funds that focused on the Internet, on technology, and on telecommunications, and aggressive growth funds that concentrated in those market sectors. Indeed, these risky sectors came to dominate the portfolios of even the more diversified traditional growth funds. The industry cooperated to the fullest, creating these risky new funds, promoting them, and selling them to a covetous public that had little interest in the more sedate value funds that were to provide a haven in the oncoming storm.

The Penalties of Timing and Selection

All of that marketing helped to enrich fund managers, who were rewarded by fees and other revenues measured at more than $250 billion for all stock, bond, and money market funds during the six-year boom and bust of 1997–2002 alone. But it cost fund owners far more than those onerous fees. By jumping into the market late in its bull run when stocks were at their highest levels rather than regularly investing in good times and bad, investors paid a huge timing penalty. By picking the wrong funds at the wrong time, they paid an even larger selection penalty.

First, consider the timing penalty. With the Standard and Poor's 500 Index generally languishing under the 300 level during 1984–91, investors purchased equity funds at a $15 billion annual rate. But after the index rose above 1,200 in 1998, on the way to its high of 1,527 in 2000, investors poured money into equity funds at a $230 billion annual rate— fifteen *times* as many dollars. Putting so little money into equity funds when stocks were cheap during the early years and then acting on the apparently irresistible impulse to invest so much money when stocks were dear has cost fund investors additional hundreds of billions of dollars.

Next, consider the selection penalty. Here the industry's responsibility is far greater. During the bubble, we created and promoted growth funds and sector funds that favored overpriced NASDAQ stocks—the "new economy," technology, and the Internet. At precisely the wrong time, investors poured over $460 billion into these highly risky funds and withdrew nearly $100 billion from the conservative value funds favoring NYSE stocks—"old economy" stocks that, bless them, both lagged the market as the bubble inflated and held fairly steady as it burst.

Fund owners, of course, must accept a large part of the responsibility for their own costly foolishness. Nonetheless, fund managers, too, must accept their own substantial share of the responsibility for those counter-productive patterns of adverse timing and selection that played havoc with the returns earned by the very investors that they had a duty to serve.

Adding Up the Score

When we combine the penalty that fund owners paid as a result of the cost-induced performance lag of the average *fund,* and then leverage that penalty with the timing and the selection penalties paid by the average fund *investor,* shareholder losses reached truly stunning proportions. While it is not possible to calculate with precision the amount by which the returns earned by fund owners have lagged the returns reported by the funds themselves, it is possible to estimate that lag. The best way to do so is by comparing the *dollar-weighted* returns earned by fund shareholders as a group with the *time-weighted* returns reported on a per-share basis, the conventional way of calculating fund returns. As Table 7.3 shows, the average fund investor lagged the average fund by 3.3 percentage points per year.*

When this shortfall is added to the 2.8 percentage-point shortfall of the average fund to the stock market itself, the gap grows to 6.1 percentage points—only 7.1 percent for the average fund investor, compared to the 13.2 percent return that was available simply by owning the stock market itself but (1) paying no management, marketing, nor administrative costs; (2) owning the entire market and eschewing any decisions on fund selection; (3) never guessing about the timing of share purchases; and (4) making no redemptions—just buying and holding, and staying the long course.

When we compound the performance of the average stock fund investor, then, the yawning gap between the annual return earned by the average fund and the return of stock market itself grows into a chasm of mind-numbing proportions. Specifically, while $10,000 invested in the stock market earned a profit of $109,800, the average investor earned a profit of just $29,700. Together, the cost penalty, the timing penalty, and the selection penalty consumed an amazing 73 percent of the profit available simply by buying and holding the stock market itself, leaving the average fund stockholder with a mere 27 percent of the total. Investors have paid a staggering price for the excessive costs and excessive marketing focus of the mutual fund industry.

---

*A crude example: Assume a fund's assets rise from $100 million to $110 million during a given year, without cash flow, and its asset value rises from $10 per share to $11, a 10 percent *time-weighted* return. Next, assume that $100 million was invested on the last day of the year at the $11 price. The fund's average assets were $150 million, but its gain remained at $10 million, a 6.6 percent *dollar-weighted* return, or 3.4 percentage points less than the time-weighted return.

Table 7.3. The stock market, the average equity fund, and the average fund investor. Total return on initial investment of $10,000: 1985–2004.

	Annual return	Final value	Profit
Stock market	13.2%	$119,800	$109,800
Average fund	10.4	72,900	62,900
Average fund investor	7.1%*	$39,700	$29,700
Investor shortfall to fund	3.3%	$33,200	$33,200
Investor shortfall to market	6.1%	$80,100	$80,100
Share of market return earned by average fund investor	54%	33%	27%

*During the 1993–2003 decade, fund shareholders in the two hundred largest equity mutual funds, accounting for about 85 percent of all equity fund assets, earned a dollar-weighted return of 6.5 percent, which lagged the 9.8 percent time-weighted return of the average fund by 3.3 percentage points per year. As shown above, if we assume that a similar lag also applied over the two decades ended 2004, the dollar-weighted return earned by the typical fund *investor* averaged 7.1 percent per year.

Salesmanship Versus Stewardship

We can thank the fund scandals for illuminating what went wrong in mutual fund America, focusing public attention on the extent to which fund managers have placed their own interests ahead of the interests of the fund shareholders they serve. Long before the scandals came to light, the triumph of the interests of fund managers over fund owners had been obvious, as salesmanship gradually took precedence over stewardship, as fund investors increasingly relied on market timing, as managers imposed excessive costs on fund investors, and as the industry came to focus on asset-gathering as its highest priority, using the classic marketing strategy of product proliferation.

What went wrong in mutual fund America, then, can be easily, if imperfectly, illustrated by the truly shocking lag in the returns earned by equity fund shareholders compared to the returns that were essentially there for the taking simply by owning the stock market itself. The huge gains that were forsaken by fund investors, importantly the result both of the profits that managers arrogated to themselves and of the speculative funds they created and marketed at the peak of the bubble, totaled in the many hundreds of billions of dollars. More difficult to measure is the harmful impact of the breach in the bond of trusting and being trusted that was once the very essence of capitalism. In both ways, fund owners have been irreparably harmed by the pathological mutation from the owners' capitalism of the fund industry at its humble beginnings to the managers' capitalism of the recent era. What went wrong in mutual fund America can be largely explained by that mutation. Why it went wrong is the province of the chapter that follows.

CHAPTER 8

Why Did Mutual Fund America Go Wrong?

"Losing Our Way"

Just as in corporate America, the failure of governance lies at the heart of why mutual fund America lost its way. Similar to corporate America, while the deterioration came gradually, it gathered enormous momentum during the booming stock market of the last two decades of the twentieth century, culminating in the now-familiar market mania and its aftermath. Further, like our corporations, our mutual funds are essentially organized as republics, with supreme power vested in their shareholders, members of a democracy who exercise their power by electing directors to represent their ownership interests.

But there the similarities end. For mutual funds are organized by managers who have only nominal, if any, ownership positions in the fund's shares. The rewards these managers seek rarely have any relationship to the amount of the capital that they invest in the funds, which usually is modest to a fault. (A mutual fund can be registered with the Securities and Exchange Commission with a mere $100,000 in initial capital.) Rather, the manager's prime focus is to earn an entrepreneurial reward, not from the returns earned by the fund itself, but from the profits the management company can make from the advisory fees paid to it by the fund, under a contract drawn by the manager, in which the manager—here a virtual dictator—represents both parties. As Warren Buffett has wisely observed, "negotiating with one's self seldom produces a barroom brawl."[1]

So it is in the manager's interest:

1. To build the largest possible amount of fund assets, because fees rise as assets grow.
2. To charge the highest fees that traffic will bear, limited only by loose regulatory constraints and even looser competitive norms.
3. To create the largest possible number of funds, appealing to the widest imaginable range of investor objectives, and offering participation in whatever stock market trends are currently in vogue, in effect always having a "product" that is in demand.
4. To charge the maximum feasible amount for marketing and distribution, the better to encourage stockbrokers, fund salesmen, and independent advisers to offer the funds to their clients.
5. To utilize the brokerage commissions generated by the fund's portfolio transactions to acquire marketing support and investment research, thereby obtaining these services without spending a single dollar out of the manager's own pocket.

Fund Managers Versus Fund Owners

The central question is the extent to which these goals of the fund managers parallel the goals of the fund owners. The answer: each of the five manager goals listed above is in fact antithetical to the interests of the investor:

1. As fund assets grow beyond a certain level—a level that varies with the fund's objectives and policies—no actively managed fund is exempt from the problem that large size can leave funds muscle-bound, their investment choices limited, and their transaction costs onerous. While advisory fees may grow more slowly than assets (at least when rates are scaled down as assets increase), the manager has a vested interest in arrogating the economies of scale to his own benefit rather than to the benefit of the fund owners.
2. The higher the fee to the manager, the lower the return to the fund owner, the virtual tautology that was described in the previous chapter.
3. While fund choice, at first glance, may seem an unalloyed benefit, investors have paid a huge financial penalty for freedom of choice, also described earlier.

4. Marketing costs money, and in the world of mutual funds all of those costs are ultimately paid—knowingly or unknowingly, willingly or unwillingly—by the fund owner. And when the investor buys a fund because the broker or salesman has a vested interest in selling it, he may well be not only buying the wrong fund but buying it for the wrong reasons at the wrong time.

5. While paying for research and distribution with brokerage commissions may be "free" to the manager, those commissions and other transaction expenses directly reduce the net returns earned by the owners of the fund.

To be sure, there is one goal—and it is a major one—in which the interests of owners and managers converge. Just as the fund investor seeks to earn the highest reasonable returns on his assets, so the fund manager seeks to provide them. Good performance enriches the shareholder with additional wealth, and it enriches the manager with higher fees. If the returns attract the attention of the marketplace, substantial flows of new investments into the fund engender even higher fees. While the benefits are parallel, however, they are rarely proportionate. Managers' profits normally rise far faster than their fees, and the inflow of new cash to manage can leverage that profitability many times over.

Whatever the case, the same conflict of interest that exists between the owners of corporate America and its managers also exists between the owners of mutual fund America and its managers. Other factors held constant, the more the managers take, the less the investors make. But that conflict is radically different in degree, in that fund managers claim a far higher portion of fund profits than business managers claim of corporate profits. The conflict is also radically different in kind, for the giant institutional owners of investment America hold substantial influence over corporate America that they may exercise to protect their own interests, whereas the relatively small individual owners of funds are virtually powerless in mutual fund America.

In corporate America, share ownership is highly concentrated among relatively few shareholders. With its 52 percent ownership, the earlier-described Institutional 100 holds potential control of our corporations, albeit without yet utilizing the rights and accepting the responsibilities of that ownership position. In mutual fund America, however, ownership is widely diffused, with funds owned largely by some 95 million American families, not a hundred of whose combined fund holdings could possibly reach even a fraction of 1 percent of fund shares outstanding.

Given this widespread ownership, it is simply impracticable to rely on shareholder democracy to ensure that mutual funds are run principally in the interest of their owners. But another factor moves shareholder democracy from an impractical idea to an impossible dream: the peculiar—indeed unique—governance structure of the industry that makes shareholder rights an illusion and gives the manager a dictatorship position, holding power that is virtually impregnable.

A Study in Corporate Incest

Consider how nearly all fund organizations operate. Even when their assets are valued in the hundreds of billions of dollars, fund complexes do not manage themselves. Each complex hires an external management company—with its own separate set of shareholders—to manage its affairs. The management company operates the fund, distributes its shares, and supervises and directs its investment portfolio. It unilaterally determines at the outset what fees it will charge. It decides when to create new funds, and it decides what kinds of funds they will be. When a fund is badly run, the company replaces the portfolio manager, but with one of its own employees. And when a fund outlives its usefulness, it is the management company that decides how to dispatch it to its well-deserved demise. It may simply liquidate it, or, much more likely, merge it into another fund with a better past record, but a fund that it also just happens to manage, and buries the record of the deceased fund in the dustbin of history.

What's more, this typical management company graciously provides the fund's officers, who are paid employees of the company, not the fund. Further, while the executives of the manager usually have a miniscule ownership position in the funds they run, they place themselves on the fund board, and until recent years, also selected most of the funds' "independent" directors, who by law must now compose at least 75 percent of the board. In the typical case, furthermore, the chairman of the board of the management company also serves as—you guessed it—the chairman of the board of the mutual fund.

Given the Gordian knot that secures the rope that binds the fund to its manager, it is impossible to imagine that at even one of the typical fund's four board meetings per year the less-well-informed independent directors can challenge the authority of the steeped-in-the-business management company minority. Small wonder that an early law review article about this industry's structure was, as I recall, entitled: "Mutual Funds: A Study in Corporate Incest."[2]

A Profession Becomes a Business

Almost since the industry's inception in 1924, this incestuous structure has been the norm. Despite its noble preamble that called for the primacy of the interests of fund shareholders, the Investment Company Act of 1940 codified the industry's structure, albeit also permitting another form of structure that enabled funds to operate on an at-cost basis. In fact, the very first mutual fund, Massachusetts Investors Trust (MIT), was organized in 1924 as a business trust, retaining its own trustees and staff and relying on a completely separate firm to distribute its shares through stockbrokers.* The incestuous structure of the industry that the act permitted both enabled and facilitated the industry's transformation. *Once a profession with elements of a business, mutual funds became a business with elements of a profession.*

Force One: The "Bottom Line" Society

Three principal forces contributed to this transformation. One force, of course, was societal change, characterized in the first chapter as the shifting of our worship from the towers of the cathedral to the towers of commerce, and the development of a "bottom line" society. "What's the bottom line?" is not only an irritating maxim used by the narrowly focused members of the business and investment fields but a revealing abstraction about our society, one that prizes money over achievement, measures our worth by how much we earn and spend, and erodes the virtuous circle of trusting and being trusted on which in the long run our society so keenly depends.

---

*I call that structure the Alpha (original) fund model. It was abandoned by MIT in 1969 in favor of the prevailing management company holding structure, what I call the Omega (final) fund model, now used universally, with only one Alpha firm exception, The Vanguard Group. Box 8.1 recounts a brief but revealing history of these two structures.

Box 8.1 The Alpha and the Omega—Comparing Two Mutual Fund Models

The U.S. mutual fund industry began with the formation of the first mutual fund, Massachusetts Investors Trust (MIT), on March 21, 1924. It was a truly *mutual* mutual fund, organized, operated, and managed not by a separate management company with its own commercial interests but by its own trustees. That original *Alpha* mutual fund model, however, was quickly eclipsed by today's *Omega* model, a very different modus operandi that encompasses not only individual *funds* but fund *complexes;* managed not by their own trustees but by external management companies. While this model prevails today, it must not be the final stage of mutual fund development. The Omega structure has served the interest of fund managers, but it has disserved the "national public interest and the interest of investors" that is demanded by the Investment Company Act of 1940.

MIT—From Alpha to Omega

The MIT example enables us to measure what happens when the model changes. For in 1969, MIT and its sister funds abandoned that Alpha model, converting to the Omega model.

Under its Alpha model, MIT was a remarkable success. Until 1975, it was the largest stock fund in the industry, a truly amazing half-century of preeminence built in part on its being the lowest cost of all funds, with a minuscule expense ratio of just 0.19 percent in 1969. MIT was a fund that stood for trusteeship without salesmanship. Its portfolio was broadly diversified and invested for the long term. It held to its own high standards and prospered, a success story for the idea that the Alpha model worked.

Then, in 1969, MIT "demutualized." It became one of the crowd, adopting the conventional external management structure. The costs borne by its shareholders soared. Its 0.19 percent expense ratio doubled again and again, reaching 1.22 percent in 2003. Unsurprisingly, given the inverse relationship that we know exists between costs and returns, its investment performance eroded accordingly. This prototypical mutual fund, widely diversified among about one hundred blue-chip stocks, continued to provide returns to its shareholders that closely paralleled, but regularly lagged, those of the Standard & Poor's 500 Stock Index. But while MIT provided 91 percent of the annual return of the Index during its forty-five-year Alpha phase, it realized just 86 percent of the Index return during the thirty-five-year Omega phase that followed.

The sharply higher costs and distinctly lower returns provided to its fund investors under the Omega model stifled the firm's growth. In 1969, the Massachusetts Financial Services group of funds (of which MIT became a charter member) accounted for 7 percent of fund industry assets. Currently the MFS share is just 1 percent, an amazing 85 percent decline.

Vanguard—From Omega to Alpha

Even as MFS moved to its externally managed Omega structure in 1969, the stage was being set for another firm to take precisely the opposite action. Only a few years later, the Wellington group of funds, operated by Wellington Management Company, was pondering whether its own Omega structure was the optimal one for the funds' shareholders.

After an intense study, the fund directors agreed to form a new subsidiary company, actually owned by the funds themselves, to administer their affairs on an at-cost basis. Named *The Vanguard Group*, the new company was organized on September 24, 1974, the first step toward the complete Alpha model that was achieved soon thereafter, encompassing distribution and investment management as well.

Managed solely in the interests of its fund owners, Vanguard flourished. From an average of 0.66 percent in 1975, the expense ratio of its funds tumbled by more than 60 percent to 0.23 percent in 2004. Armed with these lower costs, and with Vanguard directors dictating changes in the investment strategy of its flagship Wellington Fund, its shareholders were rewarded accordingly. Under its Omega structure in 1944–74, for example, this balanced fund produced only 75 percent of the annual return of its bond-stock-index benchmark. Under its new Alpha structure during the subsequent thirty years—1974 to 2004—Wellington Fund produced 107 percent of the benchmark return, a remarkable reversal of fortune that enriched its shareholders.

That artistic success was rewarded with commercial success. From 1961 to 1984, largely under Wellington Management's aegis, the firm's share of fund industry assets had tumbled from 6.7 percent to 1.7 percent. Thereafter, under Vanguard's aegis, that share has risen to almost 11 percent, a positive turnaround even more striking than the negative reversal in the business fortunes of MFS.

Despite this remarkable rise in market share, Vanguard's Alpha structure remains unique in the mutual fund industry. Why? Because its success was measured in enhanced returns to its fund *owners*, rather than to its fund *managers*. Yet despite the relative failure of MFS in costs, in performance, and in market share, the *manager's* owners reaped enormous financial gains—in excess of $1 billion in 1999–2003 alone.*

* SunLife of Canada acquired MFS in 1982, and has owned the firm ever since.

This devolution is hardly limited to the mutual fund field. It is reflected all across our society, as one profession after another has taken on the defining attributes of a business. During my half-century-plus career in the fund industry, I've seen this field move from being primarily a profession of investment management to becoming largely a business of product marketing. The same transition—albeit in a very different way—has taken place in the medical profession, where the human concerns of the care-givers and the human needs of the patient have been overwhelmed by the financial interests of commerce, our giant medical care complex of hospitals, insurance companies, drug manufacturers and marketers, and health maintenance organizations (HMOs).

Consider too how the profession of public accounting became dominated by the business of consulting. Think about the increasing dominance of "state" (publishing) over "church" (editorial) in journalism, as well as about the rise of commercialism in law and architecture that has eroded traditional standards of conduct. In all, professional relationships with clients have been increasingly recast as business relationships with customers. In a world where every user of services is seen as a customer, every provider of services becomes a seller. When the provider becomes a hammer, the customer becomes a nail.

Please don't think me naive. I'm fully aware that every profession has elements of a business. Indeed, if revenues fail to exceed expenses, no organization—even the most noble of faith-based institutions—will long exist. But as so many of our nation's proudest professions—including trusteeship, medicine, accounting, journalism, law, and architecture—gradually shift their traditional balance away from that of trusted profession and toward that of commercial enterprise, the human beings who rely on those services are the losers.

Late in 2003, Roger Lowenstein made a similar observation, bemoaning the loss of the "Calvinist rectitude" that had its roots in "the very Old World notions of integrity, ethics, and unyielding loyalty to the customer."[3] "America's professions," he wrote, "have become crassly commercial . . . with accounting firms sponsoring golf tournaments" (and, he might have added, mutual fund managers not only doing the same thing but buying naming rights to stadiums as well). "The battle for independence," he concluded, "is never won." And so it is as well in the trusteeship of other people's money.

Force Two: Big Business and Entrepreneurship

The second major force in the industry's transformation was the rise of mutual funds to become "big business." The quantum growth in fund industry assets from $2 billion in 1950 to $8 trillion in 2005 has been both cause and effect of the shift in the industry's prime focus from stewardship to salesmanship. For a tiny industry whose birth in 1924 was quickly followed by tough times, the Depression and then World War II, stewardship seemed essential. But in the easy times thereafter—an era of almost unremitting economic prosperity—salesmanship became the winning strategy. The most powerful force behind the change was the emergence of mutual fund management as one of the most profitable businesses in our nation. Entrepreneurs could make big money managing mutual funds.

In 1958, the whole dynamic of entrepreneurship in the fund industry began to change, taking an unfortunate direction for mutual fund shareholders. In the industry's early years, funds were run by small, privately held professional firms that could make a tidy profit by managing money but could not capitalize that profit by selling shares of the company to outside investors. The SEC maintained that the sale of a management company was the sale of a fiduciary office, and that the profits reaped by the manager from the sale represented an illegal appropriation of fund assets. If such sales were allowed, the SEC feared, "trafficking" in advisory contracts would follow, a gross abuse of the trust of fund shareholders.

But a California management company challenged the SEC's position. In the ensuing court battle, the SEC lost. As 1958 ended, the regulatory wall that had prevented public ownership of management companies since the industry began thirty-four years earlier came tumbling down. A rush of initial public offerings followed, with the shares of a dozen management companies quickly brought to market. Investors bought the shares of these companies for the same reasons that they bought Microsoft and IBM, and, for that matter, Enron: because they thought that their earnings would grow, and that their stock prices would rise accordingly. Business growth quickly took center stage in the mutual fund industry.

Observing this change in 1967, economist and Nobel laureate Paul Samuelson sized it up pungently: "There was only one place to make money in the mutual fund business—as there is only one place for a temperate man to be in a saloon—behind the bar and not in front of it . . . so I invested in a management company."[4] When he realized that public ownership of management companies would not only be a boon for the managers who worked behind the bar, as it were, but be a bane for the fund owners who enjoyed their libations in front of the bar, he was wiser than he could have imagined.

Despite being an industry insider—president from 1967 to 1974 of Wellington Management Company, a fund manager that had itself gone public in 1960—I shared Samuelson's insight with considerable concern. In a 1971 speech to my senior associates, I sounded the alarm: "All things considered, it is undesirable for professional enterprises to have public stockholders. This constraint is as applicable to money managers as it is to doctors, or lawyers, or accountants, or architects. In their cases, as in ours, it is hard to see what unique contribution public investors bring to the enterprise. They do not add capital; they do not add expertise; they do not contribute to the well-being of our clients. *Indeed, it is possible to envision circumstances in which the pressure for earnings and earnings growth engendered by public ownership is antithetical to the responsible operation of a professional organization.*" [5] And so it has proved to be.

This is not to say that I had the gift of perfect foresight. To the contrary, my idea was merely a recognition of the obvious: The fund industry had developed a structure that would favor the interests of managers over the interests of owners, a direct contradiction of the stated purposes expressed in the 1940 act.

Force Three: Fund Managers Become Subsidiaries

The third major force in the industry's transformation, and a rather unrecognized one at that, was the growing control of mutual fund management companies by large financial conglomerates. As the concept of publicly held management companies gained acceptance, and as substantial earnings growth materialized, giant banks and insurance companies, eager to take the new opportunity to buy into the lucrative fund business, began to acquire fund managers, often at huge multiples of their book value. (These conglomerates also had a voracious appetite for privately held fund management firms.) During the past decade alone at least forty fund managers have been acquired. Indeed, the ownership of some fund firms actually has been transferred from one owner to another numerous times, producing the very trafficking that properly concerned the SEC a half-century earlier. Currently, among the fifty largest fund managers, only eight remain privately held, plus mutually owned Vanguard. Forty-one firms are publicly held—six directly by public investors and thirty-five by giant financial conglomerates. Of these management company subsidiaries, twenty-two are owned by U.S. banks and insurance companies, six by major brokerage firms, and seven by foreign financial institutions. (Twenty-three of these firms are included in the list of institutional managers presented earlier in Table 4.2.)

When a corporation buys a business, fund manager or not, it expects to earn a "hurdle rate" on its capital. If the cost of acquiring a fund manager were, say, $1 billion, and the hurdle rate were 12 percent, the acquirer would require at least $120 million of annual earnings. In a bull market, that may be an easy goal for a fund manager. But when the bear market comes, we can expect its parent organization to undertake actions like these:

1. Maintaining existing management fee rates, or even increasing them;
2. Adding new types of fees, such as distribution fees;
3. Slashing management costs; or even
4. Getting its capital back by selling the management company to another owner, at a profit if possible.

The change in the mutual fund industry from profession to business was clearly accelerated by the shift in control of a major portion of the industry, first from private to public hands, and then from independent firms to subsidiary units of financial conglomerates. The staggering aggregations of managed assets that resulted from these combinations—often hundreds of billions of dollars under a single roof—surely serve the interest of the fund manager. With size came burgeoning fees that helped support the costly battle to build market share, and the ability to market the "brand name" of the fund complex across the nation.

On the other hand, conglomeration has hardly served the interest of the fund owner. Giant size and the search for growing profits are unlikely to make the money management process more effective, nor to drive investor costs down, nor to return the industry to its original mission of stewardship and service.

Nor has the change improved investor returns. In fact, the reverse is true. The record shows that funds operated under the aegis of financial conglomerates have provided distinctly inferior returns compared to the returns achieved by funds managed by privately held firms. For example, a study prepared using Morningstar data for Fidelity Investments tracked the performance rankings of the funds managed by the industry's fifty-four largest firms versus their peers over the decade ended in 2003. Its findings

Table 8.1. Average mutual fund performance of the 54 largest firms: Public versus private (100 = best).

Performance rankings	Top ten performers (1–10)		Bottom ten performers (54–45)	
	Fund group	Structure	Fund group	Structure
Private firms (13) 71%	Dodge & Cox	Private	J.P. Morgan	Public
	First Eagle	Private	Pioneer	Public
	Calamos	Private	BlackRock	Public
	So. Eastern/Longleaf	Private	American Express	Public
	Royce	Private	Nations Funds	Public
	American Funds	Private	Aim	Public
Public firms (41) 47%	Harris Associates	Private	Merill Lynch	Public
	Vanguard	Private	Trusco Capital	Public
	PIMCO	Public	Delaware	Public
	T. Rowe Price	Public	Strong	Public

Source: Report prepared by Geoffrey H. Bobroff and Thomas H. Mack for Fidelity Management using Morningstar data for the ten years ended 2003.

were astonishing. All eight of the top performing fund groups were privately held, and all ten of the bottom performing firms were publicly held. (See Table 8.1.) Among the thirty-four lowest ranking firms, only two were private. Thirty-two were publicly held, including thirty that were owned by conglomerates. It's hard to imagine a clearer confirmation of the theory that public ownership is antithetical to fiduciary duty.

Losing Our Way

The rise of the "bottom line" society, the soaring profitability of fund management, and the shift from private ownership of managers to public ownership and then to conglomeration—in all, the move of the fund industry from profession to business—have created a new mutual fund industry, one that has surely lost its way. In the industry's hierarchy of values, it is salesmanship, marketing, and the interests of fund managers that now dominate. Stewardship, management, and the interests of fund owners are now subservient. All of these developments have taken place as fund independent directors, although charged by law to protect the interests of fund owners, stood by seemingly powerless, overwhelmed by an industry structure that puts the fund manager in the driver's seat.

Let's consider just five manifestations of this massive change in the industry's direction, and how they contributed to what went wrong in mutual fund America:

1. The focus on a broad "product line" of funds, many of them equity funds that assume outsized risk.
2. The driving out of traditional conservative management practices and the driving in of aggressive individual portfolio managers, characterized by a "star system."
3. The shrinking time horizons reflected in soaring fund portfolio turnover.
4. The stubborn unwillingness to acknowledge, and act on, the inherent limitations on the amount of assets that can be effectively managed.
5. The swift creation of new funds on demand, and the equally swift burial of the casualties.

The "Product Line"

When I entered the mutual fund industry fifty-four years ago, the focus was on sound management. Aggressive marketing had yet to rear its ugly head. It was a tiny industry overseeing about $2 billion of assets, and there were just seventy-five mutual funds, sixty-six of which were essentially large-cap blend funds, holding widely diversified portfolios of blue-chip stocks and providing returns that generally tracked the returns of the stock market itself, as measured by the Standard & Poor's 500 Index. Most fund managements ran but a single fund, either a stock fund or a balanced fund but not both. (In those days, the two groups rarely fraternized.) In short, this was an industry in which we sold what we made.

What a difference a half-century makes! Today, there are 4,400 individual equity funds with assets totaling $4 trillion. But only 579 of the 4,204 funds large enough to be tracked by the Morningstar statistical service resemble those earlier large-cap blend funds that characterized their blue-chip forebears. The remaining 3,625 funds include 2,484 diversified equity funds investing in one of the other eight "style boxes," making bets away from the total market—on large-cap growth stocks, or small-cap value stocks, or mid-cap blend stocks.* Another 455 funds invest in specialized industry segments; technology, telecommunications, and computers are (or were!) the most popular examples. And 686 are "international" funds, an odd locution that applies largely to funds that invest in a wide variety of

---

*The nine style boxes are represented by a grid with the size of the companies in a fund's portfolio—large-, mid-, or small-capitalization—represented on the vertical axis, and the dominant investment style—growth, blend, or value—represented on the horizontal axis.

foreign markets, albeit sometimes with a seasoning of U.S.-based companies. In general, these other fund categories assume risks that are significantly higher than the market-like funds of yore.

In 1950, an investor could throw a dart at the miniscule fund list and have nine chances out of ten of picking a fund whose returns would parallel the returns of the market itself. Today, the investor's chances of doing so have plummeted to just one out of seven. For better or for worse, "choice" rules the day. Selecting mutual funds has become an art form, and the fund investor is the bearer of that selection risk.

One important counterpoint to this trend is worth noting. While unmanaged index funds, essentially representing the entire U.S. stock market through the Dow Jones Wilshire Total Stock Market Index or the Standard & Poor's 500 Index, didn't enter the field until 1975, they have enjoyed remarkable investor acceptance. Providing the nth degree of diversification, these index funds now represent one-seventh of equity fund assets, and since 2000 have accounted for more than one-third of equity fund cash inflow.

While all those years ago most fund shareholders owned the stock market through a single fund, today it is common for an investor to own three or four equity funds or even more, in effect creating a diversified portfolio of funds and managers that, depending on the results of the selections, is all too likely to produce a return that more or less parallels that of the stock market itself, but only before the deduction of costs. (After costs are deducted, of course, the return is apt to fall well short.) Most of today's managers now run funds of all types and objectives, including literally scores of equity funds under a single roof. Nineteen of the twenty-five largest management companies have more than thirty equity funds in their "product line." Fidelity, the present record holder, operates 164 different equity funds.

As the industry introduced new funds that were more and more performance-oriented, speculative, specialized, and concentrated—funds that behaved increasingly like individual stocks—it attracted more and more investors for whom the long term didn't seem to be relevant. (As noted earlier, the average investor now holds funds for slightly more than four years, a 75 percent reduction from the average holding period of sixteen years in the 1950s.) As the old "buy and hold" mantra turned to "pick and choose," freedom of choice became the industry watchword. "Fund supermarkets," with their "open architecture" that enabled investors to select from a master list of 3,000 funds or more, made it easy to move quickly from one "product" to another at the "point of sale." (My flagrant use of quotations

marks here is a tribute, if a sad one, to the triumph of marketing termi-
nology in the way the industry looks at itself.)

While it became easy to move money around, it was also costly. Yet because the cost of these transactions was hidden in the form of "access fees"
paid to these supermarkets for their "shelf space," it didn't appear costly to
do so. These fees are paid by the funds themselves, and therefore borne by
the fund's shareholders as a group. As a result, swapping funds appears to be
"free," a tacit encouragement for shareholders to trade from one fund to another. (While picking tomorrow's winners based on yesterday's performance
may seem attractive in theory, there are no data that suggest that the strategy works in practice. In fact, the data suggest quite the contrary.) The costs
of swapping funds place a heavy burden on a fund's returns, unknowingly
shared by all of the investors in the fund whether they are traders or not.

From Investment Committee to Portfolio Manager

The vast changes in fund objectives and policies have been accompanied by equally vast changes in how the mutual fund themselves are
managed. A half-century ago, the major funds were managed almost entirely by investment committees, but the demonstrated wisdom of the collective was soon overwhelmed by the perceived brilliance of the individual.
The "Go-Go" era of the mid-1960s, and then the "new economy" bubble
of the late 1990s, brought us hundreds of ever-more-aggressive "performance funds," and the new game seemed to call for freewheeling individual
talent. The term *investment committee* virtually vanished, and *portfolio manager* gradually became the industry standard, the model for some 3,387
funds of the 4,204 stock funds currently listed in Morningstar. ("Management teams," consisting primarily of multiple managers who run discrete
units of larger portfolios, are said to run 807 funds. No manager is listed
for ten funds.)

The coming of the age of the portfolio manager, whose tenure lasted
only as long as he or she produced performance, moved fund management
from the stodgy old consensus-oriented investment committee to a more
entrepreneurial, free-spirited, aggressive, and less risk-averse investment
approach. Before long, the managers with the hottest short-term records
were vigorously marketed by their firms and publicized in the media, becoming celebrities on talk shows. These managers were dubbed "stars,"
and a full-fledged star system gradually came to pass. A few portfolio managers actually *were* stars—Fidelity's Peter Lynch, Vanguard's John Neff,

Legg Mason's Bill Miller, for example—but most proved to be comets, illuminating the fund firmament for but a moment in time and then flaming out. Even after the devastation of the 2000–2002 bear market and despite the stunning fact that the average manager's tenure in a given fund is now but five years, the portfolio manager system remains largely intact, and the continuity provided by the latter-day investment committee remains but a quaint memory.

From Investment to Speculation

The broadening of the fund "product line," the coming of more aggressive funds, the move from investment committee to portfolio manager, and the burgeoning emphasis on short-term performance have had a profound impact on mutual fund investment strategies, most obviously in soaring portfolio turnover, consistent with the general trend of institutional investing that was discussed in Part I. In 1950, mutual fund managers didn't *talk* about long-term investing. They just *did* it. That's what trusteeship was all about. But over the next half-century, that basic tenet was turned on its head, and short-term speculation became the order of the day.

The long-term focus held the fund fort for as long as it could. Indeed, during each of the twenty years from 1945 to 1965, the annual portfolio turnover of equity funds averaged a steady 17 percent, suggesting that the average fund held its average stock for about six years. But turnover then rose steadily, and the average fund portfolio now turns over at an average rate of 110 percent annually. This means that the average stock is now held by the average fund for an average of just eleven months, compared to that earlier six-year standard that prevailed for decades.

While I've discussed this issue earlier, it's important to emphasize that turnover *rates* don't tell the full story of the role of mutual fund portfolio activity. By industry definition, fund turnover is based on the lesser of portfolio purchases and portfolio sales as a percentage of average assets. So at a 100 percent rate, today's manager of a $1 billion equity fund would sell $1 billion of stocks in a single year, and then reinvest that $1 billion in other stocks, $2 billion in all. Even as more competitive, and increasingly electronic, markets have slashed *unit* transaction costs, however, it's impossible to imagine that today's elevated turnover levels, in which trades often take place between two competing funds, can result in a net gain to fund shareholders as a group. The *dollars* involved are enormous. In 2004, with assets averaging $3.9 trillion, equity funds executed total portfolio transactions of $4.6 trillion. Funds sold $2.2 trillion of stocks, and bought $2.4 trillion, with many of these trades simply reflecting the transfer of a stock position from one fund to another. These data suggest an asset-weighted turnover rate of 56 percent, a rate that rises to an estimated 65 percent for actively managed funds (excluding low-turnover index funds). Given the costs of those transactions, it's inconceivable that the millions of fund owners as a group reaped any net benefit.

If a six-year holding period can be characterized as long-term invest-ment, and if an eleven-month holding period can be characterized as short-term speculation, the typical mutual fund manager today is no longer an investor, but a speculator. But fund marketers revel in the wide range of performance that arises from this change, for each large fund family seems to always have at least a few funds that appear to be performing well, leav-ing aside the fact that so many investors, lured in before that performance falters, actually end up losing money.

This combination of the idea that funds are akin to stocks, to be held as part of an ever-changing portfolio, and the development of funds follow-ing strategies focused more on short-term speculation than on long-term investment is what has gotten the industry into the unfortunate position in which it finds itself today. Of course the fund investors themselves are hardly blameless in this state of affairs, for they are not required to buy what the industry wants to sell, nor can the industry control when they buy it. Particularly in the era of the recent market bubble, investor greed came to the fore at the culmination of a great stock market blow-off, a "new economy," and a new millennium.

The daily, even momentary, swings in stock prices were covered in the newspapers and on the air, and were at the forefront of the minds of other-wise rational investors. In a blaze of bandwagon-chasing of hot funds, envy of the returns being earned by fund speculators, and a desire to achieve easy wealth without (perceived) risk, investors lost their perspective. Fund own-ers paid a high price for their foolishness, yes, but fund managers must have had some understanding, as Say's Law expresses it, that supply cre-ates its own demand. Given the economics of the fund industry, there was little resistance against succumbing to the temptation to supply whatever the marketplace might demand.

"Nothing Fails Like Success"

As the assets of an actively managed equity fund grows, the challenges of implementing its investment strategy increase. And when the assets grow exponentially, so too do the challenges: First, the number of stocks available for the portfolio manager to select shrinks. (A $1 billion fund might have a realistic investment universe of 2,500 stocks; a $20 billion fund, perhaps 250.)* Second, portfolio transaction activity tends either to become more expensive as average trade size increases or to diminish, limiting (for better or worse) the portfolio manager's ability to act on price fluctuations and changes in corporate valuations.

Finally, these limits drive the growing fund's investment returns ever closer to simply tracking the return of the stock market itself. As investors pour their money into funds with records that suggest that the manager has the skill to generate superior returns, these superior returns inevitably dissipate. "Nothing fails like success" for the fund shareholder. But while giant size is a bane for the investor who seeks outstanding returns, it is a blessing for the manager's pocketbook. Exceptional growth generates exceptional fees, and the manager is enriched handsomely. The conflict between the interest of the fund owner and the interest of the manager posed by fund size (illustrated in Box 8.2) could hardly be more stark.

It is only in rare cases, therefore, that managers summon the courage to close their funds to additional investments. The temptation to earn more fees drives firms to allow—and indeed often to encourage—their funds to grow beyond their ability to be effectively managed, and the fleeting pressure to serve the fund owner is overwhelmed. Today, only 32 of the 3,570 domestic equity mutual funds in existence are completely closed to the acceptance of any new capital, with another 184—just 5 percent of the total— closed to all but existing shareholders. Even in a business in which the average asset base of the fifty largest equity funds has burgeoned in a decade from $7.1 billion to $32.7 billion, fund closings remain a rare event. The manager's interest in ever-higher fees carries the day, and outweighs the shareholder's interest in sustaining superior returns. "Nothing succeeds like success" for the fund manager.

---

*For a $1 billion fund, for example, a 5 percent holding would be $50 million. But for a $20 billion fund, it would be $1 billion. Then, a 5 percent holding would represent more than 10 percent of the shares of any stock with a market capitalization of less than $10 billion, so large that it would be costly and time-consuming to acquire or liquidate. Only about 250 of some 6,000 publicly traded U.S. stocks have market capitalizations of more than $10 billion.

Box 8.2 Fund Size and Fund Performance— the Magellan Example

Fidelity's Magellan Fund provides the classic example of the interaction of fund size and fund performance. In its early years, the fund turned in an astonishingly successful record, outpacing the Standard & Poor's 500 Stock Index from 1978 through 1983 by a remarkable average of 26 percentage points per year. Even after its assets burgeoned from a mere $22 million to $1.6 billion, the fund's annual return remained highly superior, averaging 3.5 percentage points per year above the 500 Index from 1984 through 1993. By then, its assets had grown to a staggering $31 billion (on its way to a high of $110 billion), and the excess returns came to an abrupt halt. Magellan has fallen short of the 500 Index for eight of the following eleven years, lagging by an average of 2.1 percentage points per year, an incredible reversal of the good fortune its investors had enjoyed decades earlier.

Right along with the fund's swelling assets, the management costs borne by Magellan's shareholders were also swelling—$400 thousand of management fees and expenses in 1978; $17 million in 1984; $166 million in 1991; $500 million in 1996; and $763 million in 2001. *In the early years, small fees for large returns. In the later years, awesome fees for faltering returns.* The fund's asset growth was a bonanza for its managers, but a disaster for its owners.

Furthermore, the larger the fund grew, the more it came to resemble an index fund. In 1978–82, return of the S&P Index itself explained 82 percent of Magellan's return. But by 1997–2004, it explained 97 percent, and since 2000, an amazing 99 percent. Essentially, the fund had become an expensive Standard and Poor's 500 Index Fund. I'm *not* arguing that such a change is bad. (After all, I'm an indexer.) But I *am* arguing that the $5.3 billion total of fees and costs paid by Magellan's owners over the past decade constitutes a waste of the fund's corporate assets. From the vantage point of the investors who are paying them, such fees are patently absurd. From the standpoint of the managers who are raking them in, however, such fees are the soul of rationality. "We made the fund large," the argument seems to be, "and even if we can no longer provide superior returns, we deserve to be paid for our ancient success." That line of reasoning may appeal to fund managers, but it is an insult to fund owners.

Ultimately, of course, the owners began to respond. They are leaving Magellan in droves, withdrawing net redemptions of $10 billion in 2000–2003, and another $12 billion in 2004–5 (through February). The fund's assets now total $57 billion, or only one-half of their peak level. But it is inconceivable that Magellan Fund will ever again repeat even a hint of the remarkable success it achieved more than two decades ago.

New Funds Are Born . . . Old Funds Die

Part of the extraordinary telescoping of holding periods by fund shareholders can be laid to the change in the character of our financial markets, especially during the boom and bust of the stock market bubble of 1997–2002, and to their own opportunism, gullibility, and counterproductive emotions. But by creating new funds to match the market fads of the moment, this industry too must assume much responsibility for the unwise choices made by so many fund investors. It's worth reiterating that investors have paid a high price for the fund industry's departure from its time-honored and sound tenet "we sell what we make" to its new and opportunistic tenet "we make what will sell." That new tenet accurately reflects the fund industry's eagerness to jump on the bandwagon of the latest market whims.

The Great Bull Market was an important factor in making the 1990s a banner period for fund formation. During that decade, the fund industry enjoyed a baby boom. Some 1,600 new equity funds alone were born, a 200 percent increase in the number of equity funds (722) that were in existence at the decade's outset, and twelve times the 130 equity funds created on average in each of the decades of the 1950s, 1960s, and 1970s. Capitalizing on the stock market's mania to attract investors, the new funds created by the industry during the 1990s typically carried higher risks than their predecessors. In the latter part of the decade, as "new economy" stocks led the market upward, fund managers formed 494 new technology, telecom, and Internet funds, and aggressive growth funds favoring these sectors.

The industry created these funds, and proceeded to market them with unprecedented vigor and enthusiasm, both through stockbrokers and through advertising. At the market's peak in March 2000, the forty-four mutual funds that advertised their performance in *Money* magazine bragged about amazing rates of return that averaged +85.6 percent during the previous twelve months alone. The ads seemed to work. The lion's share of the $650 billion of new money that was invested in equity funds during 1998–2000 alone was invested in the new breed of aggressive growth funds. Most of the money, of course, poured into those winners of yesteryear *after* they led the market upward. They would also soon lead the market on its downward leg, with their shareholders suffering losses measured in the hundreds of billions of dollars. (In fact, in the five years since then, nine of the forty-four funds were merged out of existence. The remaining thirty-five funds have provided a cumulative return of −29.6 percent, precisely double the −14.8 percent loss on the S&P 500.)

After the fall, the faddish trends of new fund formation began to unwind. Record numbers of funds went out of business, usually merged into other better-performing funds that were members of the same fund family. During 1994–2004, more than 800 equity funds vanished into thin air, largely members of that aggressive breed focused on the stocks of the new economy. While the conservative equity funds of six decades ago were, as the saying goes, "built to last," their aggressive new cousins seemed "born to die." While 10 percent to 20 percent of funds went out of business during most previous decades, the failure rate soared to 36 percent during the 1990s. It is even higher now. Should present fund dissolution rates continue over the remainder of the decade, some 2,500 of today's 4,500 equity funds—*more than one-half*—will no longer exist.

Why Mutual Fund America Went Wrong

The answer to the question of why mutual fund America went so wrong—why the mutual fund scandals took place, why the powerful impact of fund costs was ignored, why the marketing ethic came to permeate the industry—is not complicated. The mutual fund industry lost its way because of the triumph of managers' capitalism over owners' capitalism. The heart of the problem lies in the industry's flawed fund governance system, in which fund directors who lacked any real power to protect fund owners ceded virtually unfettered dominion over the funds to managers whose goal was to earn entrepreneurial rewards by building giant fund empires.

The development of these forces that would sap the returns earned by fund owners and enrich the returns of fund managers was no secret. In 1996—almost a decade ago—in a speech before the Society of American Business Editors and Writers, I warned that the "spirit of trusteeship, professional competence and discipline, and a focus on the long term, are rapidly losing their role of the driving force—in the long run, the *life* force of this industry."[6]

In the aftermath of the fund scandals, the three principal points I made then seem even more relevant today:

- The industry's traditional focus on trusteeship, implying placing the interest of fund shareholders as our highest priority and charging a reasonable price for our services, is being supplanted by a focus on asset-gathering—on distribution—as we worship at the shrine of the Great God Market Share, the exorbitant cost of which is borne by our own fund shareholders.

- The industry's traditional focus on professional competence and discipline has moved from long-term investment to what is really speculation, with rapid turnover in our investment portfolios (averaging almost 100 percent per year!), funds concentrating on ever-narrowing segments of the stock market, and far too many gunslinger portfolio managers.
- And the industry's traditional focus on the eminent suitability of mutual funds for long-term investors is quickly becoming a focus on investing in fund portfolios for the short term—a second level of speculation—and, even more baneful, a focus on enticing fund shareholders to use their mutual funds as vehicles for rapid switching, either for the purpose of market timing or for the purpose of jumping on the bandwagon of the latest hot fund. And that's called speculation, too.[7]

These long-standing problems were an open secret in an industry whose leaders were all too happy to have them kept under wraps. Yet even today, after the spotlight of the scandals that illuminated their depth and severity, even after two decades in which excessive costs sapped the returns earned by mutual funds, causing them to lag substantially the returns available in the financial markets in which they invest, even after a historic episode that drained hundreds of billions of dollars from the savings of opportunistic fund investors, the industry has yet to meaningfully react. But knowing what went wrong in mutual fund America, and why it went wrong, is not enough. It is time to fix the system. It will not be easy, but the next chapter offers a menu of suggestions as to how to begin the monumental task.

How to Fix Mutual Fund America

"Organized, Operated, and Managed"
for Shareholders

If a flawed governance system lies at the heart of why the mutual fund industry went wrong, then the governance system must be fixed. In that same 1996 speech with which the previous chapter concluded, I described the central goal of the reforms we will need, urging this industry to move to a system in which "the focus of mutual fund governance and control is shifted . . . to the directors and shareholders of the mutual funds themselves, and away from the executives and owners of mutual fund management companies [where it almost universally reposes today], who seek good fund performance to be sure, but also seek enormous personal gain."[1] It is high time to shift from managers' capitalism to owners' capitalism in mutual fund America.

Back to Basics

The starting point for considering how to fix mutual fund America is the reiteration of the lofty words of the preamble to what is essentially the mutual fund industry's constitution, the Investment Company Act of 1940: "the national public interest and the interest of investors" require that mutual funds be "organized, operated, and managed . . . in the best interests of their shareholders, *rather than* in the interests of advisers, underwriters or others."[2]

Note that the law of the land says nothing about balancing the interests of managers and fund owners. If you visualize a scale, the law would have *all* of the weight placed on the shareholder side, and *none* of the weight on the side of the fund management company. Yet today's reality is precisely the reverse: almost none of the weight lies on the shareholder side; practically all of it rests on the management company side. Doubtless most industry leaders believe that the imbalance that exists today has been a positive, a prerequisite to the fund industry's unarguably enormous asset growth. Since the passage of the 1940 act, mutual fund assets have grown from $450 *million* to $8 *trillion,* an incredible 18,100-fold. Fund leaders point to that growth and argue, "We must be doing something right."

Such a facile assertion of causality, however, ignores two facts:

1. During the first four decades that followed the passage of the act, the industry's focus was largely on sound investment policies and prudent funds with long-term strategies and objectives; the scale fairly evenly balanced the directly competing interests of managers and owners.
2. More than 95 percent of that 18,100-fold growth has come since 1982, a period dominated by the longest and strongest bull market in common stocks in all human history.

The truth is that the industry's growth can be largely explained by the industry's great tradition during its formative years, and the Great Bull Market that followed. Together, these elements served to cover the multitude of sins that gradually developed.

One doesn't even need to read beyond the second page of the 1940 act to understand its unequivocal message. It's all there in the preamble on page two: *The shareholder is king.* I believe that the act got it right. After all, it simply reflected the British common law of fiduciary duty—the obligation of the trustee to place his clients' interest first—which goes back at least eight centuries. Alas, however, the drafters of the act not only failed to define just what they meant by the "national public interest and the interest of investors," but they permitted, as we now know, a governance structure that would later fly directly in the face of the national public interest and the interest of investors.

Ironically, just as in corporate America, it took a series of industrywide scandals in mutual fund America to focus the powerful spotlight of public attention on the conflict between the interests of managers and the inter-

ests of owners. When attorney general Eliot Spitzer, in his tireless advocacy of consumers' rights, clearly identified one serious manifestation of the
existence of this conflict in September 2003, his spotlight revealed an ever-
widening circle of fund managers who were implicated in illicit late trading and unethical time-zone trading practices. Soon thereafter, the Securities and Exchange Commission threw its considerable weight into the
fray. The U.S. Congress quickly joined in, as committees of the House of
Representatives and, later, the Senate held extensive hearings on "Mutual
Funds: Trading Practices and Abuses that Harm Investors."

Yet even earlier, the House had raised serious questions about mutual
fund practices. At hearings before the House of Representatives on March
12, 2003, my testimony included this statement about the failure of fund
independent directors: "Fund independent directors in actuality have only
two important responsibilities: Obtaining the best possible investment
manager and negotiating with that manager for the lowest possible fee. Yet
their record has been absolutely pathetic . . . [for they follow] a zombie-
like process that makes a mockery of stewardship. Able but greedy managers have overreached and tried to dip too deeply into the shareholders'
pockets, and directors haven't slapped their hands. They have failed as well
in negotiating management fees. 'Independent' directors, over more than
six decades, have failed miserably."[3]

I immediately told the committee members present that the words in that
indictment were not mine; they were the words of investment oracle Warren Buffett, taken directly from his chairman's letter in the then-recently
published 2002 annual report of Berkshire Hathaway. I quickly added that
I agreed strongly with him. I could easily have added that like the corporate
CEOs described in my opening chapter, "never has so much been paid by so
many to so few [mutual fund managers] for so little."

Senator Fitzgerald Stands on Principle

After the scandals came to light, the Senate's turn came. The
subcommittee on Financial Management, the Budget, and International Security took the lead, under the inspired and principled direction of Senator
Peter G. Fitzgerald (Republican, Illinois). At a hearing held on November
3, 2003, his opening statement made it clear that the senator had done his
homework. He expressed his deep concern not only about the scandals but
about the way the fund industry operates. "It's time for a wholesale re-
examination of how mutual funds are organized and managed," he said.

The governance structure of a typical mutual fund is a study in institutionalized conflict of interest. Until we eliminate the conflicts, lots of mutual funds will continue to engage in behavior that benefits fund managers at the expense of fund shareholders. . . .

Surprisingly, federal law not only allows this incestuous relationship, but codifies it. The law apparently places faith in the false conceit that fund directors can bargain at arm's length with themselves. . . . The fund industry's institutionalized conflicts of interest have cost Americans dearly. The recent scandals merely highlight that in trying to serve two masters, many fund directors have all too often preferred the investment advisory firms with which they are associated over the mutual fund shareholders whom they should theoretically be trying to protect.

"The mutual fund industry," he continued, "is now the world's largest skimming operation—a $7 trillion trough from which fund managers, brokers and other insiders are steadily siphoning off an excessive slice of the nation's household, college and retirement savings." At the conclusion of his remarks, Senator Fitzgerald was also kind enough to refer both to my work and to Vanguard's unique "at-cost" operating structure: "Relatively few have questioned the industry's practices or fees, let alone its bizarre governance structure, and too few have listened to industry reformers like John Bogle, who has been sounding the alarm for years. Until now that is. The current scandal gives us the opportunity to re-think the whole mutual fund industry. . . . We ought to consider facilitating the creation of more mutual funds that are truly mutual—ones where, like Vanguard, the funds actually own the firm."[4]

Reshaping the Fund Board

In my four appearances before congressional committees, I repeated over and over a wish list of governance changes that would, in the aggregate, initiate a reversal of the industry's version of managers' capitalism and lead toward the establishment of the ideal system of owners' capitalism. To balance at long last the scale that I described earlier, there is an urgent need for more heft on the fund side of the scale, beginning with the enactment of federal legislation that both requires and enables fund directors to serve solely the interests of fund shareholders. In particular, the powers of the *fund* organization must be strengthened so that it can deal, independently and at arm's length, with the *management* organization, just as the 1940 act mandated when it was enacted into law sixty-five years ago. My platform for reform includes these "four horsemen" of governance reform:

1. No more than one management company director on the fund board. Indeed, if loyalty is one of the cardinal duties of a corporate director, one might ask how even *one* such director can be permitted to serve, given his obviously conflicting duty of loyalty to the management company that pays his salary.
2. An independent chairman of the fund board to lead the directors.
3. A dedicated fund staff, reporting to the board chairman, with responsibility to evaluate independently the investment performance and marketing results of the manager, the reasonableness of fees paid, and any other relevant information that the board may require.
4. A federal statute of fiduciary duty for fund directors.

Congress being Congress, political parties being political parties, and lobbyists and money being, well, lobbyists and money, legislative change was not in the cards. Enacting federal legislation is a tortuous process, and the will simply was not there to take up arms against the sea of fund industry troubles, and by opposing, end them. Happily, however, under the strong leadership of then newly appointed chairman William H. Donaldson, a reinvigorated Securities and Exchange Commission acted with all deliberate speed to accomplish by regulation what legislation was not ready, willing, or able to do.

The SEC quickly tackled and successfully resolved the first three of the issues listed above. On board independence, while the commission did not go quite as far as I would have liked, it did approve a rule raising the existing requirement that at least a *majority* of the board be independent to a *supermajority* of 75 percent, an essential step toward greater fund independence. It also honored my third proposal, approving a rule that "requires funds to explicitly authorize the independent directors to hire employees and to retain advisers and experts necessary to carry out their duties . . . to help them deal with matters beyond their expertise . . . and to ensure that independent directors are better able to fulfill their role of representing shareholder interests."[5] There was little industry opposition to these two rules, and both will take effect no later than January 2006. In addition, the new SEC rules call for an annual board self-assessment and separate sessions of independent directors. It had earlier required the appointment of a chief compliance officer for the funds, and board counsel independent of the manager. These rules are also vital building blocks in the establishment of a better fund governance structure. They will enable, and implicitly encourage, directors to act with greater authority and independence.

An Independent Chairman, a Fiduciary Duty Standard

My second proposed reform, the requirement of an independent board chair, was, well, a horse of a different color. Industry opposition was strong, strident, and of course well financed. Edward C. Johnson Jr., chairman of both the Fidelity mutual funds and Fidelity's management company (who would be required under the rule to relinquish his fund title) lobbied hard, going public with a strident op-ed piece in the *Wall Street Journal* that plaintively implored investors, "If a ship I was sailing on were headed for an iceberg, I'd want one—and only one—captain giving orders."[6] Alas, Johnson forgot that in the fund business there are *two* ships. He also ignored the fact that the captain of the fund ship giving orders about the fees the fund should pay was also the captain of the management company ship that raked in all those fees. In fact, the independent chairman rule simply acknowledged that it was necessary and appropriate for the principals (the fund owners) to be represented by an agent (the fund chairman) who represented solely their own interests.

When the independent chairman rule was approved by a narrow 3–2 vote of the commission, the industry, ever irrepressible, turned its efforts to overturning it. It succeeded in placing an amendment in the Consolidated Appropriations Act, 2005, that required the commission to reexamine the issue during the year. (The dissonance of mixing the federal budget with the self-serving interests of the fund industry gave new resonance to the old saw "There are two things that you should never watch being made: sausage and legislation.") Not content with that amendment, the U.S. Chamber of Commerce went to court with a direct challenge to the validity of the SEC rule. Investors can only hope that the commission stays the course on a decision that, despite its almost universal unpopularity in the fund industry, is wholly consistent with the public interest and the interest of investors, just as the 1940 act demands.

As to the final issue—a federal standard of fiduciary duty—the SEC lacks the power to accomplish that worthy goal, and federal legislation would be required. While the provision was included in Senator Fitzgerald's omnibus mutual fund reform bill, it has gained little traction. Fulfillment of this vital standard will demand a long, hard struggle, which will doubtless be vigorously opposed not only by the fund industry but also by the states themselves.

Ever since the adoption of our U.S. Constitution, corporate charters have been the exclusive province of the states, and Delaware and Maryland, homes of so many fund charters, could well lead the state opposition. Such federal preemption of state law, furthermore, would fly in the face of those political interests that purport to believe deeply in the new federalism ("power to the states") and oppose assigning new responsibilities to the national government ("power to Washington, D.C."). But with the rise of the fund industry to its preeminence as the largest of all American financial institutions, I continue to believe that we need to put "meat on the bones," as it were, of the policies of the 1940 act. To require that funds are operated strictly in the interests of their owners, we need to add to the statute an explicit standard of fiduciary duty, as well as provisions that define the fulfillment of that standard.

Change Is in the Air

As the winds of change begin to blow, there are vital issues that need to be placed on the table if we are to fix what went wrong in mutual fund America. These five major items should be on the SEC agenda:

1. *Management company compensation.* Way back in 1966, in "Public Policy Implications of Investment Company Growth" (PPI), a report to the House Committee on Interstate and Foreign Commerce, the SEC vigorously recommended legislative changes presciently designed to restore a better balance of interest between shareholders and managers. After considering the burgeoning level of fund fees (then at an annual level of a mere $134 million), the effective control advisers held over their funds, and "the absence of competitive pressures, the limitations of disclosure, the ineffectiveness of shareholder voting rights, and the obstacles to more effective action by the independent directors," the SEC recommended the adoption of a "statutory standard of reasonableness . . . *a basic fiduciary standard that would make clear that those who derive benefits from their fiduciary relationships with investment companies cannot charge more for services than if they were dealing with them at arm's length.*" [7]

The SEC described reasonableness as a "clearly expressed and readily enforceable standard [that] would not be measured merely by the cost of comparable services to individual investors or by the fees charged by other externally managed investment companies . . . [but by] the costs of management services to internally-managed funds and to pension funds and other non-fund clients." (There is an enormous disparity in these costs. See Box 9.1.) If the standard of reasonableness does not "resolve the problems in management compensation that exist . . . *then more sweeping steps might deserve to be considered.*"[8]

The fund industry fought—and, as we now know, won—its battle against the "reasonableness" standard, and fund expenses have soared to astonishing levels. The *unweighted* expense ratio of 0.87 percent for the average equity fund that concerned the commission in 1966 has risen by 79 percent, to 1.56 percent. For those who think that *asset-weighted* expense ratios are a better test, the increase was from 0.51 percent to 0.92 percent—an even larger 80 percent increase. Total fees and operating costs paid by equity funds have risen from the $134 million that troubled the commission in 1966 to some $37 billion in 2004. Yet even now, nearly four decades later, "more sweeping steps" have yet to be considered.

The 79 percent increase in fee rates (expense ratios) and the 28,000 percent explosion in fee dollars suggest that the industry's defeat of the "reasonableness" standard has come at a cumulative cost of scores of billions of dollars to mutual fund investors. As the relationship of these numbers makes clear, "basis points" no longer represent a proper standard for considering fund fees. *Basis points are mere basis points, but dollars are real dollars.* By looking at rates rather than dollars in periodic private litigation against fund managers, the courts have given the managers a license to charge fees that could easily be regarded as a waste of corporate assets under state law. Recall the earlier example of fees of $5.3 billion paid over the past decade by giant Magellan Fund to Fidelity, its adviser, despite the Fund's poor returns relative to the S&P 500 (162 percent versus 212 percent). We must urgently reexamine the whole notion of management fees, their relation to value added (or subtracted), whether "basis points" have lost their original meaning, and whether, at long last, more sweeping steps to resolve the problems of manager compensation should be considered.

2. *Disclosure of compensation to fund managers, officers, and directors.* Full and fair disclosure has been—and must always be—the hallmark of our system of financial regulation. But only a small part of the reason that

Box 9.1 Fees Paid by Pension Clients

The proposed study of management fees ought to include an investigation of why the advisory fees paid by mutual funds dwarf the fees charged
to pension plans by those very same advisers. While the fees paid by pension funds are rarely made public, the $166 billion California Public Em-
ployees' Retirement System provides full disclosure of what it pays its
managers. Consider these three cases in which mutual fund managers
were also managing portfolios for Calpers during 2002:

Mutual fund fees versus pension fund fees

	Assets (million)		Fee rate		Fee (thousand)	
Manager	Mutual fund*	Calpers	Mutual fund*	Calpers	Mutual fund	Calpers
AllianceBernstein	$2,700	$902	0.97%	0.08%	$27,000	$710
Capital Guardian	22,200	590	0.40	0.10	88,000	570
Putnam Investments	11,000	675	0.47	0.06	52,000	420
Average	$12,000	$720	0.61%	0.08%	$56,000	$600

Source: Calpers and Lipper.
* Respectively, AllianceBernstein Large Cap Growth, American Funds New Perspective, and Putnam Voyager.

While Calpers does not disclose the stocks in these portfolios, it is not
unreasonable to assume that similar portfolios are held by both the pension account and the mutual fund. So how is it that those giant mutual
funds managed by the very same advisers—with assets averaging seventeen times as large as the pension accounts—are paying fees that average
more than seven times the *rate (0.61 percent versus 0.08 percent)* and
nearly one hundred times the *dollars* ($56 million versus $600,000) paid
by relatively small Calpers? While the array of services provided to the
fund may be broader, there is no way that factor alone could account for
these enormous differences.

How can such extreme differences exist? Some possibilities: (1) While
the advisers control their mutual funds, they don't control Calpers.
(2) Unlike the Calpers trustees, the independent fund directors have failed
to negotiate with the adviser on an arm's length basis. (3) Given the high
fees generated by the funds, managers are happy to use marginal pricing
when they seek to attract new pension clients. (The added costs incurred
in managing additional assets are extremely low.) (4) The fund directors
are not given the information about the fees paid by the adviser's pension
clients, a shortcoming that a recently proposed SEC rule would rectify.

(*continued*)

Box 9.1 *Continued*

There may also be a fifth reason: While Calpers negotiates seemingly rock-bottom rates, it offers its managers incentive fees under which the adviser may earn much larger fees, *but only if it produces superior investment returns.* AllianceBernstein, for example, received an extra $3,600,000 in incentives from Calpers in 2002, and Capital Guardian received an extra $930,000. (It is not clear whether Putnam failed to offer an incentive fee, or simply failed to earn one.) But such incentive arrangements are anathema to fund managers. The directors of the mutual funds served by these managers have failed to demand similar "pay for performance" schemes. Apparently, arm's length bargaining comes into play only when truly independent trustees control both the choice of managers and the level of fees, and are dedicated to giving the pension plan beneficiaries and fund shareholders a fair shake.

"The Cost of Conflicts of Interest"
A landmark 2001 article in *The Journal of Corporation Law* confirms the amazing disparity between the fees paid to investment managers by the funds that they operate and control compared to the far lower fees paid by the pension funds that they do not operate and control.[9] "Mutual Fund Advisory Fees: The Cost of Conflicts of Interest" concludes:

> Fund advisors are feasting on a complex, poorly disclosed fee structure that is out of kilter with free market price levels. . . . That this aberration exists in the most regulated of all corners of the securities business demonstrates powerfully the consequences of watered-down fiduciary standards, weak, misguided regulation, Congressional indifference, and either poor advocacy on the part of investors' lawyers or excessive judicial deference to fund managers' contentions.
> . . . The gap between prices charged funds for advisory services versus prices fetched elsewhere in the economy for those same services represents the bill paid by fund shareholders for the advisory conflict of interest that is both the fund industry's hallmark and its stigma. That tab . . . translates into fund shareholders being overcharged to the tune of nearly $9 billion-plus annually—a staggering number . . . The SEC should require that fund shareholders receive most favored nations treatment when it comes to fees for advisory services. Fund independent directors need to demand that advisors identify and quantify what they charge for rendering investment advice . . . to non-fund clients . . . [and explanations of] how service differences rendered to their captive and free market customers justify such price disparities.

disclosure works is that it informs the investing public. Even more important, in my view, is this simple fact: *disclosure modifies behavior.* That is, if their actions have to be disclosed, most managers will think twice before they take advantage of their shareholders. Yet the mutual fund industry alone has somehow been able to operate in an isolated enclave in which management company officers and directors are virtually exempt from the same kinds of full disclosure requirements that apply to *all* other publicly held companies in the nation.

As a result, when mutual fund executives are employed by a separate management company that is either privately held or owned by a financial conglomerate, their compensation is hidden behind a corporate veil, with no thought given to piercing that veil. Even the disclosure rule recently approved by the commission would require the disclosure only of how, but not how much, portfolio managers are compensated. Such a limited disclosure is essentially no disclosure at all. The commission should require not only the disclosure of the dollar amount of each portfolio manager's compensation (including his or her share of the profits of the management company itself) but also comparable compensation data for the five highest-paid executives of the company. There is no rational reason for exempting fund executives from the spotlight of public disclosure applicable to their counterparts in regular corporations, indeed the very information demanded by the security analysts that fund managers employ. It is brazen hypocrisy for fund industry leaders to object to such even-handed treatment. *The playing field ought to be leveled.*

While we're about it, we should also require that fund directors, executives, and portfolio managers report the extent to which they "eat their own cooking" by investing in the shares of the funds they manage. While the new rule requires that fund portfolio managers disclose their holdings of fund shares, there is no requirement that they disclose their fund share transactions. And there is no requirement that other management company officials disclose either figure. That information gap needs to be eliminated.

A similar information gap also exists with respect to the holdings of fund directors. Somehow our powerful industry lobbyists persuaded the SEC to exempt directors from disclosure of the precise number of shares they own, the standard for all other public corporations. Rather, fund directors need now only disclose the *range* of their holdings both for the fund and for all funds in the group: $10,000 or less; $10,000 to $50,000; $50,000 to $100,000; over $100,000. What earthly good is it for an investor to know only that a given director has spread a modest $100,000 (or is it more?) among one hundred or more funds in the group? If such information is better than no disclosure at all, it is only barely so. The sooner we revise the regulations to provide full and accurate disclosure of management compensation and ownership of fund shares, the better.

It is time for the SEC and its staff to stiffen its back against the powerful influence of the Investment Company Institute. While they deny that they are doing exactly that, industry leaders seem hell-bent on resisting meaningful reform. (On the proxy disclosure issue, for example, the ICI's official position was that they endorsed the SEC proposal, *except for* the requirement that funds disclose their proxy votes.) I continue to be mystified by the basis for the ICI's influence, publicly stating in the *New York Times,* that "the ICI's influence over the SEC staff is completely disproportionate to the intellectual weight of its arguments."[10]

3. *Incubator funds: a license to steal?* Even as the statistical evidence mounts that the simple rate of return earned by a fund is the principal factor on which investors rely in making their choices ("Oh, what fools we mortals be!"), there has been little information provided as to whether those records are credible. While investors assume that the rates of return earned by funds presented in advertising, in shareholder reports, and in prospectuses are accurate, that record is too often sheer illusion. Returns reported by giant funds, for example, often include the superior records achieved when they were tiny, returns that melt away as investors, salivating over the past records, pour their money in and the funds reach a size that virtually precludes future superiority.

The commission apparently deems it neither inappropriate nor improper for a fund manager to continue to promote as "real" a fund's record after circumstances have radically changed. While that policy is unfortunate, the SEC ought to at least have a zero-tolerance policy toward illusory records that are manufactured out of thin air, often part of a pervasive pattern in which managers form a host of "incubator funds." Such funds are typically owned only by insiders, have tiny asset bases, and are aggressively managed. Once born, if they hit the jackpot, they are offered to the public and aggressively marketed. If they don't hit the jackpot, they're given a decent, but inevitably quiet, burial.

Fund managers who engage in such actions don't always get away with them. In 1999 and 2000, the SEC fined Van Kampen and Dreyfus for materially misleading the public in ads touting the performance of formerly incubated funds. During the funds' incubation period, the managers granted them outsized allocations of "hot" initial public offerings, which were quickly sold on the open market for a huge profit—a strategy that was largely responsible for the funds' prior returns averaging 64 percent annually. When the managers then offered these funds for sale to the public, they advertised their returns prominently, but without disclosing that the performance was due almost exclusively to this practice, which was impossible to replicate going forward. Van Kampen was fined $100,000; Dreyfus, $950,000.

A recent Wharton School paper described fund incubation as a "strategy for enhancing return histories . . . the process of running lightly-capitalized, self-funded investment accounts in a semi-private environment."[11] The paper reported that the return earned by funds emerging from incubation was 18 percent per year above the average return of funds that were discarded. In one example, the paper cited an incubated fund that produced a three-year annualized return of 28.79 percent, winning Morningstar's highest "five-star" rating. Some firms created a whole range of incubator funds, most likely as part of a carefully conceived marketing strategy. In the past decade alone, 128 such funds have come and gone, performing sensationally enough to make it out of the incubator, only to return to mediocrity, or even worse, thereafter. The paper also found that the funds that survived to be publicly offered suffered from "severe return reversal" (that is, plummeting post-incubation returns).

The firms that participated in this strategy started large numbers of incubation funds in order to, in the paper's words, "upwardly bias investors' estimates of their ability, and thereby attract additional inflows," killing them when they fail to repeat their success after they enter the tough real world of investing. Such behavior is hardly consistent with "organizing, operating, and managing" funds in the interest of their shareholders. Rather, it is directly consistent with organizing funds in the sole interest of their promoters, a direct contradiction to the act's purposes. Incubation funds have everything to do with the business of marketing, and nothing to do with the profession of management. The commission must put the kibosh on the promulgation of the returns earned on these funds during their incubation period.

4. *401 (k) plans.* Recent press reports have described clandestine payments from fund managers to plan consultants and pension clients, often in the form of fee rebates. The complex relations between the administra-

tive costs borne by the company and the amounts shifted to the plan participants, the costs assumed by the fund sponsor and their relation to the advisory fees the assets generate, and the sources of any compensation to pension consultants—sometimes from the company sponsoring the plan, sometimes from the manager selling it—all deserve prompt and careful study. Most 401(k) plan arrangements are unregulated, and industrywide guidelines for fair practice do not seem to exist.

An editorial in *Barron's* in November 2003 probably only scratched the surface when it said: "There is one more unrecognized mutual fund scandal disguised as the regular order of business. Ever since Congress invented the 401(k), employers who sponsor retirement plans have been making deals with mutual-fund management companies. We can find little disclosure in this area; employees are not told how much money, if any, changes hands between employers and fund managers to give one management company exclusive access to thousands of employees. But it is clear that most employers, even the biggest and most generous, offer one and only one family of funds in their defined-contribution plans. And it is clear that some employers have chosen fund families with high fees and expenses, making their employees captive customers and unwitting sharers of their savings with fund families implicated in the mutual-fund abuses."[12] This area should be a high strategic priority for the commission, and the work has begun with its May 2005 report on the fees paid to pension consultants.

5. *An economic study of the mutual fund industry.* Entitled "The Economic Role of the Investment Company," my Princeton thesis all those years ago was my youthful attempt to undertake an economic study of the industry.[13] While the SEC studied the industry in 1953, again in 1966 in the PPI study, and once again as part of the *Institutional Investor Study Report* in 1971, I know of no comprehensive studies that have taken place since then. The dramatic changes in the industry over the ensuing thirty-four years have yet to be evaluated.

In 1995, I wrote to the SEC's chief economist calling for an economic study of the fund industry. He wrote back, essentially saying: "Great idea! But the industry will never give us the data." Today, there's far too much at stake to accept such a cavalier refusal. In order to facilitate our understanding of how the fund industry actually works, we need a comprehensive economic study that would evaluate the role of mutual funds and their managers in the context of our national economy and of the public interest.

It's time to "follow the money"—to account for the sources of industry's direct revenues paid by shareholders (management fees, administrative fees, distribution fees, sales loads, out-of-pocket fees, and so on), and the indirect revenues utilized by fund managers, including brokerage commissions. It's also time to account for the uses of these revenues—for administration, marketing and distribution, investment management, and other major cost centers, including soft dollars. In today's information vacuum, legislative and regulatory policy is operating in the darkness of ignorance. It ought to operate in the light of knowledge.

We also need to understand much more about the radical changes in fund investment policies, including soaring portfolio turnover rates and the relationship between fund size and fund performance. In Warren Buffett's words, "a fat wallet is the enemy of superior returns," a conclusion clearly manifested in the earlier Magellan Fund example and reinforced throughout the entire industry.[14] Why is it, then, that so few fund managers limit the amount of assets they manage in a single fund or in a fund complex? What's more, we need to be able to quantify with far greater precision the extent to which fund managers enjoy economies of scale, as well as the extent, if any, to which these economies have been shared with fund owners.

One major fund manager, for example, has failed to share *any* of these economies with shareholders. Although the assets of American Century's original fund have grown 286 times over—from $18 million in 1967 to $5.1 billion in 2004—the fund's expense ratio in 2004 remains exactly what it was in 1967: 0.98 percent. The assets of all of its equity funds have now grown to $68 billion, but their average expense ratio in 2004 was 1.0 percent, or 2 percent *higher* than its sole tiny equity fund thirty-seven years ago. Result: fees paid by their equity fund investors have risen from $149,000 in 1967 to $650 million in 2004.

Finally, such a study should examine the economic consequences of the growing conglomeration of the industry. The acquisition of fund managers by giant banks and financial conglomerates places the interests of fund shareowners a further step removed from the industry's original roots, when the principals of the industry's privately owned managers interfaced with, and were directly responsible to, the fund directors. As the data in chapter seven suggest, measured by the comparative investment returns provided by the subsidiaries of these goliaths, conglomeration has ill served fund shareholders.

Temporary Problem or Permanent Morass?

The five issues discussed above are among the major manifestations of the reality that mutual funds are businesses run primarily for their managers, to the direct disadvantage of their owners. Mutual fund America, it turns out, manifests the same aberrational pattern that we have observed throughout the financial services industry and in corporate America. Each issue deserves careful study at the public policy level.

These problems will not be easy to resolve. Witness a recent paper by a Federal Reserve economist entitled "Mutual Funds: Temporary Problem or Permanent Morass?"[15] The paper argues that, despite the obvious conflicts of interest between fund owner and fund managers, there is "one and only one reasonable objective [for the manager]: *to maximize [the manager's] own profit*." The record is clear that such profit maximization has indeed been the goal of nearly all managers. The management company has been driving the mutual fund automobile, and the fund shareholder has been consigned to the back seat, often to the rumble seat, and sometimes even to the trunk. But, as a legal matter, the 1940 act places the shareholder in the front seat, and indeed raises the question as to whether the manager should even be allowed to ride in the fund car itself.

I, for one, am not willing to consign the mutual fund industry to a permanent morass. I have too much love for the great potential of this industry to serve our nation's families effectively to accept the conclusion of the Federal Reserve paper. It is simply unacceptable that mutual funds should continue to be mired in any morass that puts the interests of managers ahead of the interests of the shareholders even for a moment, let alone permanently. Just as the law demands, national policy demands that the mutual fund industry operate in the interests of the public and of investors.

What Is the Public Interest?

The drafters of the Investment Company Act of 1940 did not define what they meant by the "national public interest and the interest of investors." So let me take a stab at what might be considered a reasonable definition of those interests:

- Funds should provide a sound repository for long-term investing.
- Funds should offer a productive medium to accumulate assets for retirement.

- Funds should work to enhance the efficient functioning of our capital markets.
- Funds should be constructive participants in corporate governance.
- Funds should fully and fairly disclose their risks, returns, and costs.
- Fund directors should be independent, conflict-free, and fully empowered to act solely on behalf of fund shareholders.
- Funds should offer prudent stewardship of shareholder assets.

Those seven attributes are wholly consistent with self-evident implications of the act's statement of purpose. It is now time to write them into the law.

If the implicit fiduciary duty standard of the 1940 act had been explicitly observed by industry participants, and if the structure I outlined earlier had been in effect, we would not now need to be discussing more regulation to protect our investors against late trading and market timing with new compliance guidelines; nor to eliminate "breakpoint" violations; nor to reform management fee structures; nor to ensure "best execution" of portfolio transactions; nor to eliminate soft-dollar abuses; nor to define the role and functions of fund directors and trustees. We are discussing these issues because the fund industry has not measured up to the central principle of the 1940 act—the overriding duty to serve fund owners rather than fund managers and distributors.

Funds must measure up to their owners' interests by operating, at all times and in every way, in a manner that serves those interests. What catalysts might be needed to create this change? One possibility is suggested by the series of events that precipitated the creation of Vanguard in the autumn of 1974: a great bear market; poor fund performance; overly zealous marketing of overly speculative funds; the prospect of large cost savings; and a board with a strong leader.

In the Vanguard case, the leader was the chairman of our independent director group—the late Charles D. Root Jr., whose remarkable service in the cause of mutualization deserves a full chapter in industry history. He was willing to support a radical proposal by the person who had just been deposed as head of the management company but continued to serve as chairman of the funds, a person that just happened to be me. And so, after months of trial and tribulation, the deed was done, as the funds first assumed responsibility for their own administration and shareholder recordkeeping, and shortly thereafter, for their distribution and some of their investment management activities. As noted in chapter eight ("Alpha and Omega"), what we described as the "Vanguard Experiment" in mutual fund governance has far exceeded both the firm's and the industry's expectations for minimizing costs and producing optimal shareholder returns. At the same time, Vanguard's achievements as a business enterprise have surely been beyond the wildest dreams, not only of its skeptics but of its early advocates, and its market share of industry assets has continued its relentless rise.

The "Mutual" Mutual Fund

It will be no easy task to create new *mutual* mutual fund organizations that are designed to fulfill the principles set forth in the 1940 act. For there would be no economic incentive to invest the capital, the time, the effort, and, for that matter, the headaches and the heartaches, with no possibility of earning a return on these investments of blood, sweat, and capital. Even Vanguard rose, phoenixlike, from the ashes of an existing fund group in which the relationship between the manager and the directors had deteriorated.

Of course funds cannot be born by themselves, nor in their early years can they thrive alone. Like babies, they require parents who nurture them as they grow and become adults. But there is a point at which, like children, mutual funds grow up. They become perfectly able to operate on their own—for better or worse—and to live independent lives without parental supervision. Yet while the earliest mutual funds reached their maturity in the late 1940s and 1950s, they remain in the thrall of their parents, with Vanguard the sole exception. Now that the industry's oldest fund has celebrated its eightieth birthday, isn't it high time for large, established fund groups to stand on their own?

Powerful economic interests, to say nothing of human inertia, stand in the way of the urgent change that is needed in the fund industry. But all is not lost. Despite the recalcitrance of fund managers and entrepreneurs—to say nothing of those financial conglomerates that control such a large portion of fund assets—there is another avenue toward change: awakening the investing public. If investors demand change, the industry will have to respond. In my 1999 book, *Common Sense on Mutual Funds: New Perspectives for the Intelligent Investor,* I offered some ideas about what might prompt investors to demand a fair shake.

Trial and error is one possibility. Investors who get badly burned by a long period of equity under-performance, or even (and much more memorably!) by a significant plunge in stock prices, will not soon return to the industry's fold. Investors buying hot funds, experimenting with market timing, and shopping and swapping funds with untoward frequency will one day learn, through painful experience, that these short-term approaches have been not only unproductive, but counterproductive.[16] [Unless, of course, they could, in Attorney General Spitzer's words, "bet on the horse after the race was over."]

Whether by luck, by grace, or by wisdom, the scenario I described in 1999 almost precisely anticipated what was about to happen: the 50 percent plunge in stock prices; the painful and costly experience of fund investors who bought hot "new economy" funds; the market-timing scandals; and the corrosive effect of excessive fund costs, all engendered by the near-absence of countervailing power held by the mutual funds themselves vis-à-vis their managers. Yet by and large, fund investors have so far remained passive and quiescent.

Consistent with the historic patterns, fairly strong cash inflows returned to the fund industry as the stock market recovered some of the lost ground. But fund investors have become increasingly selective, generally shunning speculative funds and managers engulfed by scandal, and favoring more prudent funds operated by lower-cost managers.

Awakening the Investing Public

Investors, then, are closer than ever to demanding the fair shake they deserve. But as a group they still seem oblivious to the benefits of having funds run in their own interest. We have a long way to go, for without a massive swell of investor action—whether by placing political pressure on legislators, or "voting with their feet"—it will be nigh on impossible to fix what went wrong in mutual fund America. Investors can no longer simply shrug off the actions of fund managers who have betrayed their interest, or imposed excessive fees and charges, or lured them into the wrong funds at the wrong time, or simply provided too many years of inadequate and uncompetitive returns. If the last-line investor neither knows, nor cares, about his or her own economic interests, all of the forces of government and regulation and all of the calls for reform will be insufficient to bring about the necessary change.

If you are a mutual fund investor, you need to begin to look after your own economic interests. First of all, you need information.

- Full disclosure not only about fund expense ratios but about the actual dollar amounts of the annualized expenses you will incur, something easily presented in fund statements at each year end.
- Full disclosure about the transaction costs incurred by the funds—not only the brokerage commissions, but also the bid-ask spreads and the market impact costs, with the total presented on an annualized basis as a percentage of your own investment in the fund; and full disclosure about the tax consequences of high-turnover strategies.
- Full disclosure about the impact of sales charges on your annual investment return. You should also know the extent to which your broker or adviser is receiving extra compensation or brokerage commissions as a quid pro quo for offering the funds that are recommended to the investor, and whether your manager is buying "shelf space" in one of the new supermarkets.

As it stands today, very little of this information is available. Fund managers have no interest in allowing you to understand that you may be paying as much as 2 or 3 percent of your assets each year in the search for superior returns—an amount that essentially precludes not only superior returns but even mediocre returns, and virtually insures inadequate returns. So long as mutual fund costs remain at today's high levels, few fund investors will come anywhere near capturing 100 percent of the market's returns. The record is clear that in the mutual fund industry, *you get what you don't pay for.*

Fund managers also don't want you and other fund investors to understand the debilitating effect of compounding those costs. Thanks to mutual fund marketers, most investors are well aware of the magic of compounding returns. But few investors, again thanks to the industry, are aware of the tyranny of compounding costs. Yet costs, as we have seen, can siphon off three-quarters of the return that an investor could otherwise earn over an investment lifetime simply by buying and holding the entire stock market.

As a fund investor, you are entitled to information about risk, too. While risk measures are vaguely complex, simply knowing the volatility (standard deviation) of an equity fund's returns relative to the stock market is essential knowledge; the same is true for the volatility and investment quality of a bond portfolio, so that when you seek investment-grade bonds you don't end up with junk. In all, information about risks and costs is meaningful and essential. On the other hand, information about the past returns earned by funds—especially short-term returns—is close to meaningless. In mutual funds, alas, the past is all too rarely prologue.

Seven Pillars of Wisdom

If the fund industry is to be the investment medium by which the industry reaches its potential, its investors need wisdom, too. Indeed, if information is essential, wisdom is priceless. These are seven pillars of wisdom every investor should have:

- Wisdom to realize the importance not of past returns in the stock and bond markets but of the *sources* of those returns.
- Wisdom to know that specific-security risk and market-sector risk and manager risk alike can be greatly mitigated—indeed ultimately eliminated—by diversification, leaving only stock market risk remaining.
- Wisdom to know that market risk itself, without adding those other risks to it, is quite large enough.
- Wisdom to know that there are powerful odds against "beating the market" and against successful market timing, and that for each investor who succeeds, another must fail (with success mitigated and failure accentuated by costs and taxes).
- Wisdom to know what we *don't* know. In these uncertain, even dangerous, times, we do not know how our world will look tomorrow, let alone a decade or a generation hence.
- Wisdom to realize that an appropriate balance between stocks and bonds is the most prudent course.
- Wisdom to know that *not* investing is a surefire way to fail to accumulate the wealth necessary to ensure a sound financial future.

A Fair Shake

It is well within the power of our policy makers—our legislators and regulators—to ensure that such information is readily available, but we also need a special investor advocacy commission dedicated solely to the education of investors to spread that information far and wide. Building investor literacy is essential,* but we also need investor wisdom,

---

*The National Council for Economic Education has been working to educate our nation's students on economic and personal finance issues. Expanding the reach of such organizations to educate more of our young people on issues like compound interest, the importance of costs, and the basics of investing would go a long way toward eliminating the trial-and-error process that has cost American investors so dearly.

a rare commodity, one too often acquired only through the hard experiences of life. For the unwise, investing in the financial markets can be a hugely expensive way to acquire wisdom. Surely a strong, respected, and independent advocacy commission would be a good start.

Armed with knowledge and empowered with wisdom, investors will, finally, come to invest in funds in which they are assured, first and foremost, of a fair shake. Funds with low expenses, low portfolio turnover, and low (if any) sales charges; funds that are tax efficient; funds that are well diversified; and funds that are run by managers whose character is attested to by the way that they, yes, organize, operate, and manage the funds they offer in the interest of their fund owners rather than in their own interests, overseen by a strong and independent board of directors. Funds, in short, that enable the investor to "stay the course" for a lifetime.

The mutual fund industry, too, must play a role in its own repair, beginning with a healthy dose of introspection, so far, conspicuous by its absence, that recognizes the weaknesses it has developed in its modern era. Painful as it may be to hear the industry described as the "world's largest skimming operation" (Senator Fitzgerald) or as a "giant fleecing machine" (Attorney General Spitzer),[17] those charges are not without some validity. After all, the managers receive their fees before the owners receive their returns; the more the managers take, the less the investors make. There is simply no denying that fund owners are at the bottom of the financial services food chain.

It is not only our public servants who recognize this truth. Listen to these blunt words from Jack R. Meyer, former chief executive of Harvard Management Company, shortly before he left his post there after leading an increase in the university's endowment fund from $6 billion to $27 billion in ten years. "The investment business is a giant scam. Most people think they can find managers who can outperform, but most people are wrong. I will say that 85 percent to 90 percent of managers fail to match their benchmarks. Because managers have fees and incur transaction costs, you know that in the aggregate they are deleting value. Most people should simply have index funds to keep their fees low and their tax down. No doubt about it."[18]

While Meyer could be considered an industry outsider, Fidelity's Peter Lynch could be considered the consummate insider. Yet their views seem to coincide. When he relinquished his responsibilities in 1990, Lynch, the successful longtime manager of Magellan Fund, publicly stated that most investors "would be better off in an index fund."[19]

In a sense, Meyer and Lynch are simply stating the obvious: the all-market index fund or the Standard & Poor's 500 Index fund is a far better way of investing than searching through a seemingly endless list of the products of the marketing-driven, asset-gathering machine that characterizes today's mutual ·fund industry. Other types of equity funds may approach that simple ideal, and certainly some few will surpass it. But the odds against their success are enormous.

This wholly realistic but too often ignored view is shared by many independent and respected voices. In 2004, even the editorial opinion page of the *Wall Street Journal*—the paradigm of conservatism—joined the chorus:

> Will fund customers keep supporting the enormous overhead required to sustain ineffectual, unproductive stock picking across an array of thousands of individual funds devoted to every investing "style" and economic sector or regional subgroup that some marketing idiot can dream up? Not likely. A brutal shakeout is coming and one of its revelations will be that stock picking is a grossly overrated piece of the puzzle, that cost control is what distinguishes a competitive firm from an uncompetitive one.[20]

The Coming Shakeout

When that brutal shakeout begins, as it will, and fund owners start to move their money to where their common sense and their simple prudence dictate, the days of managers' capitalism in mutual fund America will be numbered, and the days of owners' capitalism will begin. Investors will seek out and select funds whose independent directors, operating as their faithful fiduciaries under new and clearly defined responsibilities, put them in their rightful place in the driver's seat of the fund industry. Fund owners will be rewarded accordingly, and fairly.

But the shakeout may go even further, and include the mutualization of at least part of the American mutual fund industry. No longer would large fund families contract with external management companies to operate and manage their portfolios. They would perform those functions in-house and run themselves. Mutual fund shareholders would, in effect, own the management companies that oversee their funds. They would retain their own officers and staff, and the huge profits now earned by external managers would be diverted to the shareholders. They wouldn't waste their own money on costly marketing campaigns designed to bring in new investors at the expense of existing investors, nor would they start opportunistic funds at the drop of a hat. With lower costs, they could either receive higher returns or assume lower risks, or both. They might even see the merit of market index funds.

Regardless of the exact structure, conventional or mutual, an arrangement in which fund shareholders and their directors are in working control of a fund—as distinct from one in which fund managers are in control—will lead to funds that are truly "organized, operated, and managed" in the interests of their shareholders. Such funds will enhance economic value for fund shareholders by providing investors with a higher share of the rewards of investing, and thereby will be the most successful in drawing the attention—and the dollars—of those millions of fund owners who are looking for a fair shake. And as that momentum develops, what went wrong in mutual fund America will be fixed, why it went wrong a mere memory.

Early in 2003, Justin Fox, a young journalist for *Fortune* magazine, asked me if I was optimistic about this outcome. I responded: "No, I'm not optimistic. I'm *certain*. Why? Because investors may ignore their own economic interests for the rest of my lifetime, and Justin, they may even ignore them for the rest of yours. But I guarantee you that investors will not ignore their own economic interests *forever*."[21]

PART **FOUR**

Conclusion

This tenth and final chapter returns to the theme of the introduction: the importance of capitalism—corporate America, investment America, and mutual fund America alike—in contributing to the proper functioning of our society and to our strength as a nation. Here, I call for a federal commission to undertake a sweeping examination of two vital aspects of our new world: One, a major displacement of the direct ownership by the shareholders of our corporations in favor of a new system of "agency ownership" dominated by financial intermediaries, largely mutual funds and pension funds that hold shares for the benefit of their owners and beneficiaries. Two, the faltering state of our nation's public, private, and individual retirement systems, the backbone of the nation's savings.

In summing up the substance of my book—what went wrong in each of these three major elements of capitalism, why it went wrong, and how to fix it—I call on the wisdom of some of the sagest minds of present and past, including Henry Kaufman, Felix Rohatyn, Alan Greenspan, Warren Buffett, Adam Smith, Joseph Schumpeter, John Maynard Keynes, Joseph Stiglitz, and Louis Brandeis, all of whom, one way or another, have shared so many of my concerns.

I conclude by emphasizing that my ideas for limited government in-volvement through such a federal commission are wholly consistent with the kind of federalism espoused by Alexander Hamilton, Henry Clay, Abraham Lincoln, and Theodore Roosevelt, among our nation's greatest leaders. Following their principles will enable us, using Thomas Paine's words, "to begin the world anew."

10

American Capitalism in the Twenty-first Century

"To Begin the World Anew"

Traditional capitalism has made a superb contribution to America's economic and social greatness. In the recent era, however, it has gone off track, moving away from its original concept of ownership power to a new concept of manager power, in corporate America, in investment America, and in mutual fund America alike. But our system can be fixed, and I remain steadfastly optimistic about our country's ability to right itself.

It is incumbent both on our business leaders and on our financial leaders to go well beyond the reforms described throughout this book, some already instituted and some on the way to being instituted. The scandalous actions of our managers have generated powerful reactions. Congress has enacted the Sarbanes-Oxley Act to improve corporate financial practices. Powerful investment bankers have been sanctioned and fined for their unethical behavior that has undermined the integrity of the financial markets. Fines and fee reductions have been assessed against mutual fund managers for their malfeasance. Criminals are on their way to jail. The Securities and Exchange Commission, while late to the game, has moved vigorously to protect investors, and has already adopted rules that should help to rectify the failings of the mutual fund industry.

At the same time, leaders of great repute in the business community, the investment community, and the mutual fund community have stood up and spoken out, making a positive difference. Consider, for example, the eminent financier, economist, and historian Henry Kaufman. In his remarkable book *On Money and Markets,* he said:

> Unfettered financial entrepreneurship can become excessive—and damaging as well—leading to serious abuses and the trampling of the basic laws and morals of the financial system. Such abuses weaken a nation's financial structure and undermine public confidence in the financial community. . . . America's weak regulatory system is an outgrowth of a larger imbalance, with deep roots in the American past, between the power of the state and the power of business. . . . Only by improving the balance between entrepreneurial innovation and more traditional values—prudence, stability, safety, soundness—can we improve the ratio of benefits to costs in our economic system. . . .
>
> Senior management, more than any other group in modern American finance, must hammer home the central truth about financial behavior: Breaking the rules is not merely a breach of ethics and the law—it is poor business. . . . Trust is the cornerstone of most relationships in life. Financial institutions and markets must rest on a foundation of trust as well. . . . When financial buccaneers and negligent executives step over the line, the damage is inflicted on all market participants . . . and the notion of financial trusteeship too frequently lost in the shuffle. . . . That is why the large majority of ethical and responsible market participants must not tolerate the transgressions of the few abusers. And regulators and leaders of financial institutions must be the most diligent of all.[1]

Kaufman is not alone. Felix Rohatyn, the widely respected former managing director of Lazard Freres, is another of the wise men of Wall Street who have spoken out. "I am an American and a capitalist and believe that market capitalism is the best economic system ever invented. But it must be fair, it must be regulated, and it must be ethical. The last few years have shown that excesses can come about when finance capitalism and modern technology are abused in the service of naked greed. Only capitalists can kill capitalism, but our system cannot stand much more abuse of the type we have witnessed recently, nor can it stand much more of the financial and social polarization we are seeing today."[2]

Alan Greenspan Adds His Voice

To those two strong, unflinching voices, I add Federal Reserve chairman Alan Greenspan, who echoed them in his opening remarks in a speech at a 2004 conference sponsored by the Federal Reserve Bank of Atlanta:

Recent transgressions in financial markets have underscored the fact that one can hardly overstate the importance of reputation in a market economy. . . . Rules cannot substitute for character. In virtually all transactions, we rely on the word of those with whom we do business. . . . A reputation for honest dealings with a business or financial corporation is critical for effective corporate governance. Reputation and trust were valued assets in freewheeling nineteenth-century America. Throughout much of that century, laissez-faire reigned, and caveat emptor was the prevailing prescription. . . . A reputation for honest dealing was thus particularly valued.

Even those inclined to be less than scrupulous in their private dealings had to adhere to a more ethical standard in their market transactions, or they risked being driven out of business. To be sure, the history of business is strewn with Fisks, Goulds, and numerous others treading on, or over, the edge of legality. But they were a distinct minority. . . . Over the past half-century, the American public has embraced the protection of the myriad federal agencies that have largely substituted . . . implied certifications of integrity for business reputation. As a consequence, by the 1990s the value of trust so prominent in the nineteenth century appeared to have fallen to a fraction of its earlier level. But the corporate scandals of recent years have clearly shown that the plethora of laws of the past century have not eliminated the less savory side of human nature. . . . I hope and anticipate that trust and integrity again will be amply rewarded in the marketplace as they were in previous generations. There is no better antidote for the business and financial transgression of recent years.[3]

Each of these illustrious individuals underscores that an undesirable and fundamental shift has taken place in capitalism that simple tinkering with rules will not remedy. The problems are much deeper, and concern the very soul of capitalism itself—the vital power that animates, pervades, and shapes capitalism, as I noted in the introduction to this book, and draws its energies into a unity.

Yet strong words, even from three such distinguished members of the financial pantheon, will not be enough. We must cross the financial Rubicon, taking the critical stride that remains—and it is not an easy one—by establishing a culture focused on serving the interests of the owners of our nation's corporations and mutual funds as our highest priority, and affirmatively recognizing the duty of our fiduciaries and trustees to honor that responsibility.

This process must begin with a return to the original values of capitalism, to that virtuous circle of integrity and trust and trustworthiness discussed at the outset. When ethical values go out the window and service to those whom we are duty-bound to serve is superseded by service to self, the whole idea of the capitalism that has been a moving force in the creation of our society's abundance is soured. In the era that lies ahead, the trusted businessman, the prudent fiduciary, and the honest steward must again be the paradigms of our great American enterprises.

"Business Ethics"

Our ethics—"our system of moral principles of human conduct," as the dictionary defines it—never was perfect, and never will be perfect. But striving for the best that is in us must be the eternal goal of our citizens, and our business and financial *managers* are no exception. To restore our public reputation as *leaders,* we could all do worse than reflect, as we start each day, on how best to pass through the gates of righteousness.

Indeed, if "business ethics" is not to remain a contemptuous oxymoron, we all might begin our work each day with some notion of righteousness—of stewardship, if you will, for it is pretty much the same thing. Perhaps in doing so we can begin to redefine a new "bottom line" for our society. Rather than prizing financial profit above all else, we must work to become a society that reverses the priorities of the litany that I recited at the start of this book, once again celebrating achievement over money, character over charisma, substance over form, virtue over prestige, and so on.

The idea that values are intimately embedded in the practice of business was hardly anathema to the worldly economists of the ages. Late in the eighteenth century, even before Adam Smith extolled, in *The Wealth of Nations,* the virtues of the invisible hand of competition and the essential nature of personal advantage and self-interest in making the world's economic system work, he wrote *The Theory of Moral Sentiments*. In that remarkable book he called for "reason, principle, conscience, the inhabitant of the breast, the great judge and arbiter of our conduct, who shows us the real littleness of ourselves, the propriety of generosity, of resigning the greatest interests of our own for yet the greater interests of others, the love of what is honorable and noble, the grandeur and dignity of our own characters."[4] Adam Smith with us again, but here as the apostle of virtue.

Joseph Schumpeter identified a similar spirit. Nearly a century ago, he described for us the motives of the successful entrepreneur: "The joy of creating, of getting things done, of simply exercising one's energy and ingenuity . . . the will to conquer, the impulse to fight, to succeed, not for the fruits of success, but for success itself."[5]

In the 1930s John Maynard Keynes followed suit, reminding us that numbers are only numbers, quantities on a scoreboard that are only one measure—and, truth told, hardly the best measure—of an enterprise. Keynes emphasized that it was the merest pretense to suggest that an enterprise is "mainly actuated by the statements in its own prospectus, however candid and sincere . . . based on an exact calculation of benefits to come." Rather, the key to success is "animal spirits—a spontaneous urge to action rather than inaction," warning that "if animal spirits are dimmed and the spontaneous optimism falters, leaving us to depend on nothing but a mathematical expectation, enterprise will fade and die."[6]

These three economists—surely among the greatest in history—are all sending us the same message, advising us to put the greater interest of others and the dignity of our own characters first, and our own self-interest second; to put enterprise and animal spirits first, and managing for the bottom line second; to put the joy of creating and the will to conquer first, and the mindless conformity of greed last.

The Founding Fathers

Even more is at stake than improving the *practices* of governance and investing, as we are clearly doing today. We must also establish a higher set of *principles*. This nation's founding fathers believed in high moral standards, in a just society, and in the honorable conduct of our affairs. Those beliefs shaped the very character of our nation. If character counts—and I have absolutely no doubt that character *does* count—the ethical failings of today's business model, the financial manipulation of corporate America, the willingness of those of us in the field of investment management to accept practices that we know are wrong, the conformity that keeps us silent, the greed that overwhelms our reason, all erode the character that society will require of us in the years ahead.

Of course the successful enterprises that endure must generate profits for their owners. They will do that best when they take into account not only the interests of their stockholders but the interests of their customers, their employees, and their communities, and the interests of our society. These are not new ideals for capitalism. Again, hear Adam Smith: "He is certainly not a good citizen who does not wish to promote, by every means of his power, the welfare of the whole society of his fellow citizens."[7] So it is essential that the owners of corporate America speak up, speak out, and demand that our corporations and our fund managers represent our interests rather than their own—the owners first, the managers only second.

We also would do well to honor by our actions the words of the giant who was, all those years ago, first in the hearts of his countrymen. In his farewell address in 1796, president George Washington reminded us that "virtue or morality is a necessary spring of popular government" (and, I would add, of corporate government), warning that "reason and experience both forbid us to expect that national morality can prevail in exclusion of religious principle."

The Highest Hurdle

The change in the nature of corporate ownership constitutes one of today's greatest challenges. It's all well and good to fly the banner for owners' capitalism, but today only one-third of corporate America is held directly by principals (the direct owners) with the remaining two-thirds held by agents (the financial managers), creating a vicious circle in which corporations own and control, or heavily influence, how their own shares are voted. The challenge is to force our financial intermediaries to honor the traditional standards of fiduciary duty, with their actions dictated solely by the interests of those whom they serve as stewards—fund managers serving fund owners, pension trustees and managers serving plan beneficiaries, trust officers serving the families whose estates they manage, and so on.

In the mutual fund industry, by contrast, the direct ownership of shares by investors is the prevailing modus operandi. But despite the noble purposes of the 1940 act, the law has allowed fund managers to maintain a moat around their management company fortress that is both wide and deep, almost invulnerable to attack by shareholders, no matter how ill served they have been. We must continue to enhance the power of fund directors so they can honor the duty the law demands: to ensure, as the act says, that mutual funds are "organized, operated, and managed" in the interest of their shareholders, rather than in the interest of their managers.

Mutual funds, of course, are both *owners*—as shareholders of corporate America—and *owned*—by their own shareholders. Funds have the latent power and the fiduciary duty to be the driving force in investment America. Yet like pension funds, they have largely ignored active corporate governance. Part of the reason is that our institutions have become largely short-term speculators rather than long-term investors, far more a rent-a-stock industry than an own-a-stock industry. Another reason is the conflicts of interest these institutions face because they own the stocks of the very companies that they serve as managers, receiving billions of dollars of advisory fees and administrative fees from these companies, year after year.

With the convergence of mutual fund and pension fund management described in chapter four, we find yet another challenge. The acquisition of so many investment managers by giant publicly held banks and other financial conglomerates has both complicated and compromised the ownership of corporate America by creating a circularity in which, to an appreciable extent, the owners are the owned. Through the pension plans and savings plans they have created for their employees, America's corporations own huge positions in their own shares and in the shares of other corporations similarly situated. The task of cutting that Gordian knot to eliminate the obvious conflicts is as challenging as it is essential.

A Call for a National Commission

The route investment America must take to return to our traditional standards of fiduciary duty and service to investors is not an easy one. It begins with a return to our institutional roots as investors rather than traders. The present core of truly long-term investors—including index funds and disciplined managers who emphasize buy-and-*hold* strategies based on fundamental intrinsic values, rather than buy-and-*sell* strategies focused on ephemeral stock prices—must organize to make their will felt, and attract others to follow.

But that is not enough. Because the direct owners of stocks of years past (the principals) have been supplanted by today's institutional managers (their agents) who have a duty to serve them, we urgently need a national policy to resolve this unprecedented situation. We need to change the rules of the game to require that institutional investors exercise the responsibilities of corporate citizenship on behalf of their clients.

I like the idea of Robert Monks that I cited earlier: "Government involvement . . . that guarantees the nation's citizens the neglected rights of ownership of their stocks . . . a clear and consistently enforced public policy that gives all owners' representatives, the intermediary investment institutions and their fund managers, the clear fiduciary requirement . . . [to act] under trustee and fiduciary laws for the *sole* purpose and *exclusive* benefit of their beneficiaries' interests."[8]

The accomplishment of that task cannot be left to the fainthearted, and will require the appointment of a national commission composed of our wisest, most respected, and best-informed citizens. The federal government will likely need to preempt the multiple state laws under which our corporations have been chartered ever since our nation's founders left that power with the individual states.

It may even entail federal charters for fiduciary institutions, and perhaps even for business corporations, something today's federalists would doubtless vigorously oppose. (Ironically, as noted earlier, those who believe that the power of the states should be ascendant are now defined as "federalists," the diametrically opposite philosophy of their eighteenth-century counterparts who favored more power for the federal government.) There is a third school of thought that can bridge that gap, a school that, while it cherishes the beliefs that the separation of the economy from the state is as essential for capitalism as it is for liberty, also understands that from time to time the people's government must step in and work to solve novel and complex problems. This is one of those times.

A Third Tradition

Today, America's political parties are philosophically divided between a so-called liberal tradition favoring the use of the national government to foster equality and social justice, and a so-called conservative tradition favoring limited national government in the name of protecting liberty, freedom, and personal responsibility. According to David Brooks of the *New York Times*, however,

> Through much of American history there has always been a third tradition, now dormant, which believed in limited but energetic govern-

ment in the name of social mobility and national union. This third tradition was founded by Alexander Hamilton, embraced by Henry Clay, taken up by Abraham Lincoln and brought into the 20th century by Theodore Roosevelt. . . . Hamilton came from nothing and spent his political career trying to create a world in which as many people as possible could replicate his amazing success. [He] looked around after independence and saw a country destined to become the greatest empire of the earth, and sought to liberate and stir Americans to exploit the full range of their capacities.

Hamilton believed in using government to enhance market dynamism by fostering more equitable competition. He believed government could usefully promote social revolutions . . . rejecting the formula, assumed too often today, that you can be for government or for the market, but not for both. He saw entrepreneurial freedom, limited but energetic federal power, and national greatness as qualities that were inextricably linked. It was always the cause America represents—universal freedom— that was uppermost in Hamilton's mind, spurring individual initiative, but also gathering the fruits of that energy in the cause of national greatness.[9]

The Governance Issue

Were Alexander Hamilton alive today, he would surely be aware that it's high time to restore the integrity of our system of capitalism, and to rethink the nation's investment process. In today's wrongheaded version of capitalism, corporate managers are in charge of our business wealth, almost unchecked by the gatekeepers; and the investment community is too heavily focused on short-term stock prices and too lightly focused on long-term intrinsic corporate values to challenge their domain. The impetus that will reverse that focus is not yet clear.

Given the vicious circle in which corporations, in important degree, own themselves, our investment intermediaries have proven reluctant to use their latent power. Further, even for those intermediaries who have the motivation to exercise it, hopelessly archaic proxy rules serve to handcuff the exercise of that power. And the prospects seem increasingly dim for opening even a tiny crack in the rigid regulatory doorway that precludes owners from their rights of ownership by denying them reasonable access to corporate proxy statements. With mutual fund managers firmly ensconced in the driver's seat of the governance of the funds themselves, we are captives of a system in which both corporate directors and fund directors seem not only unwilling but unable to take on the role and responsibility of the gatekeeper as a steward, one who holds the interests of the shareholder as his highest priority.

As a respected voice on investment issues, Warren Buffett has few peers. His long experience in value investing has given him wisdom and insight into corporate governance that are soundly based on fiduciary duty. He despairs of the problems that remain unresolved both in corporate America and in mutual fund America, as evidenced by the excerpts in Box 10.1 from his letters to shareholders in past annual reports of Berkshire Hathaway Inc. These views are a refreshing and independent echo of my own analysis of the issues, as presented in these pages.

The Wealth of the Nation

One of the central problems that flows from today's managers' capitalism is the failure of owners to capture their fair share of the rewards of our financial system. "Skimming" and "fleecing" and "giant scam" or not, far too large a share of the munificence created by our corporations goes into the pockets of their senior executives, Wall Street titans, and institutional managers. Further, while pension fund trustees are duty-bound to serve the interest of the corporation's employees whose pensions are at stake, too often pension plans are operated in the financial interest of the corporation itself.

As discussed in detail throughout this book, the mathematics of investing are fairly simple: The more the managers of corporations, investment bankers, and mutual funds *take*, the less the last-line investors *make*. The profits of the financial industry—the firms engaged in the creation, distribution, and management of assets—have soared from 15 percent of all corporate profits in 1975 to 29 percent in 2003. Part of this increase resulted from the growth in the assets managed by financial intermediaries, driven by a great bull market. Another large part of the profit grab is attributable to the costly, and finally counterproductive, marketing programs that seek to persuade investors to dream the impossible dream of easy wealth, easily achieved. Yet the eternal reality remains: the stock market is a commoditized system in which each advantage seized by one money manager represents a sacrifice, by definition, in the form of a disadvantage incurred by another. Before they deduct their costs, all investors as a group are average. After that deduction, their clients earn, as they must, returns that are well below average.

Box 10.1 Warren Buffett on Directors:

The respected voice of Warren Buffett, filled with wit and wisdom, has been a common sense beacon on the subject of director responsibility in corporate America and mutual fund America alike. The excerpts from his Chairman's Letters that follow illustrate the high standard of director conduct he advocates.

Corporate Directors
Both the ability and fidelity of managers have long needed monitoring. Indeed, nearly 2,000 years ago, Jesus Christ addressed this subject, speaking (Luke 16:2) approvingly of "a certain rich man" who told his manager, "Give an account of thy stewardship; for thou mayest no longer be steward." Accountability and stewardship withered in the last decade, and the behavioral norms of managers went down. . . .

Most CEOs are men and women you would be happy to have as trustees for your children's assets or as next-door neighbors. Too many of these people, however, have in recent years behaved badly at the office, fudging numbers and drawing obscene pay for mediocre business achievements.

Directors should behave as if there was a single absentee owner, whose long-term interest they should try to further in all proper ways. This means that directors must get rid of a manager who is mediocre or worse, no matter how likable he may be. If able but greedy managers over-reach and try to dip too deeply into the shareholders' pockets, directors must slap their hands. Over-reaching has become common but few hands have been slapped.

Why have intelligent and decent directors failed so miserably? The answer lies not in inadequate laws—it's always been clear that directors are obligated to represent the interests of shareholders—but rather in what I'd call "boardroom atmosphere." It's almost impossible, for example, in a boardroom populated by well-mannered people, to raise the question of whether the CEO should be replaced [or] to question a proposed acquisition that has been endorsed by the CEO, particularly when his inside staff and outside advisors are present and unanimously support his decision. (They wouldn't be in the room if they didn't.)

Compensation committees too often have been tail-wagging puppy dogs meekly following recommendations by consultants, a breed not known for allegiance to the faceless shareholders who pay their fees. This costly charade should cease . . . CEOs have often amassed riches while their shareholders have experienced financial disasters. . . . Directors should stop such piracy.

(*continued*)

Box 10.1 *Continued*

The acid test for reform will be CEO compensation. Managers will cheerfully agree to board "diversity," attest to SEC filings and adopt meaningless proposals relating to process. What many will fight, however, is a hard look at their own pay and perks. It would be a travesty if the bloated pay of recent years became a baseline for future compensation. Compensation committees should go back to the drawing boards.

Mutual Fund Directors

For the most part, a monkey will type out a Shakespeare play before an "independent" mutual-fund director will suggest that his fund look at other managers, even if the incumbent manager has persistently delivered substandard performance. When they are handling their own money, of course, directors will look to alternative advisors—but it never enters their minds to do so when they are acting as fiduciaries for others.

The hypocrisy permeating the system is vividly exposed when a fund management company—call it "A"—is sold for a huge sum to Manager "B." Now the "independent" directors experience a "counter-revelation" and decide that Manager B is the best that can be found—even though B was available (and ignored) in previous years. Not so incidentally, B also could formerly have been hired at a far lower rate than is possible now that it has bought Manager A. That's because B has laid out a fortune to acquire A, and B must now recoup that cost through fees paid by the A shareholders who were "delivered" as part of the deal. Just as compensation committees of many American companies have failed to hold the compensation of their CEOs to sensible levels, mutual fund company directors have failed as well in negotiating management fees. Fund directors have many perfunctory duties, but in actuality have only two important responsibilities: obtaining the best possible investment manager and negotiating with that manager for the lowest possible fee.

Year after year, at literally thousands of funds, directors had routinely rehired the incumbent management company, however pathetic its performance had been. Just as routinely, the directors had mindlessly approved fees that in many cases far exceeded those that could have been negotiated. Sadly, despite the lapdog behavior of independent fund directors, "boardroom atmosphere" almost invariably sedates their fiduciary genes.

[Fund] directors have failed . . . in negotiating management fees. If you or I were empowered, . . . we could easily negotiate materially lower management fees with the incumbent managers of most mutual funds. And, believe me, if directors were promised a portion of any fee savings they realized, the skies would be filled with falling fees. Under the current system, though, reductions mean nothing to "independent" directors while meaning everything to managers. So guess who wins?

[Before the recent scandals], many fund-management companies had followed policies that hurt the owners of the funds they managed, while simultaneously boosting the fees of the managers. These management companies were earning profit margins and returns on tangible equity that were the envy of Corporate America. Yet to swell profits further, they trampled on the interests of fund shareholders in an appalling manner.

So what are the directors of these looted funds doing? As I write this, I have seen none that have terminated the contract of the offending management company (though naturally that entity has often fired some of its employees). Can you imagine directors who had been personally defrauded taking such a boys-will-be-boys attitude? To top it all off, at least one miscreant management company has put itself up for sale, undoubtedly hoping to receive a huge sum for "delivering" the mutual funds it has managed to the highest bidder among other managers.* This is a travesty. Why in the world don't the directors of those funds simply select whomever they think is best among the bidding organizations and sign up with that party directly? The winner would consequently be spared a huge "payoff" to the former manager who, having flouted the principles of stewardship, deserves not a dime. Not having to bear that acquisition cost, the winner could surely manage the funds in question for a far lower ongoing fee than would otherwise have been the case. Any truly independent director should insist on this approach to obtaining a new manager.

A great many funds have been run well and conscientiously, despite the opportunities for malfeasance that exist. The shareholders of these funds have benefited, and their managers have earned their pay. Indeed, if I were a director of certain funds, including some that charge above-average fees, I would enthusiastically make the two declarations I have suggested. Additionally, those index funds that are very low-cost . . . are investor-friendly by definition and are the best selection for most of those who wish to own equities. . . .

The blatant wrongdoing that has occurred has betrayed the trust of so many millions of [fund] shareholders. Hundreds of industry insiders had to know what was going on, yet none publicly said a word. It took Eliot Spitzer and the whistleblowers who aided him to initiate a housecleaning. We urge fund directors to continue the job. Like directors throughout Corporate America, these fiduciaries must now decide whether their job is to work for owners or for managers.

Source: Warren E. Buffett, Chairman's Letter, Berkshire Hathaway 2002 and 2003 Annual Reports, February 21, 2003, and February 27, 2004. Reprinted with permission.

---

* An apparent reference to Richard Strong, whose contretemps are described in chapter seven. After being barred from the securities industry for life, Mr. Strong sold his management company to Wells Fargo Bank for an estimated $400 million. Again, as in the example of Putnam's Mr. Lasser in chapter seven, "nothing succeeds like failure."

As Table 7.3 showed, the potential long-term destruction in the wealth of our nation's families reaped by the croupiers of our society over the past two decades has been devastating, consuming enormous portions of this wealth. Over an investment lifetime the impact of those costs is absolutely staggering. Today, when a twenty-one-year-old begins a career, the remaining life expectancy is sixty-two years for a man and sixty-seven years for a woman. Consider the impact of investment costs over sixty-five years: $1,000 invested at the outset of the period, earning an assumed annual return of, say, 8 percent, would have a final value of $148,780—*the magic of compounding returns.* Even assuming an annual intermediation cost of only 2½ percent, the return would be reduced to 5½ percent. At that rate, the same initial $1,000 would have a final value of only $32,465—*the tyranny of compounding costs.* The triumph of tyranny over magic is reflected in a stunning reduction of almost 80 percent in accumulated wealth for the investor. The lost $116,315 has been consumed in what seemed to be small increments, year after year, by our financial system.

What is more, such a shocking waste of the wealth of our nation's families surely understates the damage done to them, for it is measured in nominal dollars. Even if we are lucky enough to hold inflation to just 2½ percent per year in the future, the resulting net nominal return of 5½ percent is nearly halved, to a return of just 3 percent in real (inflation-adjusted) terms. If we further reduce that real return by the taxes passed through to investors (at least for those who do not own their funds in tax-deferred retirement accounts) by tax-inefficient mutual funds and tax-disastrous hedge funds, the result is not pretty—perhaps an average return of 1 to 1½ percent, or even less. (Remember that, like costs, taxes are deducted each year in current dollars, but their negative impact is felt at the end of the long period, in real dollars.) Only a moment's reflection is necessary to suggest that merely reporting past mutual fund performance in terms of real dollars would send a wake-up call—if not sound an alarm—to fund investors.

The Relentless Rules of Humble Arithmetic

In 1914, in *Other People's Money,* Louis D. Brandeis, later to become one of the most influential justices in the history of the U.S. Supreme Court, railed against the oligarchs who, a century ago, controlled investment America and corporate America as well. He described the self-serving financial management of the day, which "trampled with impunity on laws human and divine, obsessed with the delusion that two plus two make five,"[10] and predicted (accurately, as it turned out) that the widespread speculation would collapse, "a victim of the relentless rules of humble arithmetic." He then added this unattributed quotation, perhaps from Sophocles: "Remember O Stranger, arithmetic is the first of the sciences, and the mother of safety."

The more things change, the more they remain the same. While the history of the era that Brandeis described is not repeating itself today, paraphrasing Mark Twain, it rhymes. Our investment systems—our government retirement programs, our private retirement programs, indeed, all of the securities owned by our stockowners as a group—are plagued by the same relentless rules. Since the returns investors receive come only *after* the deduction of the costs of that system of financial intermediation (even as a gambler's winnings come only from the chips that remain after the croupier's rake descends), the relentless rules of that humble arithmetic devastate the long-term returns of investors.

How much do those intermediation costs take from investors? No one knows the exact amount. But consider just a few of the cost centers. In the past five years alone, revenues of investment bankers and brokers came to an estimated $1.3 trillion; direct mutual fund costs came to about $250 billion; annuity commissions to some $40 billion; hedge fund fees to about $60 billion; fees paid to personal financial advisers maybe another $20 billion. Even without including, say, banking and insurance services, total financial intermediation costs came to nearly $2 *trillion,* an average of $400 billion per year, all directly deducted by the croupiers from the returns that the financial markets generated before passing the remainder along to investors.

Of course some of these costs create value (for example, liquidity and market efficiency). But by definition, those costs cannot create above-market returns. The fact is the reverse: The costs of investing are the direct cause of below-market returns, a dead weight on the amount investors earn. *In investing, you get what you don't pay for.* We must develop a far more efficient way, a lower-cost way, to offer investment services.

A Flawed Private Retirement System

Since 1970, our national policy has been to increase savings for retirement by providing tax-sheltered accounts such as individual retirement accounts (IRAs) and defined-contribution pension, thrift, and savings programs (usually 401(k) plans). The present administration in

Washington seems determined to further extend the reach of these tax-advantaged vehicles, along with the amount that each family may invest in them each year. But it is not at all clear that such policies have been, or will be, effective in raising our national savings. Indeed, according to government statistics, America's savings rate is at an all-time low.

It will be a challenge to improve the savings rate with tax incentives. First of all, some 24 million of our families have annual incomes below the poverty line (about $19,000). Another 22 million families have incomes between $19,000 and $35,000. Even for those at the very top of that scale, however, after the deduction of federal, state, and Social Security taxes, only about $28,000 remains. Under the best of circumstances, incomes at those levels leave little room for a family to save. At the other end of the scale, there are 30 million families earning more than $75,000 per year, families who are highly likely to save all they can for the future—for their children's education, a new home, a comfortable retirement, and so on—even if tax deferral did not exist.

Further, it is not at all clear that the tax incentives already created for investors have led to substantial accumulations of wealth. Only about 22 percent of our workers are participating in 401(k) savings plans; only about 10 percent have IRAs, plus about 9 percent who have both. And even after a quarter-century of availability, the average 401(k) balance is now a modest $33,600, and the average IRA $26,900—hardly enough capital adequate to form the foundation for a comfortable retirement. It short, today's reliance on tax-advantaged savings (let alone tomorrow's, under even more liberal terms), however valuable to our well-to-do citizens who can afford it, does little but further raise the ever-widening gap between our wealthiest families and our families most in need. This growing diversion of wealth is not only a destructive force leading toward the creation of a "two nation" society—rich versus poor—but represents an unwelcome departure from the basic principles of our Declaration of Independence and our Constitution.

But even our defined-benefit pension plans are now at risk, largely because of unrealistically high assumptions of prospective rates of return that ignored, one might say, the relentless rules of humble arithmetic. The future for our pension plans is fraught with challenges that can only be described as truly awesome. A recent report by Morgan Stanley's respected accounting expert Trevor Harris (with Richard Berner) put it well: "Years of mispriced pension costs, underfunding, and overly optimistic assumptions

about mortality and retirement have created economic mismatches between promises made and the resources required to keep them. Corporate
defined-benefit plans as a whole are as much as $400 billion underfunded.
State and local plans, moreover, may be underfunded by three times that
amount [$1.2 trillion]. Those gaps will drain many plan sponsors' operat-
ing performance and threaten the defined-benefit system itself, especially
if markets fail to deliver high returns, or if interest rates remain low."[11] A
more recent estimate by the Pension Benefit Guaranty Corporation places
the deficit of single-employer plans at $450 billion, and the deficit of multi-
employer plans at $150 billion.[12]

It's time to align both our private pension system and our government
pension systems with those relentless rules, just as we must do with the retirement savings of our families, whether they are investing directly in mutual funds or in defined contribution savings plans.

Social Insecurity?

At the heart of our nation's retirement system is Social Security,
the federal system that has efficiently provided a generous and uninterrupted
stream of income to a major portion of America's retired wage earners and
their families for more than seven decades. The Bush administration aims to
resolve the so-called crisis in the system by a partial "privatization" of the system, under which participants would divert a portion of their tax payments
into personal retirement accounts. Given the importance of retirement savings in our prosperous society, these issues demand at least as much recognition in a book on capitalism in America as do our private and state pension
and savings funds. After all, something like $1.5 trillion is on the books of
the Social Security Administration's balance sheet, in the form of special
interest-bearing notes issued for that purpose by the federal government.

These notes constitute what is called the "trust fund," described only a
few years ago as a "lockbox" holding these savings, leaving aside that these
notes are essentially money that the U.S. Treasury owes to itself, assets that
will be drawn down as the benefits paid out to beneficiaries exceed the Social Security taxes paid into the fund by wage earners. That drawdown is
generally expected to begin in about 2018, finally exhausting the trust
fund in about 2050. Thereafter, other factors held equal, those taxes would
fund about 70 percent of the expected benefit payments.

Unless offset by general tax revenues, the potential reduction in payments about a half-century hence would represent a failure to keep the ex-

isting commitments of the Social Security system. But it is too early to describe the system as in a "crisis." The fact is that a few simple—and, if undertaken promptly, relatively painless—steps would cure what would otherwise later become a serious problem.

It may sound simple. But it *is* simple. Like a family whose expenses exceed its revenues, the solution is obvious. Either income must go up, or expenses must go down, or a little of each must occur. In Social Security, then, we must do some combination of:

a. Increasing revenues, taking such steps as raising the amount of wages subject to payroll taxes, and perhaps making a small increase in the tax itself; and/or

b. Reducing expenses, by modifying or trimming cost-of-living adjustments and accelerating the present modest increase planned in the retirement age, and even raising the age as longevity increases. (Bringing state and local government employees fully into the system would also help.)

What about Personal Savings Accounts?

Only when we establish a sounder footing for Social Security— including figuring out how to finance the reduction in contributions to the trust fund engendered by the implementation of "personal savings accounts"—can we turn to consideration of how a system of personal savings accounts should work. First, contributions to personal accounts should be limited to a relatively small proportion of an individual's present contribution, perhaps 4 percentage points of the present 12.4 percent total tax on employees and wage earners, up to a $1,000 maximum per family, leaving the remaining 8.4 percent to provide the guaranteed benefits. (This now appears to be what the administration will recommend.)

Second, future benefits must be reduced commensurately for those who choose this option. Here again, the administration has suggested that regular benefits would be reduced by an annual return of 3 percent plus the inflation rate. So if the inflation rate were 2.5 percent, private account holders would profit only to the extent that the stock market return exceeded 5.5 percent, hardly a slam dunk. Polls indicate that, despite the favorable odds that stocks will provide a higher return than that benchmark over long periods of time, about five-sixths of covered beneficiaries would decline this tradeoff. Those beneficiaries who realize that stocks are risky and volatile, who can't accept the emotional strain, and who would rather not relinquish part of their regular Social Security income may even be making a good judgment by staying in the present system.

The administration's notion of providing personal savings accounts that would enable those covered by Social Security to invest those monies in mutual funds of their own choice is theoretically attractive. But it ignores the profound negative impact that this diversion of capital would have on the contributions to the existing Social Security system. On the other hand, the administration deserves great credit for its courage in recognizing the debilitating arithmetic of mutual fund investing and therefore recommending very low cost index funds as the underlying investment of these private accounts. Simply put, the administration seems to have concluded, properly, that the retirement savings of American families are too important to the wealth of our nation to be entrusted to the wiles of the mutual fund industry.

It is now expected that the administration's privatization proposal will be modeled on the remarkably successful Federal Employees Thrift Plan,* in which government employees invest regularly in a series of broad market index funds (and/or a special U.S. government bond) at a direct cost of about 0.05 percent (five basis points), and, given the nature of indexing, essentially zero portfolio turnover costs. The all-in cost of that soundly conceived thrift plan, then, is not only a tiny fraction of the 2½ to 3 percent all-in cost for the average equity fund—taking into account the sales charges, advisory fees, operating expenses, and portfolio turnover costs— but well below the cost of the lowest-cost index mutual funds. What is more, by limiting investor choices to a small number of broadly diversified index funds, the plan also implicitly recognizes the need to prevent investors from making the inevitable, hasty, and costly errors associated with the timing of their investments and in the selection of their funds.

However, I believe even further simplification would enhance the value of the savings plan to its participants:

1. Offer only a single equity fund, modeled on an all-stock-market index fund, such like the S&P 500 fund in the Federal Thrift Plan, but perhaps with some additional international exposure.

* This $150 billion investment pool, essentially a tax-deferred 401(k) plan for federal employees, is administered by the Federal Retirement Thrift Investment Board on their behalf.

2. Since basic Social Security benefits are measured in fixed-dollar, inflation-adjusted returns, allow neither fixed-income nor other equity options. Such a policy should obviate the confiscatory penalties that investors create for themselves by unfavorable market timing and bad fund choices.

3. Allow *no* escape hatches, either to exit the program, or to reenter it, thus muting the counterproductive emotions of investors that get in the way of the accumulation of substantial wealth. Instead of fruitlessly striving to add to the equity account in the exuberance of a market high, or panicking and exiting in the deep pessimism that marks a market low, the idea is to buy and hold the entire stock market for Warren Buffett's favorite holding period: Forever.

4. In order to provide a sound transition from the years of accumulating assets to the years of distributing income, gradually move the individual account into bonds as retirement approaches. For example, make a 10 percent allocation to bonds ten years before retirement age, and increase it by an additional 10 percent each year until it reaches 100 percent at retirement.

The magic, if such it be, of the program I've described for private accounts is simply that it eliminates all of the bells and whistles—the excessive costs, the excessive choice, the excessive investment changes—that have bedeviled mutual fund investors. With these strictures, I believe that the returns earned by those Social Security participants who chose to open personal savings accounts would be greatly enhanced. But, for all the discussion about these personal accounts, public policy should recognize the obvious fact that if Social Security investments in stocks simply replace, as they must, the investments of other market participants in stocks, society as a whole is neither better nor worse off. (This relentless rule of humble arithmetic too is eternal.)

However the proposed personal accounts are structured and however broadly they may be utilized by our citizens, they cannot by themselves resolve the problems surrounding the shortfall in accomplishments of our other retirement systems. Social Security itself must be fixed, but prompt action also must be taken to repair the damage to our defined-benefit systems—both public and private—and the inadequate accumulations in our defined contribution thrift and savings system—individual and corporate alike—that were described earlier in this chapter.

"The Ownership Society?"

Whatever the case, the administration should acknowledge that rather than helping to create an "ownership society," its proposal actually represents a further extension of today's "intermediation society," in which financial institutions have largely replaced individual owners of stocks. In the pooled personal savings account, which could well become the largest financial intermediary in history, participants would have almost none of the traditional benefits of ownership such as choice of securities and exercise of voting rights. There is a significant difference between owning a business and participating in a pool that holds shares *in all of America's businesses.*

So it is essential that we appoint a group of our wisest, most experienced, and most independent citizens to serve as trustees of the new "Social Security Savings Fund," acting *as faithful fiduciaries of the participants who select this option.* If we can only disengage both the strident demands of the political right and the angry protestations of the political left, and make the changes in the traditional system that I've suggested, the newly secure Social Security system that I have described here will work for its participants and for the nation. "It's not politics, stupid, it's common sense."

Since our society has an enormous and compelling stake in the self-sufficiency of its older citizens, it hardly seems too much to ask that the same federal commission that must be created to consider our "intermediation society" also assume the responsibility for evaluating what might be done to give our "investment society" a fair shake, and thereby strengthen the retirement-plan system whose assets constitute, with real estate, the lion's share of our nation's savings. Fixing the financial system so that it operates in the interests of owners rather than in the interest of managers, just as existing mutual fund law demands, is clearly in the public interest. Under a U.S. Constitution that created a union designed "to promote the general welfare and secure the blessings of liberty to ourselves and our posterity," the federal commission I have described has both the right and the responsibility to focus on those lofty goals.

Other Voices, Same Conclusions

To some, my evaluation of what went wrong in corporate America, in investment America, and in mutual fund America may seem radical and extreme, perhaps even heretical, undermining a good system that has created so much value for our citizenry. Others may agree that something has gone wrong, but then engage in endless debate about why it went wrong and how serious and widespread the wrongs were. And of course, like any disturbance in the status quo, many other voices will be raised in protest against any need to fix the system, arguing against any particular approach that should be followed—much like white blood cells attacking an intruder—or, more likely, trusting the participants in the financial markets to fix the system themselves, without any government intervention.

Fortunately, other voices have been raised to deal with the plain facts, voices of persons of great reason and integrity. In this chapter, we've already heard from Justice Brandeis, from Henry Kaufman, from Felix Rohatyn, and from Warren Buffett. Another is Peter G. Peterson, co-chairman of the Conference Board Commission on Public Trust and Private Enterprise. In his 2004 best seller *Running on Empty: How the Democratic and Republican Parties Are Bankrupting Our Future and What Americans Can Do About It,* the legendary Pete Peterson, railing as ever, and railing *accurately* as ever, articulately demands fundamental changes in our Social Security system.

To that distinguished list we can add Joseph Stiglitz, Nobel laureate in economics and former chief economist of the World Bank. In his seminal essay "Evaluating Economic Change" in the Summer 2004 edition of *Daedalus,* Stiglitz articulately describes the "erosion of moral values" in our corporations, our accountancies, our banks, and our mutual funds. He too believes that executive compensation, incentives, and distorted financial information, taken together, constitute compelling evidence that, in his words, "the pursuit of self interest does not necessarily lead to over-all economic efficiency."[13] He forcefully expresses his concern that "shareholders' lack of information makes it virtually impossible for them to ensure that the managers to whom they have entrusted their wealth and the care of the company will act in their best interests." Extensive excerpts from his essay are included in Box 10.2. His extraordinary intellect and his wide credibility buttress my own message that it is time for a change, time for a new world that is not only different in degree, but different in kind from the world of today, a new world that returns capitalism to its traditional ownership roots.

"To Begin the World Anew"

The need to change the rules of the game in corporate America, in investment America, and in mutual fund America—essentially reaf-

Box 10.2 Joseph E. Stiglitz: "Evaluating Economic Change"

The Erosion of Moral Values

Many are concerned by the seeming erosion of moral values, exhibited so strikingly in the corporate scandals that rocked the country in the last few years, from Enron to Arthur Andersen, from WorldCom to the New York Stock Exchange—scandals that involved virtually all our major accounting firms, most of our major banks, many of our mutual funds, and a large proportion of our major corporations.

Of course, every society has its rotten apples. But when such apples are so pervasive, one has to look for systemic problems. This seeming erosion of moral values is just one change . . . that does not seem to indicate progress. Economists have traditionally been loath to talk about morals. Indeed, traditional economists have tried to argue that individuals pursuing their self-interest necessarily advance the interests of society. This is Adam Smith's fundamental insight, summed up in his famous analogy of the invisible hand.

Markets do not lead to efficient outcomes, let alone outcomes that comport with social justice. As a result, there is often good reason for government intervention to improve the efficiency of the market. Just as the Great Depression should have made it evident that the market often does not work as well as its advocates claim, our recent Roaring Nineties should have made it self-evident that the pursuit of self-interest does not necessarily lead to overall economic efficiency.

The executives of Enron, Arthur Andersen, WorldCom, etc. were rewarded with stock options, and they did everything they could to pump up the price of their shares and maximize their own returns; and many of them managed to sell while the prices remained pumped up. But those who were not privy to this kind of inside information held on to their shares, and when the stock prices collapsed, their wealth was wiped out. At Enron, workers lost not only their jobs but also their pensions. It is hard to see how the pursuit of self-interest—the corporate greed that seemed so unbridled—advanced the general interest.

Fiduciary Responsibility

Advances in the economics of information (especially in that branch that deals with the problem that is, interestingly, referred to as "moral hazard") help explain the seeming contradiction. Problems of information means that the shareholders have to delegate responsibility for making decisions, but their lack of information makes it virtually impossible for them to ensure that the managers to whom they have entrusted their wealth and the care of the company will act in their best interests. The

(*continued*)

Box 10.2 *Continued*

manager has *a fiduciary responsibility.* He is supposed to act *on behalf of others.* It is his *moral* obligation. But standard economic theory says that he should act in *his own interests.* There is, accordingly, *a conflict of interest.*

In the 1990s, such conflicts became rampant. Accounting firms that made more money in providing consulting services than in providing good accounts no longer took as seriously their responsibility to provide accurate accounts. Analysts made more money by touting stocks they knew were far overvalued than by providing accurate information to their unwary customers who depended on them.

Changes may produce new conflicts of interest and new contexts in which the pursuit of self-interest clashes with societal well-being. When people see others benefiting from such conditions, a new norm of greed emerges. CEOs defend their rapacious salaries by referring to what others are getting; some even argue that such salaries are required to provide them the appropriate incentives for making "the hard decisions."

Financial Innovations

Some financial innovations have made it more difficult to monitor what a firm and its managers are doing, thus worsening the information problem [by providing] distorted information to investors; costs could be hidden, and revenues increased. With *reported* profits thereby enhanced, share prices also increased. But because share prices were based on distorted information, resources were misallocated. And when the bubble to which this misinformation contributed broke, the resulting downturn was greater than it otherwise would have been.

Curiously, stock options were heralded as providing better incentives for managers to align their interests with those of the shareholders. This argument was more than a little disingenuous: in fact, the typical stock-option package, especially as it was put into practice, did not provide better incentives. While pay went up when stock prices went up, much of the increase in the stock price had nothing to do with the managers' performance; it just reflected overall movements in the market. It would have been better to base pay on relative performance.

Precisely this kind of myopia was evidenced in the competitive struggles of the 1990s. Those investment banks whose analysts provided distorted information to their customers did best. Repeatedly, the investment banks explained that they had no choice but to engage in such tactics if they were to survive.

Source: Excerpted from an article by Joseph E. Stiglitz, published in Daedalus, *the journal of the American Academy of Arts and Sciences, Summer 2004. Reprinted by permission of MIT Press Journals.*

firming the superiority of the interests of the owners to the interests of the managers—is vital and profound. The share of the rewards of capitalism arrogated to themselves by corporate executives, by Wall Street, and by mutual fund managements have created an excessive drain on the nation's wealth and on the wealth of America's families. This diversion of so much of the rewards of investing to the managers during the great two-decade-long bull market was tolerated because most investors nevertheless enjoyed positive returns; and because the link between the investors who put up their own capital and the actual ownership of the shares of our corporations had become so attenuated.

Today, the vast majority of corporate shares are held indirectly by a variety of financial intermediaries, largely the managers of pension funds and mutual funds. But by placing service to self ahead of their duty to serve those who have entrusted them with the faithful handling of their assets, our manager-agents have failed to recognize adequately their fiduciary responsibility to their owner-principals. So, in Tom Paine's phrase, it's time "to begin the world anew," time to build a better corporate and financial world in today's America. The place to begin is with a federal government commission that works to resolve the problems of our intermediation society, and fosters the development of an investment society that gives owners a fair shake. The phrase *intermediation society*, or even *agency society*, may lack the cachet of *ownership society*. But none of these characterizations capture the essence of the system we must create. Our goal must be the creation of a *fiduciary society* in which the trustees of other people's money act solely in the long-term interests of their beneficiaries. We are a long way from the perfect system that we ought to strive to create in corporate America, investment America, and mutual fund America.

Writing as Publius in *The Federalist*, no. 6, on November 14, 1787, Alexander Hamilton used words that, in the context of this day, two-plus-centuries later, should serve as a warning to us. "Have we not already seen enough of the fallacy and extravagance of . . . idle theories which have amused us with promises of an exemption from their imperfections, weaknesses, and evils incident to society in every shape?"

Hamilton answered his question with another question, this one rhetorical: "Is it not time to awake from the deceitful dream of a golden age, and to adopt as a practical maxim for the direction of our . . . conduct that we are yet remote from the happy empire of perfect wisdom and perfect virtue?" Similarly, if we citizens of today can only accept that such a happy empire of perfect wisdom and perfect virtue is also yet remote in today's flawed version of American capitalism, we can begin the hard work of fixing its shortcomings.

The time to begin to build that world anew is now.

N O T E S

Introduction

1. Edward Gibbon, *The Decline and Fall of the Roman Empire* (1776–88; New York: Random House, 2003), 11.
2. Ibid., 1137.
3. John Maynard Keynes, *The General Theory of Employment, Interest and Money* (1936; New York: Harcourt, Brace and Company, 1964), 159.
4. Dr. Bernard Lown, letter to the author, undated.
5. Quoted in David B. Hart, "The Soul of a Controversy," *Wall Street Journal*, April 1, 2005.

CHAPTER 1: What Went Wrong in Corporate America?

1. Quoted in Warren G. Bennis, "Will the Legacy Live on?" *Harvard Business Review*, February 1, 2002, 95.
2. Jonathan Sacks, "Markets and Morals," The 1998 Hayek Lecture. London: Institute of Economic Affairs, 1998.
3. James Surowiecki, "A Virtuous Cycle," *Forbes*, December 23, 2002, 248.
4. Adam Smith, *The Wealth of Nations* (1776; New York: Random House, 1994), 485.
5. Surowiecki, "A Virtuous Cycle," 248.
6. William Bernstein, *The Birth of Plenty: How the Prosperity of the Modern World Was Created* (New York: McGraw-Hill, 2004), 4 and jacket copy.
7. William Pfaff, "A Pathological Mutation in Capitalism," *International Herald Tribune*, September 9, 2002, 8.
8. Peter Schwartz and Peter Leyden, "The Long Boom: A History of the Future," *Wired*, July 1997, 115.
9. Ibid.
10. Mark Gimein, "The Greedy Bunch," *Fortune*, August 11, 2002, 64.
11. "Flotation Fever," *The Economist*, March 18, 2004, 7.
12. Conrad S. Ciccotello, C. Terry Grant, and Gerry H. Grant, "Impact of Employee Stock Options on Cash Flow," *Financial Analysts Journal* 60/2, March/April 2004, 39.

13. Quoted in Edward Chancellor, *Devil Take the Hindmost: A History of Speculation* (New York: Farrar, Straus and Giroux, 1999), 58.

14. Edward Chancellor, "The Trouble with Bubbles," *New York Times,* January 27, 2002, 13.

15. Martin Howell, *Predators and Profits* (Upper Saddle River, N.J.: Reuters Prentice Hall, 2003), passim.

16. Source for projected earnings growth, Morgan Stanley 1981–2001, author's estimate thereafter.

17. Theo Francis, "'Phantom' Accounts for CEOs Draw Scrutiny," *Wall Street Journal,* June 13, 2005.

18. Patrick McGeehan, "They Don't Need a Ticket to Ride," *New York Times,* April 11, 2004, section 3, page 1.

19. CNN/USA Today/Gallup poll, July 2002.

20. Lucian Bebchuk and Yaniv Grinstein, "The Growth of U.S. Executive Pay," Working Paper, January 2005, abstract. Updated figured obtained in author's conversation with author, and in Alan Abelson, "Street Fight," *Barron's,* April 4, 2005, 5.

21. Quoted in Bob Herbert, "The Era of Exploitation," *New York Times,* March 25, 2005, 17.

22. Steve Galbraith, "Compensatory Damage," Morgan Stanley Research, October 20, 2003, 1.

23. Ibid.

24. Peter Bernstein, "Surprising the Smoothies," *Journal of Portfolio Management,* Fall 1979.

25. Source for 1990–94 data, Min Wu, "A Review of Earnings Restatements," August 2002, published by Softrax. Source for 2000–2004 data, Diya Gullapalli, "Outside Audit: To Err Is Human, to Restate Financials, Divine," *Wall Street Journal,* January 20, 2005. (These figures will also appear in chapter five.)

26. Lucian Bebchuk and Jesse Fried, *Pay Without Performance* (Cambridge, Mass.: Harvard University Press, 2004), 125.

CHAPTER 2: Why Did Corporate America Go Wrong?

1. James Surowiecki, "To the Barricades," *The New Yorker,* June 9, 2003, 44.

2. Adolf A. Berle and Gardiner C. Means, *The Modern Corporation and Private Property* (1932; New Brunswick, N.J.: Transaction, 2002), 64–65.

3. Adam Smith, *The Wealth of Nations* (1776; New York: Random House, 1994), 800.

4. Jeff Gerth and Richard W. Stevenson, "Enron's Collapse: The System," *New York Times,* January 20, 2002.

5. As quoted in David Boyle, *The Tyranny of Numbers* (London: Harper-Collins, 2000), 38.

6. Yahoo!, press release, October 10, 2001.

7. Erin Schulte, "Stocks Surge at Midmorning as Investors Pore Over Earnings Reports," *Wall Street Journal,* October 11, 2001.

8. John C. Bogle, "Public Accounting: Profession or Business?" The Seymour Jones Distinguished Lecture at the Vincent C. Ross Institute of Accounting Research. New York: New York University's Stern School of Business, October 16, 2000.

9. As quoted in Jamin B. Raskin, "Corporate Citizenship," review of *Unequal Protection: The Rise of Corporate Dominance and the Theft of Human Rights,* by Thom Hartmann, *Los Angeles Times,* August 24, 2003.

10. Robert W. Lear and Boris Yavitz, "Boards on Trial," *Chief Executive* (October 2000), 40.

11. Enron, 1999 Annual Report.

12. Warren E. Buffett, Chairman's Letter, Berkshire Hathaway 1993 Annual Report, March 1, 1994.

13. Joseph Fuller and Michael C. Jensen, "Dare to Keep Your Stock Price Low," *Wall Street Journal,* December 31, 2001.

14. Jeffrey A. Sonnenfeld, "Expanding Without Managing," *New York Times,* June 12, 2002.

15. Ibid.

CHAPTER 3 : How to Return Corporate America to Its Owners

1. Report available at http://www.conference-board.org/knowledge/governCommission.cfm.

2. John C. Bogle, "Mutual Fund Secrecy," *New York Times,* December 14, 2002.

3. John J. Brennan and Edward C. Johnson 3rd, "No Disclosure: The Feeling Is Mutual," *Wall Street Journal,* January 14, 2003.

4. AFL-CIO Office of Investment, "Behind the Curtain," September 2004.

5. Hewitt Heiserman, *It's Earnings That Count* (New York: McGraw-Hill, 2004), xxvii.

6. The U.S. Department of Commerce's Bureau of Economic Analysis, National Income and Product Accounts, table 7.16.

7. Quoted in James Surowiecki, "Board Stiffs," *The New Yorker,* March 8, 2004, 30.

8. Mark J. Roe, "The Inevitable Instability of American Corporate Governance," Olin Center for Law, Economics, and Business Discussion Paper No. 492, September 2004, abstract.

9. Paul A. Gompers, Joy L. Ishii, and Andrew Metrick, "Corporate Governance and Equity Prices," *Quarterly Journal of Economics,* vol. 118, issue 1, February 2003.

10. Mark Gordon, Martin Lipton, and Laura Munoz, "'Restoring Trust' or Losing Perspective?" Memorandum, August 27, 2003, 2.

11. Henry G. Manne, "Citizen Donaldson," *Wall Street Journal,* August 7, 2003.

12. Ibid.

13. See *Unocal Corporation vs. Mesa Petroleum Corporation,* 493 A. 3d 946 (Delaware 1985).

14. See *Blasius Industries, Inc., vs. Atlas Corporation,* 564 A.2d 651, 659 (Delaware Ch. 1988).

15. Lucian A. Bebchuk, "The Case for Shareholder Access to the Ballot," *The Business Lawyer* 59(2003):43–66.

16. Henry A. McKinnell, Ph.D., in a letter to Jonathan G. Katz of the SEC, File No. S7-10-03, June 13, 2003.

CHAPTER 4 : What Went Wrong in Investment America?

1. Adolf A. Berle and Gardiner C. Means, *The Modern Corporation and Private Property* (New Brunswick, N.J.: Transaction, 2002).

2. "SEC, NYSE, NASD and Elliot [sic] Spitzer Settle with U.S. Investment Banks," SriMedia, April 28, 2003. http://www.srimedia.com/artman/publish/article_547.shtml.

3. This e-mail and the other private e-mails discussed below were all uncovered by the investigations by New York attorney general Eliot Spitzer, the SEC, and other federal investigators.

4. Joan Caplin and Amy Feldman, "What Would It Take to be the Worst Analyst Ever?" *Money,* April 25, 2002, 98.

5. Charles Gasparino, "Citigroup Investigation Now Leads to Door of Elite Nursery School," *Wall Street Journal,* November 14, 2002.

6. J. Bogle, "The Economic Role of the Investment Company," senior thesis, Princeton University, 1951, 94.

7. "Big Money in Boston," *Fortune,* December 1949, 116.

8. Quoted in Bogle, "The Economic Role of the Investment Company," 101

9. Benjamin Graham, *The Intelligent Investor* (1949; New York: HarperCollins, 2005), 207–8. All subsequent Graham quotes in these paragraphs from these pages.

10. Paul Krugman, "For Richer," *New York Times Magazine,* October 10, 2002, 62.

11. Ibid.

12. Graham, *The Intelligent Investor,* 228.

13. The first three points were made by John Biggs in his keynote address at the Conference on Institutional Investors as Owners, entitled "Strong Managers, Weak Boards, Passive Owners: A Fair Description?" and are paraphrased. New York: New York University's Stern School of Business, February 5, 2005.

CHAPTER 5 : Why Did Investment America Go Wrong?

1. Quoted in Warren E. Buffett, Chairman's Letter, Berkshire Hathaway 1987 Annual Report, February 29, 1988.

2. Warren E. Buffett, Chairman's Letter, Berkshire Hathaway 1996 Annual Report, February 28, 1997.

3. This and subsequent Keynes quotes from John Maynard Keynes, *The General Theory of Employment, Interest and Money* (1936; New York: Harcourt, Brace and Company, 1964), 154–55.

4. John C. Bogle, "The Economic Role of the Investment Company," senior thesis, Princeton University, 1951, 109.

5. Quotes in this paragraph from Keynes, *General Theory,* 159.

6. This and all subsequent Grant notes from James Grant, "One in 50 Billion," *Grant's Interest Rate Observer,* July 17, 1998, 2.

7. John C. Bogle, "The Silence of the Funds," speech before the New York Society of Securities Analysts, New York, October 20, 1999.

8. Author's notes.

9. Earnscliffe Research and Communications, "Report to the United States Independence Standards Board," November 1999.

10. American Institute of Certified Public Accountants, Press Release, November 19, 1999.

11. John Maynard Keynes, review of *Common Stocks as Long Term Investments,* Edgar Lawrence Smith, 1925.

12. Ibid.

13. General Motors, 2001 Annual Report.

14. "A World Awash with Profits," *The Economist,* February 12, 2005, 62.

15. Clifford S. Asness, "Rubble Logic," speech before the CFA Institute's Reflections and Insights Conference, Pasadena, Calif.: February 11, 2005.

16. Source for 1990–94 data, Min Wu, "A Review of Earnings Restatements," August 2002, published by Softrax. Source for 2000–2004 data, Diya Gullapalli, "Outside Audit: To Err Is Human, to Restate Financials, Divine," *Wall Street Journal,* January 20, 2005.

17. David Henry, "Mergers: Why Most Big Deals Don't Pay Off," *Business Week,* October 14, 2002, 60.

18. Bernstein Disciplined-Strategies Monitor, October 2003, 12.

19. Quoted in Lawrence Minard, "The Original Contrarian," *Forbes,* September 26, 1983, 42.

20. All quotes in this paragraph and the next from Robert L. Bartley, "No Profit," *The American Spectator,* December 2003/January 2004.

21. Alfred Rappaport, "The Economics of Short-Term Performance Obsession," working paper, September 2004.

22. Benjamin Graham, "A Conversation with Benjamin Graham," *Financial Analysts Journal* 32, no. 5 (September/October 1976): 20.

23. Benjamin Graham, *The Intelligent Investor* (New York: HarperCollins, 2005), 205.

24. John Maynard Keynes, *The General Theory of Employment, Interest and Money,* 155.

CHAPTER 6 : How to Fix Investment America

1. John Maynard Keynes, *The General Theory of Employment, Interest and Money* (1936; New York: Harcourt, Brace and Company, 1964), 154.

2. Burton G. Malkiel and Atanu Saha, "Hedge Funds: Risk and Return," working paper, December 1, 2004, 35.

3. Source: Securities and Exchange Commission Annual Reports.

4. Keynes, *General Theory*, 158–59.

5. Robert D. Arnott and Clifford S. Asness, "Surprise! Higher Dividends = Higher Earnings Growth," *Financial Analysts Journal* 59, no. 1 (January/February 2003): 70.

6. Roger Lowenstein, "A Boss for the Boss," *New York Times Magazine*, December 14, 2003, 42.

7. "No Democracy Please, We're Shareholders," *The Economist*, April 29, 2004.

8. Robert A. G. Monks and Nell Minow, *Corporate Governance* (Malden, Mass.: Blackwell, 1995).

9. Robert A. G. Monks and Allen Sykes, "Capitalism Without Owners Will Fail," http://www.ragm.com/hottopics/2004/ragm_sykesPolicyMakersGuide.pdf, 29–30.

10. "Getting Rid of the Boss," *The Economist*, February 6, 1993, 13.

CHAPTER 7 : What Went Wrong in Mutual Fund America?

1. For the first quotation, see Investment Company Act of 1940, http://www.sec.gov/about/laws/ica40.pdf. The second quotation is from the commission's unanimous opinion in its Vanguard decision, see The Vanguard Group, Inc., 47 S.E.C. 450 (1981).

2. Matthew P. Fink, "ICI President's Report," speech before the Investment Company Institute's General Membership Meeting, Washington, D.C.: May 22, 2003.

3. Paul G. Haaga Jr., "ICI Chairman's Remarks," speech before the Investment Company Institute's General Membership Meeting, Washington, D.C.: May 22, 2003.

4. From New York State Attorney General Eliot Spitzer's complaint against Canary Capital Partners, LLC, http://www.oag.state.ny.us/press/2003/sep/canary_complaint.pdf.

5. Reuters News Service, "Fidelity Receives Subpoena," *Houston Chronicle*, October 7, 2003.

6. Judith Burns, "Skepticism Rings Industry Cleanup," *Wall Street Journal*, December 28, 2004.

7. Hans Christian Andersen, "Fairy Tales Told to the Children—Third Booklet." In *The Emperor's New Clothes*, ed. Rosemary Lanning and Eve Tharlet (illustrator) (New York: North-South Books, 2000).

8. Dennis K. Berman and Christopher Oster, "Wells Fargo Nears Deal to Acquire Strong Financial," *Wall Street Journal*, May 26, 2004, C4.

9. "Connelly Named Fund Leader Of The Year," *Fund Action*, March 10, 2003.

10. John Hechinger, "Putnam Board Says 3 Officials Knew of Trades," *Wall Street Journal*, March 21, 2004, C1; and John Hechinger, "Putnam to Pay $110 Million, Try to Rebound," *Wall Street Journal*, April 9, 2004, C1.

11. David Swensen, *Unconventional Success* (New York: Free Press, 2005), 278–80.

12. Riva D. Atlas, "NASD Says Fund Family Paid Improper Fees," *New York Times*, February 17, 2005.

13. Swensen, *Unconventional Success*, 6.

14. "Stale Prices and Strategies for Trading Mutual Funds," Jacob Boudoukh, Matthew Richardson, and Marti Subrahmanyam, *Financial Analysts Journal* 58, no. 4 (July/August 2002): 70.

15. *Financial Analysts Journal*, November/December 2002, 17.

16. Ibid.

CHAPTER 8 : Why Did Mutual Fund America Go Wrong?

1. Warren E. Buffett, Chairman's Letter, Berkshire Hathaway 1985 Annual Report, March 1, 1986.

2. While my memory of the 44-year-old article's thesis was correct, my recollection of its title was not. The article was entitled "The Mutual Fund and Its Management Company: An Analysis of Business Incest," *The Yale Law Journal* 71, no. 1, 137.

3. Roger Lowenstein, "The Purist," *New York Times Magazine*, December 28, 2003, 44.

4. Paul A. Samuelson, quoted in *Notre Dame Lawyer* (South Bend, Ind.: Notre Dame Law School, 1969), 956.

5. John C. Bogle, "Deliverance," speech before Wellington Management Company's Partners, Boston: Wellington Management Company, September 9, 1971.

6. John C. Bogle, "Important Principles Must Be Inflexible," keynote speech before the Society of American Business Editors and Writers, Chicago: Society of American Business Editors and Writers Annual Conference, November 11, 1996.

7. Ibid.

CHAPTER 9 : How to Fix Mutual Fund America

1. John C. Bogle, "Important Principles Must Be Inflexible," keynote speech before the Society of American Business Editors and Writers, Chicago: Society of American Business Editors and Writers Annual Conference, November 11, 1996.

2. For the first quotation, see Investment Company Act of 1940, http://www.sec.gov/about/laws/ica40.pdf. The second quotation is from the Commission's unanimous opinion in its Vanguard decision, see The Vanguard Group, Inc., 47 S.E.C. 450 (1981).

3. John C. Bogle, "Mutual Fund Industry Practices and Their Effect on Individual Investors," testimony before the Subcommittee on Capital Markets, Insurance, and Government Sponsored Enterprises hearing entitled "Mutual Fund Industry Practices and Their Effect on Individual Investors," U.S. House of Representatives, March 12, 2003.

4. Senator Peter G. Fitzgerald, opening statement before the Subcommittee on Financial Management, the Budget, and International Security hearing entitled "Mutual Funds: Trading Practices and Abuses That Harm Investors," U.S. Senate, November 3, 2003.

5. Securities and Exchange Commission final rule on Investment Company Governance, September 7, 2004, http://www.sec.gov/rules/final/ic-26520.htm.

6. Edward C. Johnson 3rd, "'Interested'—And Proud of It!" *Wall Street Journal*, February 17, 2004.

7. "Public Policy Implications of Investment Company Growth," Securities and Exchange Commission, H.R. Rep. No. 89–2337, 1966.

8. Ibid.

9. Stewart L. Brown and John P. Freeman, "Mutual Fund Advisory Fees: The Cost of Conflicts of Interest," *Journal of Corporation Law* 26, 609.

10. Stephen LaBaton, "SEC's Oversight of Mutual Funds Is Said to Be Lax," *New York Times*, November 16, 2003.

11. Richard B. Evans, "Does Alpha Really Matter? Evidence from Mutual Fund Incubation, Termination, and Manager Change," job market paper, January 2004.

12. Thomas G. Donlan, "Fun Management: Which Came First, the Dragons or the Sheep?," *Barron's*, November 17, 2003, 42.

13. John C. Bogle, "The Economic Role of the Investment Company," senior thesis, Princeton University, 1951.

14. Warren E. Buffett, Chairman's Letter, Berkshire Hathaway 1994 Annual Report, March 7, 1995.

15. Paula A. Tkac, "Mutual Funds: Temporary Problem or Permanent Morass?" Federal Reserve Bank of Atlanta Economic Review, Fourth Quarter 2004, 89, no. 4, 5.

16. John C. Bogle, *Common Sense on Mutual Funds* (New York: Wiley & Sons, 1999), 392–93.

17. Eliot Spitzer, speech before *Money* Magazine's 2004 Money Summit. New York: June 8, 2004.

18. Quoted in William C. Symonds, "Online Extra: Husbanding that $27 Billion," *Business Week*, December 27, 2004, http://www.businessweek.com/@@kSYT7IYQ3RdgsQYA/magazine/content/04_52/b3914474.htm.

19. "Is There Life After Babe Ruth?" *Barron's*, April 2, 1990, 15.
20. Holman W. Jenkins Jr., "Also Stalking the Fund Industry: Obsolescence," *Wall Street Journal*, December 10, 2003.
21. Justin Fox, "Saint Jack on the Attack," *Fortune*, January 8, 2003, 112.

Chapter 10: American Capitalism in the Twenty-first Century

1. Henry Kaufman, *On Money and Markets: A Wall Street Memoir* (New York: McGraw-Hill, 2001), 304–5, 307, 313.
2. Felix Rohatyn, "Free, Wealthy and Fair," *Wall Street Journal*, November 11, 2003.
3. Alan Greenspan, "Capitalizing Reputation," at the 2004 Financial Markets Conference of the Federal Reserve Bank of Atlanta, Sea Island, Georgia, April 16, 2004.
4. Adam Smith, *The Theory of Moral Sentiments* (1759; Cambridge, Eng.: Cambridge University Press, 2002), 158.
5. Joseph Schumpeter, *The Theory of Economic Development* (Cambridge, Mass.: Harvard University Press, 1934), 93–94.
6. John Maynard Keynes, *The General Theory of Employment, Interest and Money* (New York: Harcourt, Brace and Company, 1936), 161–62.
7. Smith, *Theory of Moral Sentiments*, 272.
8. Robert A. G. Monks and Allen Sykes, "Capitalism Without Owners Will Fail," http://www.ragm.com/hottopics/2004/ragm_sykesPolicyMakersGuide.pdf, 29.
9. David Brooks, "How to Reinvent the GOP," *New York Times*, August 29, 2004.
10. Louis D. Brandeis, *Other People's Money and How the Bankers Use It* (1914; New York: Bedford Books, 1995), 45 (as are the other Brandeis quotes that follow).
11. Richard Berner and Trevor Harris, "Financial Market Implications of Pension Reform," Morgan Stanley Research, January 18, 2005.
12. Michael Schroeder, "Pension Agency Faces a New Front," *Wall Street Journal*, May 26, 2005.
13. Joseph E. Stiglitz, "Evaluating Economic Change," *Daedalus* 133/3, Summer 2004.

INDEX

Page numbers followed by *n* indicate a footnote. Page numbers followed by *t* indicate a table.